Preludes to Growth

AN EXPERIENTIAL APPROACH

Preludes to Growth

AN EXPERIENTIAL APPROACH

 THE FREE PRESS
A Division of Macmillan Publishing Co., Inc.
New York

Photograph by the author

Richard Katz

Harvard University

COLLIER MACMILLAN PUBLISHERS
London

Copyright © 1973 by Richard Katz

All rights reserved. No part of this book may be
reproduced or transmitted in any form or by any means,
electronic or mechanical, including photocopying, recording,
or by any information storage and retrieval system,
without permission in writing from the Publisher.

The Free Press

A Division of Macmillan Publishing Co., Inc.
866 Third Avenue, New York, N. Y. 10022

Collier–Macmillan Canada Ltd.

Library of Congress Catalog Card Number: 72–94013

Printed in the United States of America

printing number
1   2   3   4   5   6   7   8   9   10

To my parents, my teacher, and those who will come

Contents

Photograph by the author

Preface

THE contract for this book was signed. Months later, deep into writing, I asked myself several times and quite honestly: "Why am I doing this?" Before I signed the contract, when the book was still an idea rather than a manuscript, I could answer that question. But as I wrote more and the book realized more of its character, I had more than second thoughts. The effort required to complete the manuscript didn't make the sense it had before; partly, of course, because I hadn't realized so much effort would be required.

I spent several days wrestling with this book, seeking to recontact it. It became obvious that the author-ego trip, the fame-success syndrome, provided little of substance. It became even more obvious that the essential point was that in writing a book I was assuming a responsibility. People read a book, and at times they are affected. And with this particular book, my responsibility became even clearer, for I was asking the reader to become a participant; and perhaps this would encourage more people to try to apply the book in their lives. Could I honestly ask others—another, you— to try out what I described in the book? Did I believe in what I was writing? Did I do what I suggested you try doing? As I worked on these questions, the book changed its character. It became more an expression of what I consider to be a valuable and valid approach. It became for me a more honest and exciting undertaking. And it again made sense to write, to communicate with others about some of the experiences, techniques, and ideas I find challenging.

I can be more specific if I describe how this book relates to what I'm doing. I've always been dissatisfied with the lecture which unilaterally presents a body of material in a theoretical framework. It seems so unconnected with what concerns me most; namely, what each of us in fact *does* in his everyday life. Talking about things, creating concepts for their own sake, is interesting, perhaps; but how we live, day-to-day, is real. Reflecting on our own experience is, of course, a different matter. It can provide guidance for our daily lives.

But experience-based education is not easily developed nor neatly packaged. For a while I utilized techniques from the then new field of sensory enhancement, and tried to make sensitivity training more of an educational process. But these approaches seemed so limited and transitory. They lacked perspective and vision. I never found in them guidance for a lifetime. At the same time, I personally had become more committed to working on my inner life over time, seeking something higher, beyond myself.

Some of the original impetus for the book came from this earlier experimentation with sensory enhancement and sensitivity training. When the severe limitations of those approaches became apparent, writing this book became more a task than a challenge. But I was not prepared, nor am I now, to write comprehensively about something I'm just beginning to experience; namely, the difficult journey toward a more spiritual life. This was the paradox that nearly ended the writing. I felt I had to go beyond techniques which influenced the earliest form of the book, yet I could not go directly to that which was starting to take me beyond.

I tried to go into that paradox honestly. Where I emerged is where I am now. I can write this book because I believe it has value. From my involvement with a spiritual approach has come perspective and, at times, inspiration. I've reconsidered earlier material and tried to transform it. I've emphasized more the importance of simple honesty in our everyday life, over time; of honestly finding out who we are and facing that before we even begin to try changing ourselves. I think the book is pointing in the right direction. It might help some (re)start becoming more alive; and that is important. This aliveness could also serve as a prelude to work on spiritual issues.

Acknowledgments

$\mathcal{M}$ANY people participated in making this book.

Students and teaching fellows in my classes at Harvard and Brandeis, including Adult Education, helped to develop material which now appears in this book. For example, the discussion sections in the experiential exercises are based on their experiences with the exercises. I want to mention a few of those who helped: Judy Barker, Susan Basow, Wes Borden, Ruth Bowman, Gene Check, Rashi Glazer, Sandy Hughes, Martha Kanter, Martha Lewis, Barbara Mandelkorn, Mike Murphy, Fern Nemenyi, Cesareo Paleaz, Robert Poutasse, and especially Diane Skowbo and Bob Kaufman. Mentioning only these few is difficult because so many in my courses actually helped. Too many names for this space. They realize their collaboration.

Leading workshops at places such as Esalen, and discussions and work relationships with Dave Kolb, Jim McIntyre, and Irv Rubin at M.I.T. were early influences on my approach to experiential exercises.

Many read over parts or all of the manuscript with real interest. Susan Basow, Veda Clift, Margie Corbett, Jim Fadiman, Rashi Glazer, Mark Horowitz, Bob Kaufman, Abby Seixas, Bob Shuman, and Diane Skowbo each offered valuable comments.

A manuscript is always typed, but I now realize what that really means.

Three women collaborated with me in preparing this book for publication. Kay Chermayoff, Linda DiNorscia, and Verna Regan approached the manuscript with concern and care, working on their own time to meet certain deadlines. It made a difference to me that they were involved in the book.

Brandeis University provided financial support in preparing parts of the manuscript.

Finally, three persons, from very different points of view, gave me perspective on the book. Mary Maxwell Katz, Abe Maslow, and especially Mr. Willem Nyland each brought me closer to understanding why I was writing this book.

May I Have a Moment with

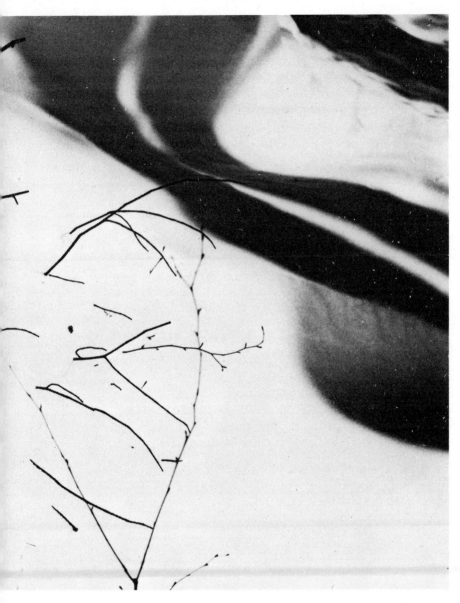

Photograph by the author

You?

$\mathcal{I}$ want to encourage you to work with this book. By putting your experiences into it, you can take something from it. But the book's form, its black-and-white print on page following page between bound covers, may discourage your participation in the book's material. And though I intentionally chose the present sequence of materials, the sequence is also meant as a jumping-off point. As you work with the book, you can easily rearrange it so it is more your book.

For example, perhaps you should read the Manual after you've had a chance to do one of the beginning exercises. The "I Am Me" and "Educating for Personal Growth" exercises are particularly important. They yield new material as you work with them more than once. And certainly that's possible. The "Overview" (Section Two) can serve as a touchstone, and perhaps it should recur throughout the book. You can easily read and reread it. The exercises can be approached in the sequence in which they're presented, or they can be viewed as constituting a resource pool from which you select certain exercises to consider certain issues. Doing an exercise toward the end of the book may encourage you to do again an exercise from the book's beginning. And you can use the case studies in different ways. The "Solo Survival

Experience" case study is a good extension of the "I Am Me" exercise, and a good counterpoint to the "Encountering" exercises—reestablishing in the latter case that encountering oneself is the basis of interpersonal encounter.

Here is one way you can get into the book, traveling between parts, dealing with material again from a new perspective:

Start with the "Now to Begin" exercises, perhaps reading parts of the Manual, such as "Perspectives on the Book," before doing these exercises; then read the entire Manual; then do the "Creative Alertness" exercises; read the Overview; then do the "Encountering" exercises, rereading parts of the Manual dealing with groups and group processes, and perhaps reading the "Solo Survival Experience" case study; do the "Creating," "Self-assessment," and "Education for Personal Growth" exercises; then reconsider the Overview, perhaps after you've read the "Education for Transcendence" case study; and, as you continue your efforts toward growing, work with the "Educating for Personal Growth" exercise and the Overview.

As you begin to recompose the book, you can generate circular sequences. You can gain multiple views of one point and one view of multiple points. Which brings us full circle. For it is your relating to the book which brings its parts to a whole and gives it a breath of life.

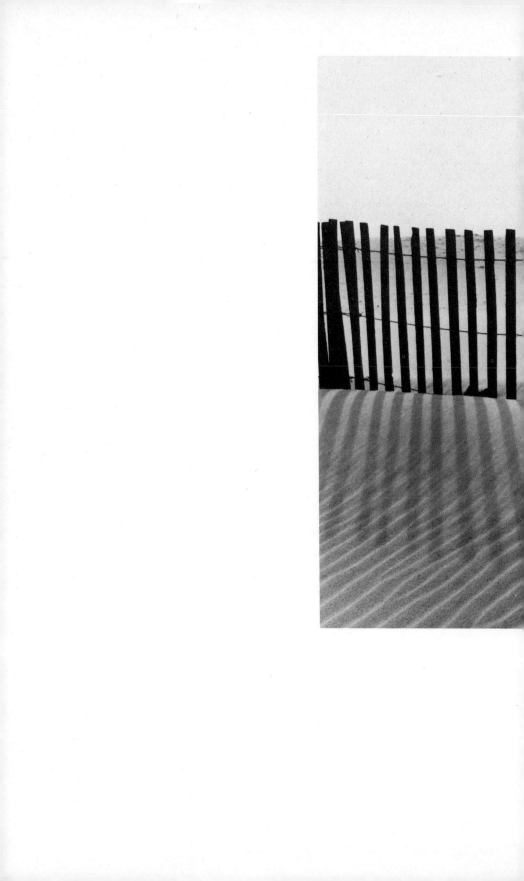

Photograph by the author

Manual

*T*HIS book has to be re-created if it is to live. The book is open-ended, waiting for your reconstruction. It invites your participation. I expect you'll use this manual to get further into the book.

Who Is This Manual For?

But immediately I'm confronted with a dilemma. Manuals are usually for the teacher or leader; they usually accompany the text or program which is for the student. Yet I believe that the learner and teacher must collaborate, and that each person must lead himself in learning. Also, when participants in a learning process have access to information about that process, they learn more.

And so this manual will be different. There will be one manual and I want it to be a manual for all those who have the book and begin to participate in it. Faculty and students, learners and teachers, we are in this together. As each of you embarks on the journey to and through the book, you can turn to the manual as you would an experienced friend. It can provide food for the self-directed traveler.

I've written the manual with the idea that all will read it. No hidden agendas which tell someone what the book really means. No secret instructions for running the experiential exercises so that they really work. The manual will be an open guide to what I hope can become an open book.

This manual is particularly oriented toward one aspect of the book —participation in experiential exercises. Often it is through these exercises that one can understand more clearly how to participate in the book. Also, they can be the hardest part of the book to work with.

Some exercises can be done on your own, others need a group context. The manual discusses in detail one group model for doing the exercises, namely, the self-directed group. The manual can also help with these exercises done by yourself. These times and experiences with yourself are the foundation of your work with the book or in a group.

Whatever the exercise or situation, try to remember: Be honest with yourself, as honest as you can about what you're doing and why, what you see about yourself, and what you can accept. That can be the heart of your own manual.

Perspectives on the Book

I'd like to describe more fully my hopes for the book and to talk about possibilities for its use. But first I'd like to say something which I feel is important but hard to communicate. It's obvious that I have a special relationship to this book; so that when I present my ideas about it, they can take on a certain significance. It's only natural for you to say, "Well, if the author doesn't know what the purpose of this book is, who does?"

But this is just the point that I want to work on. I have clear ideas about this book and its possible use. But my goal for the book is to have you take hold of it and use it to help guide your own education. My goal is to have you develop your own goals. And so before I go into my ideas, could you make a promise to yourself? Could you try taking my ideas as suggestions, using them as guidelines for developing your own approach to the book? Perhaps together we can break the unproductive pattern of the "expert" unilaterally telling others what his product is and how it should be used. As you work with the book, come back to this manual. Reread it and then see how much of a dialogue is created between us. Rewrite this chapter and its verse.

What Might This Book Encourage?

The basic purpose of the book is to help you create your own education. But I don't mean education in the usual sense, namely, acquisition of information or content learning—reading, writing, and 'rithmetic. It is rather education in a generic or classical sense. "To know thyself"—Socrates said it for many before him and for many after him. Today some call it humanistic education.

I hope that through this book you may have beginning experiences in humanistic education. Perhaps, at certain moments, you can begin to be more open and alive, coming closer to contacting yourself. This can restart your humanistic education, which is a lifelong search for understanding about yourself and your world. The search occurs only in part at schools; it is guided only at times by teachers. It involves the whole man, including his physical, emotional, and spiritual dimensions as well as his intellectual dimension. Humanistic education can evolve into education as personal growth or education for personal growth.

I see the book as providing support in your quest for self-knowledge. The larger goal is an understanding of our world, but I am convinced that this comes about only through increasing our self-knowledge. The same would apply to communicating more openly and effectively with others. This would be one of my goals, but again I think it comes about only through first being able to communicate with oneself. I believe that self-knowledge is at the heart of social, economic, and political growth. The social, economic, and political realms deserve to be changed, but if the change is to be favorable and enduring, individuals must start acting with wisdom.

From another viewpoint, in working with this book, you can learn about social science from the inside. Concepts like personality, behavior, social systems, and interaction patterns can become alive and substantial. You can begin developing and testing out social science from an experiential base, starting with your own experiences. This would be in marked contrast to the typical social scientist who is always looking in from the outside, trying to infer what those "other people" are really doing.

But we must be realistic about this book. In and of itself it will not produce personal growth. Its only promise is the promise of yourself that you can fulfill. What the book can do is to encourage experiences which could become the *beginnings* of such growth. Perhaps it can evoke moments of creative alertness, where you experience yourself and your environment more directly. These moments can help

establish a vision that there is more to you than meets the eye, that
deep within there is something beyond your apparently individualistic
self. The critical issue becomes to increase these moments of alertness
over time, and to integrate them into your daily life. This may prepare
you to begin creating moments of awareness. As these moments of
awareness increase and become integrated into your life, you are
actively engaged in personal growth.

What I've said thus far may sound too abstract and vague. Some
of this is because I'm talking more about an approach than particular
content areas. The book is more concerned with learning how to learn
than with subject matter. The important thing is how you approach
your life.

But at the same time we don't develop an approach except through
working *in a certain way* on concrete issues or subjects. I'm interested
in educational issues in the broad sense: how we learn and how we
teach, how we learn by teaching and teach by learning, how we grow.
On one level the book tries to encourage you to be more alive and
enlivening. At another level it tries to encourage persons involved in
education to vitalize the educational process. The two levels merge.
In developing yourself as a person, you can develop yourself as a
teacher or as a student. We could then work toward an education
process which is a lifelong pursuit of understanding.

I have tried to describe some of my goals for the book. And I find
myself coming back again to the central questions. What is the book
for you? How are you using it? What will it become?

THE BOOK'S CONTEXT

Sometimes knowing the context within which a book exists helps
one to understand that book. I emphasize the word *sometimes* because this book encourages you to create your own education. Locating
this book within the fields of education could distract you. Use my
remarks about the field of education as a road map and a reminder
that your special journey has not yet been charted.

The process of personal growth is at the heart of this book's approach. That process can be seen as having two major phases—
preludes and paths. The former deal more with issues in personality
and occur at more of a psychological level; the latter deal more with
the essential core beneath personality and occur at more of a spiritual
level. In the prelude phase, a person may realize he can change, but
growth remains more a possibility than a reality. As one works with
a path, over a long period of time, growth becomes realized. A person
begins a journey into more transpersonal or spiritual realms.

THIS BOOK FOCUSES ON THE PRELUDES TO PERSONAL GROWTH AND
POINTS TOWARD PATHS OF GROWTH. It is not itself offered as a path.
Some of the more classical paths are Sufism, Yoga, and Zen Buddhism.
But this is not to say that the book deals with unimportant issues.
Before one can work on a path, he must first become alive, realize he
can change and seek something more for himself. He must seek a
path before he finds it. All this must occur during the preludes to
growth. It is not an easy phase; it demands our time and energy and
commitment. Working on the preludes to growth is essential not only
because it can lead to an involvement with a path, but also because it
can lead to simply being more open and alive in our everyday life.
And that is important.

My saying that this book focuses on the preludes of growth is one
thing; what happens in using the book can be another thing. Misunder-
standings and oversimplifications can occur. For example, after doing
the experiential exercises, some persons feel they have accomplished
all the exercises could ask of them, saying "Wow, I'm really honest
now!" Others feel they had arrived before they even began the exercise; they are "already there," appearing as wise men. I would express
only this caution: Be honest and realistic, I would almost say unassum-
ing or unpretentious. Almost all the time we are fooling ourselves,
thinking we are somewhere when it's only that we wish we were
there. Still others say that nothing is happening because they already
knew what they now see about themselves in an exercise. Really?
Know it so it can be fully accepted? Sometimes you can see something
you thought you knew, *really* for the first time. And still others are
discouraged or frustrated by the feeling, "I can never be as honest as
that!" or "How can I apply this insight in my daily life?" Realizing that
everyone has these same problems can reduce frustration and create
mutual support.

In describing this book as a way to simulate the beginnings of
growth, I am purposely contrasting it to several other techniques and
approaches. This is not an encounter or sensitivity-training or T-group
book. For example the book does not emphasize the "big bang" approach to growth, as exemplified in the weekend marathon encounter
group. The emphasis is rather on day-to-day changes, changes which
in themselves may be quite small but, as they build on each other, can
produce enduring growth. Dramatic one-shot experiences too easily
lead to nostalgic recollections rather than change. Insights generated
during these intensive periods must be worked on in daily life if they
are to affect one's life.

Nor do I see the book as *merely* enhancing your senses, or allowing
you to be more expressive. It is not an approach which emphasizes

what has been fondly called the "touchie feelies," nor is it a sanction for expressing feelings merely for the sake of transitory expressiveness. Put another way, I would hope that the book is not merely a release or at worse a titillation for "hung up" middle-class Americans. We can avoid that by continually stressing the need for change in simple day-to-day situations over time, and the need for growth in those areas of contemporary life which are most pressing and distressing.

But I want to say more than "this is not merely another sensitivity-training book" or "this is not merely a collection of techniques." I think the book has a point and a point of view. It is based on an approach to growth which I believe is valid and effective. I discuss this approach in more detail in the "Overview." I am trying to present an approach which has long-term growth potential.

The book starts at a necessary beginning, emphasizing the need to see ourselves realistically and to accept ourselves as we really are. It suggests future directions, emphasizing the movement toward the transcendent and spiritual. Throughout I've kept in mind these further, transcendent realms of human potential. I hope this has given the book, which deals primarily with the first steps toward these transcendent realms, integrity and validity. I know at least that the book's approach is not a dead end nor one which leads persons to indulge repetitively in self-analysis or expressivity. It is coming from someplace and going somewhere.

One more important point. I have not conceived the book as an alternative to therapy. Though the distinction is not always clear-cut, I would consider the need to come *up to* a level of adequate functioning as a therapeutic need. For example, if a person wants to examine intensively a particular problem which is a severe obstacle, then a therapeutic setting would be more appropriate. This book speaks to those aspects of us where we function adequately, but *only* adequately. But most of us want to function more than adequately. We are seeking something more for our lives, for others, and for our environment. Put very simply, we are seeking more aliveness, understanding, significance, harmony, and sanity.

Try to accept this book for what it is without labeling it. There may appear to be similarities with other techniques, but I think that the differences are much more important. If we must label the book's approach, perhaps you can use a term like *alertness training*. But then again, why do we need a label? If we could only use the book well, labels would soon wither. If you get a small taste of the possibility that you can change in your everyday life, then the approach can be called *yours*.

Your Approach to the Book Recreates It

EXPERIMENTAL EMPHASIS. This book will appeal to your experimental side. In using this book you will be exploring new directions in education. This is not only because of its emphasis on self-knowledge as the key to knowledge rather than learning *about* things. More generally, the book presumes that in using it, you will recreate it.

I believe that one teaches best what one is. It's hard to imagine a rigid person really teaching others about flexibility. I've tried to give this book some of the characteristics that it seeks to encourage.

INVITATION TO INVOLVEMENT. As you become involved in the book, it becomes alive. Very little can happen until it begins to happen with you. As you become an active explorer, the book as existing between two covers loses its meaning and it gains in significance as an approach to learning. I've tried to program the literal book for self-destruct.

Also, I've tried to keep the book open-ended so as to encourage your participation. For example, the book does not hang together too completely. The relationships between theory and experience, thought and action are there, but they are not *too* clear and neat. I'm more interested in raising issues than in completely covering them, in asking questions than in answering them. As you engage the book, you can move it beyond itself, recreating it as your own experience. You are beginning again to create your own education.

EXPERIENTIAL EDUCATION. Throughout the book there is an emphasis on experience-based learning. We learn about something most effectively through experiencing it and reflecting on and accepting that experience. Perspective evolves. This learning process could be symbolized this way:

At the core is your own experience.

SELF-DIRECTED LEARNING. If this book is to work, you must work with it and on it. And I can't emphasize too much the *you*. The book

assumes that you can take the major responsibility for directing your
own learning. Unless you do, learning will be short-lived. I am not
saying that we must teach ourselves everything. There are people who
have wisdom and knowledge, who can teach. But the responsibility
for learning from them must finally rest with ourselves. If the wisdom
of others is to become real for us, we must struggle with it, trying to
understand it, trying to make it our own.

Weaving This Book into Your Everyday Life

In working with the book, you may begin to understand something
about yourself; but unless you build on that understanding in simple
ways on a day-to-day basis, it withers. In that case, the book has no
real impact.

Emphasis on Self-understanding

Throughout the book, I emphasize self-understanding as the key to
growth on a personal as well as political, social, and economic level.
I'm not talking about being individualistic, where all I care about is
what's in it for me. The issue is, rather, will I honestly see myself *and*
accept what I see? An honest experience of myself truly confronts
another—it challenges him to reach an honesty with himself. Compared to this, the usual method of confrontation, where one person tells
another what he thinks of him, is misguided. For it's rare that we can
face even ourselves honestly; and that's who each of us knows best.
Encounter is essentially a matter of encountering ourselves.

Who Might Use This Book?

Anyone who's interested in the humanistic approach to education
might use this book. As you seek understanding and growth, I think
this book is for you.

But since the book contains experiential exercises, where you're
invited to do things, sometimes with others, it's important to stress
your freedom of choice. Though the book begins as *you* begin working
with it, it is essential that *YOU always choose whether and how you
want to become involved* in these exercises and their applications.
I'm not interested in a forced revelation of personal life, either in the
forced aspect or the revealing quality.

The exercises I've prepared purposely emphasize more conscious,
practical, everyday issues. They do not deal specifically with fantasy
material or psychological probing. I believe that the everyday level of

functioning is critical, especially to the process of change and growth. Also, you can more easily regulate the quality of your participation when the exercises are focused on that level. You can move within an exercise to fantasy material if you are willing and able, and at your own pace.

If you're preoccupied with trying to function *at least* adequately, attend first to that issue and don't participate in the exercises, especially when they're in the group setting. If you're not ready for an exchange which may be highly emotional, then go slowly during an exercise or excuse yourself entirely. You may feel this way on a specific day or during a particular period. Use the exercises to enhance what is *merely* adequate functioning.

If you can be honest with yourself about your state, you can trust your own judgment about when and how to participate. Certainly, the views of others can also be helpful. Others may see aspects of your behavior which slip by you—for example, a defensiveness or a rigidness or an anxiousness. Try to remember, however, that rarely is someone completely unable to do the exercises. Rather, people are more or less able to participate at different times. Put more simply, we can be more or less honest with ourselves at different times.

Operational Issues in Using the Book

THE PARTS OF THE BOOK ARE A WHOLE

I have tried to put the book together in a way which invites your participation and encourages you to recreate it. I offer the structure of the book as a guide for your own use of the book.

There are three other sections in the book. Section One, the experiential exercises, explores certain themes in humanistic education and growth—for example, encountering. Section Two is an overview of the process of personal growth. Section Three contains case studies which describe applications of this approach.

The manual is primarily operational, the exercises are experiential, the overview theoretical, and the case studies descriptive. Each section is a viewpoint on the same issue—humanistic education and growth. They can shed light on each other, and through each other toward that issue. For example, the overview can give a context and perspective to the exercises and case studies. The exercises can give you the experience which makes the overview meaningful for you. The case studies can suggest extensions of the exercises and the overview into actual educational situations.

EXPERIENTIAL EXERCISES

The exercises are offered as opportunities to experience yourself in new ways, to try out more honest ways of communicating with yourself and others. During an exercise you may become willing to risk a change. You may experience a breakthrough as you lay aside a mask of interaction. Or you may experience a less dramatic but no less real moment where you experience your usual self without the usual embellishment. In doing the exercises you can turn experience into creative alertness, and your understanding can become deeper. But the exercises themselves are not magic rituals. Unless *you realize* them as opportunities for a fresh view, you may not even experience.

How do these exercises work? But first, why should they work? They may seem artificial or superficial. They are artificial only in that we need special conditions before we risk being different. The inertia of our habitual patterns is so overpowering. Unless we take ourselves in hand, as if to say: "Stop! I want more in my life, I want to be more honest," we never dare to grow. The exercises can be opportunities where you can stop for a moment and go beyond deadening habits. The exercises are superficial only if you want them to remain at that level. They can become as significant as you allow them to be; they can tell you as much as you are willing to hear.

The emphasis is not on the exercise but on the person who participates in it. Exercises themselves are not good or bad; they are only vehicles for increasing your understanding. They work because someone creates opportunities for understanding through participating in them. An exercise which seems dull or irrelevant is a failure only if you could not meet yourself during or after it. Some of the more dramatic exercises can be unproductive if you let them distract you from creating these opportunities.

The exercises are simple to execute, yet they have potential for increasing creative alertness. This is an essential paradox. To participate in the exercises you need no elaborate equipment nor prior experience with exercises nor any particular talents. The exercises are based on common sense and deal with ordinary issues. But they deal with these issues in a special manner. The exercises involve *you*. As you act and react or try something new, you are part of what is happening and it suddenly becomes real.

Ground Rules

Before beginning the exercises, it is essential that all participants accept a fundamental assumption: each person must be responsible for himself. Others in a group can certainly help you, but only when you are willing to assume responsibility for your own behavior. Specifically, since we are each experts on ourselves, we must respect another when he says "I don't want to talk about that," or "I don't want to do that." This means that each participant must seriously and at times courageously choose whether and how he wants to become involved. As each person begins to respect his own judgment in this regard, people respect each other's judgment. Then a group is composed of individuals working together, not under the yoke of group conformity.

Individual responsibility is particularly important because the exercises can at times evoke emotional issues. For example, persons doing an exercise may experience nervousness, anxiousness, embarrassment, or fear of failure. These reactions can make participation more difficult. Also, when physical touching is involved, particularly in a nonverbal exercise, sexual reactions can intensify and confuse your participation. It is so hard in our culture to touch as a sign of understanding or caring. Unlike other cultures, we complicate sex and limit touching to a sexual signal. These emotional peaks can be opportunities for significant learning provided we are willingly exploring them rather than being forced into them. And this is where responsibility for your own behavior comes in.

It is also reassuring to realize that everyone feels nervous or anxious —more or less. With all these reactions, it's best to recognize them and accept them. Otherwise you can feel particularly unprepared for an exercise when in fact nobody is ever completely prepared.

Attitude

I've talked about the importance of an open attitude toward the exercises, of an experimental · approach. A goal might be for each person to participate in an exercise so as to see himself more honestly, to learn as much as he can, to discover as much as he can accept. Then each person is embarking on a common voyage and benefits from the presence and interest of others. This is in marked contrast to a situation where someone seeks power over others, manipulating their behavior or evaluating their experiences. If you enter into an exercise honestly, your response to it can also be honest. And you really can't want anything more than that.

Preparation

Of great importance is how you prepare for each exercise. You should come ready to work; otherwise you'll be primed to maintain the comforts of the habitual. If you must expect something, expect the unexpected rather than a particular outcome. Try to marshal your energy so that you can put something into the exercise. Too often someone says, "I just want to let it all happen," when he really means, "I want to wait to see if anything will happen to me" or "I don't want to talk about what I want to happen." Think of the flower bud growing, ready to blossom. Rather than sitting back waiting for it to happen to you, let it happen by helping to create it. Be there, as fully as possible, ready, in each exercise. At the same time, don't be tense. Be receptive to something slightly new. Maintaining this apparent paradox will give you and the exercise an aliveness.

You'll need more time than the minute before the exercise begins if you hope to create this ready and receptive state. That "minute before" is beset with its own particular nervous energy. If you know what theme will be stressed in the exercise, you might spend some of your preparation time considering that theme, posing certain questions for yourself.

Laboratory Phase

In its first phase, the exercise occurs in more of a laboratory setting, a special environment which can support your trying new behaviors. The environment is at times an ongoing group. The exercises say to you: "We are all here really for one purpose: to begin generating some understanding of ourselves and others. Let's let our defenses down somewhat and try to help each other and ourselves. We can dare to change because we will try not to evaluate each other, or criticize, or make fun of first attempts to be more open."

At other times, the environment is a place where you can be by yourself. Then the exercise says essentially the same thing: "Let your defenses down a bit so you can begin to see yourself."

The exercises can give you some discipline and incentive to change. Obviously, however, the laboratory phase of the exercise is only a temporary environment. If growth is to occur, you must transform the exercises' discipline into a self-discipline; you must begin to create your own opportunities in which you feel free to experiment.

The exercises are not magic, they will work only if you work with them. Don't rush through an exercise. Stay with situations in an exercise just a little longer than what you find comfortable and easy. When you feel at a loss as to what to say or do next, don't immediately say something to fill up space and don't quickly leave the scene of ambiguity. Stay with the uncertainty; try to get into it and come through it. Often a new level of understanding can emerge.

DOING THE EXERCISES. Keep channels of communication open so that people can discuss problems they may be having with the exercises or the group. Keep group participation flexible so that persons can miss a session or two, or leave the group if they must without stigma. This is *not* to minimize the importance of commitment to the group over time, but a safety valve is necessary. And what is most difficult, keep a sensitive lookout for signs of distress, when a person may be more defensive or overwhelmed than even he realizes. I must stress *sensitive*. Because the worst thing is to convince someone who is constructively struggling with an issue that he is overwhelmed and should leave the group. We love to label other people's problems, and too often people accept that label and actually develop the problem.

Situations do arise where a person may decide not to do a particular exercise. Respect this decision without prying for reasons or motivations. But make it explicit that the person has decided not to participate. If he is then interested in discussing his reasons, he can do so. Avoid forcing someone to either leave the group or participate against his will. Talk about a strong reaction against the exercises as it is developing; this can prevent someone from being pushed into the corner.

Keep the emphasis on your understanding, not the quality or worth of the exercise. Don't waste time analyzing whether an exercise is good or bad, or discussing whether to do an exercise or how it should be done. Instead of being negative, be positive. Change what you find unproductive. Exercises aren't a convenient way to avoid a difficult or embarrassing situation. Exercises are meant to take you to meaningful exchanges, not away from them. If your discussion is a good one, keep at it—exercises shouldn't interrupt. If you do an exercise out of boredom, at least accept that you are bored. Then use the exercise as an opportunity to become unbored—that is, alive to yourself.

INSTRUCTIONS. Often persons will read the instructions for an exercise before the session begins. Therefore, especially with the briefer and simpler instructions, it's not necessary to read them aloud immediately before doing an exercise. But some instructions should be read during the exercise, for example with "Eye to Eye," "Hand Contacts Hand," "Force toward Encounter," "Space Exchange" and "Line Up and Away." Also, reading instructions to an exercise right before it begins can add something. In either case, the instructions should be read with an intention of raising the level of the exercise. Anyone who has an interest in or feeling for the exercise can do this. It's not very inspiring to hear a reading of the written instructions in monotone.

LOGISTICS. The exercises are full. I'm assuming that persons come ready to work on the exercise and start soon after their arrival. A fifty-minute exercise will use fifty minutes well. Therefore it's necessary both to prepare for the exercise and to have a good idea of who is coming each session—the group shouldn't wait for someone who will not come.

In writing those exercises done in a group, I've assumed a group of ten to fifteen people. This is an effective size. But neither the lower or upper limit is rigid. If you want to have larger or smaller groups, you'll have to modify some of the exercise structures and instructions accordingly.

Plan your sessions so that everyone can participate in the exercise without rushing through parts. For example, in "Which Role Is You? Which Is Me?" if some persons are watching the role-playing, be sure they also have a chance to assume the roles. In "Hand to Hand" or "Force toward Encounter," don't make the interactions too brief. Each exercise writeup includes approximate times for the entire exercise and its different aspects—these can help you plan.

Throughout, keep a productive balance between experience and reflection on that experience. Leave time after an exercise for a good discussion—at least ten minutes in a fifty-minute period. Continue a discussion into the next session if issues remain alive.

DISCUSSION. Unless experience is considered and examined, much of its potential for education is lost. Through reflecting on your exercise experience, you can distill from it certain of your characteristics. You can begin to paint your portrait.

One way to reflect on your exercise experience is through a discussion with others who've done the exercise with you. It's important to leave time to share ideas with your exercise mates. Immediately after an exercise, the experience is still fresh and the discussion can be alive. This group discussion shouldn't substitute for the simpler form of reflection, namely taking time out of your "busy schedule" to consider your experience, seriously and carefully, with yourself and for yourself.

For each experiential exercise, I've discussed some of the issues which can arise during and after the exercise. My written discussion is included as a gentle guide and no more. In fact you might want to read these written discussions only after you've at least begun your own discussion. Read after your discussion, the written discussion may give you leads for further consideration; read in the midst of your discussion, it might suggest a different direction; read before the exercise, it may help in your preparation. Don't feel you have to cover all the "discussion points." Use what I've written to provoke in yourself a slightly different stance toward your own experience.

I have a few suggestions about how you might conduct your discussions. First and last, the discussion should evolve from *your own experience*. The emphasis must be on what *you* saw about *yourself*.

That's really the only person you know something about. Talk about others only as a means of allowing them to talk about themselves more easily. In hearing others talk about themselves, you begin to develop perspective on yourself. Individual problems become existential issues.

It is helpful to concentrate on common-sense observations rather than inferences and assumptions. Be simple about yourself, and when you talk about others, continue to be simple. Try to make observations that are descriptive rather than evaluative. For example, you might talk about how a person presents himself, what posture and facial expression he adopts. Or, you might describe how a person makes you feel. Instead of you telling another why he is doing something, tell him how he affects you. Then each person may better explain his own behavior. You can encourage another to examine his own motivations if you don't leap to explain him away. By using common-sense descriptions, you can develop a language with a simple quality, and with this you can communicate. The goal would be to exchange facts about yourself rather than figments of your imagination. Before you evaluate someone else, pause and consider that what we criticize in someone else is usually what we don't like about ourselves.

You can help the discussion become alive by considering both the process and content levels. On the process level, try to keep the discussion simple and direct. Insist that people try to talk first about themselves, that they be specific and emphasize common sense. On the content level, you can get suggestions from my written discussion about themes or situations which might be raised in your exercise. This written discussion presents the experiences of many persons with the particular exercise.

Finally, remember there is a difference between discussing your experiences and the experiences themselves. During an experience people sometimes become so concerned with how they will describe their experience that they stop experiencing; instead they merely develop a set of descriptive words and phrases. This is unnecessary. Worrying "Will I remember what happened?" is an excellent way to stop anything from happening. You'll find that the important aspects of an experience will stay with you. You may still have trouble finding words to describe an experience, but that is a problem of ineffability, not memory.

Nonverbal Emphasis

Try to remain as nonverbal as possible while doing an exercise, especially during the laboratory phase. I say this without being too concerned that you will be overly nonverbal. The forces toward verbalizing are strong, almost overwhelming. We seem compelled at least to explain and usually to analyze (away) our experiences. Doing exercises without talking can deepen the exercise experience. The word *nonverbal* is unfortunate; I really mean *beyond words*. Certainly the nonverbal taps a deeper level of existence than the verbal mode, whether you call it mythic or archetypal or unconscious.[1]

You can do the laboratory phase of exercises such as "Eye to Eye," "Hand to Hand," "I Am Me," "Force toward Encounter," "Who Can See?" "Group Sculpture," "Group Collage," "Space Exchange," and "Line Up" without talking. With the other exercises, by attending to nonverbal dimensions and cues—gesture, posture, expressions, body tonus—you can see a lot more. For example, be alert to how your body tells you that you are tense before you "know" it. Then during the discussion, words can be used to symbolize experiences you've had. Instead of being the whole iceberg, words can be where they belong —on the visible tip.

While the nonverbal approach can lead to a more meaningful level beneath and beyond words, it can also result in just the opposite. I have often seen people hide behind the aura of silence, masking their superficiality or avoiding real communication. At other times, people engage in inferior talk, using gestures or facial expressions to develop a sign language. Then again, the nonverbal approach can complicate or confuse communication rather than deepen it. While a person is silent, his thoughts or emotions often accelerate unproductively. This sometimes occurs when touching brings a unidimensional and limiting sexual quality to an interaction. All of which suggests that simply not talking doesn't automatically deepen an experience. Like everything else we've been discussing, silence needs to be worked with.

Individuals/Groups

Some exercises are for a person alone, others for persons within a group. I suggest working in both settings if possible. If you work with a group, try to have it be a continuing group. As the group has common experiences, it gains in strength. Whether the exercise is done alone or in a group, the emphasis is on each person seeing himself as he really is.

Applications

I hope that the exercises are not merely "fun and games" or ways to "turning people on." It is relatively easy to "turn people on." It is much harder to stimulate an educational experience. If the exercises

[1] See discussions of the nonverbal realm by Ernest Schachtel, *Metamorphosis,* Basic Books, Inc., Publishers, New York, 1959. See especially Chap. 12, pp. 279–322. Also Edmund Carpenter and Marshall McLuhan (eds.), *Explorations in Communications,* Beacon Press, Boston, 1960.

are to be educational, they must become part of your life rather than a license to be different for a brief period.

You have to intentionally stress the application of exercises in daily life. People are reluctant to take that important step of transforming a laboratory experiment into a life situation. Being such a real step, it's not easy or comfortable.

Groups should meet outside of regular meeting times and places. As group members see each other going about their ordinary life affairs, the need to apply an exercise can become clearer. For then it becomes obvious that each person spends almost all his time in ordinary day-to-day situations, not in special groups.

There are certain things you might keep in mind as you seek to extend these exercises into everyday opportunities. Before you apply an exercise, first develop a relationship with the exercise. See what it lets you learn, consider how you use it. You have a chance to develop this relationship in the special environment of the laboratory phase. After you have some idea of what the exercise means for you, then apply it and extend it. As it enters the mainstream of your life, the true depth of your learning can be revealed.

It's always very important to consider your own motivation. Why are you doing this? In applying an exercise, you're not setting up a psychology experiment in which people in the outside world are your subjects. You are being experimental, that is, innovative, and trying to learn something, perhaps by working with others. If others are involved in your application, you should be able to talk with them afterwards and gain the benefit of their impressions. This is not always practical or desirable, but your attitude in making the application should never rule out that possibility.

It is counterproductive for your own growth to charge blindly into the world, forcing your exercises on your environment and on other people. For example, I wonder where growth is when you unilaterally wrench encounter from another. It's important to realize not only where you are but where others are. When "love" is forced on someone, it ceases to be love: it becomes a vehicle for power and manipulation. Try to be clear about what you want and need, and try to be sensitive to what others want and need. If you can clarify your motivations, you can even purify them.

Recreate the exercises. Work on them, build from them. Emphasize the substance of the exercise, not its form; the principles involved, not the literal details. Apply with imagination, in an organic way. You can't just import an exercise from the laboratory to the outside world. Merely repeating some of the exercises might make others unnecessarily uptight or hostile. Wearing a blindfold or looking and touching in unusual ways can be accepted in the laboratory phase of an exercise; it can put people off when done in the street. And the object is to learn, enlisting the help of others; not to be diverted and constantly harassed by them.

At the start, create opportunities in supportive environments. Pick a situation where you don't have to maintain a certain image. As an example, let's consider someone who tends to be shy and wants to see himself more fully by expressing and accepting his outgoing side. If your boss needs to have you as a shy person, don't try to be outgoing —at least at first—when working with him. Seek a situation where others will allow you to be different without being disappointed or critical or surprised. Sometimes it's best to try new behaviors with strangers, since they usually don't know what to expect from you and therefore don't demand that you be a certain way. As you begin to accept your usually unexpressed side, you can try expressing it with a broader range of people and in a greater variety of settings. Then you are becoming more yourself.

The application of an exercise may appear less dramatic than when you first worked with the exercise in the laboratory phase. This is deceptive. It is always harder to change where it really matters, in your day-to-day activities. These changes are simple and substantial, and that is very dramatic.

Finally, you should think carefully about what you want to learn, where you need to grow. Don't just think of an exercise to apply. First consider your life, letting the issues of importance emerge. Create opportunities so you can deal more honestly with what is important for you.

The less these exercises are integrated with what you do every day, the less meaningful they become. They have to be reshaped and re-conceived so that they are at home in the ongoing situations of your life. You have to work with the material of your daily life and bring that material into focus through an exercise. You create your own exercises. But now I'm not talking about exercises which are irrelevant and unimportant breaks in your day. Rather, I'm talking about an attitude, an approach to your life. Throughout your day, you try and risk being more yourself. You intentionally create opportunities to see yourself more honestly. This is pointing toward life as an exercise in self-discovery.

OVERVIEW

The "Overview" presents the theoretical foundation for the book's approach. It is an essay which is in part a theory of personal growth, in part a set of assumptions about growing. It discusses both the book's primary and present focus and the future directions toward which it can point. With this essay, I've tried to place the book in perspective. I feel this is particularly important for the experiential exercises. Without some perspective, it is hard to move through and beyond the exercises toward real growth.

Case Studies

The "Case Studies" report on applications of humanistic education. They describe attempts or programs or institutions in which growth is occurring. The case studies are in process in that they emphasize unsettled issues. They are experimental in that they emphasize research done to discover things rather than to justify a position. Finally, they are practical in that they emphasize the nature and characteristics of a growth environment.

I won't describe the "Overview" or the "Case Studies" at length because their format is more familiar. But it would be unfortunate if the more familiar form led to a too-familiar response. I've tried to make both sections suggestive. If you approach them actively, questioning and considering, they can be just that. Try to avoid the deadening-end of the passive reader.

Understructure

The book is not highly structured. I've tried to make the book's structure flexible so that you can create your own structure. But also, I have a clear and strong aim. I've had experiences where a course I taught or a group I ran wandered in confusion not because it lacked structure but because it lacked an aim. I have tried to make my aim clear and I don't feel it will limit you. Rather, it will give you something to work on. Put simply, I expect you will use the book to see yourself more honestly. This is where I stand. As you develop your own aims, you generate self-discipline. This self-discipline is what gives freedom substance; without it, freedom is merely chaos.

The deemphasis on a formal structure has certain implications. Self-directed learning can emerge more forcefully. So can frustration and confusion—"What are we doing?" "What should we be doing?" But this is an inevitable relationship. Try to work with the confusion, realizing it primarily as a phase of the self-directed process.

Who's the Leader? We All Are

Many of the experiential exercises in their laboratory phase occur in group settings. In most every group, leadership is an issue. There might be one leader, several leaders, or a series of leaders at different times in a group's history. In the usual educational setting, the leadership issue is more or less resolved. *More or less* is a helpful term these days when leadership is being redefined even in that most clearly resolved of situations, the military enterprise. But again, in the usual classroom, leadership resides more in the teacher than in the student. And from this more power and authority is usually placed in the teacher's hands than in the student's.

This book offers a very different educational model, intentionally challenging our usual assumptions. A goal of this book is to encourage self-directed learning. You must be the final judge of whether you are learning: it is *your* experience that is at the core; it is the application of exercises in *your* life that is critical; it is what happens in *your* day-to-day living that is the ultimate criterion of change. The book's emphasis on an instrumented approach to learning can make us all "experts." I purposely selected experiential exercises which are simple to do and which require no particular expertise. They ask only that you make a serious effort and try to be open to your new experiences.

We're reexamining the balance of responsibility, expertise, and power which normally characterizes the teacher-student relationship. And it's not easy to share either responsibility, expertise, or power. But if you're basically not qualified to run exercises for an experiential group, that's probably the last thing you want to do—at least it should be. You have a straightforward and valuable option. Encourage each person to develop his power for directing his own learning, to accept responsibility for this self-direction, and to realize his reservoirs of expertise; for each person knows how to lead himself.

Some of the dilemmas in using this book are now more explicit. Who is the teacher? Who is the leader? But I would not ask these questions for too long. I think it is more productive to ask: "How can we together create an environment for learning and growth?" "How can we in learning teach each other?"

A first step is to discuss your questions, confusions, and ideas about leadership; to share them with each other, *including* the traditional leader. These questions will probably resurface continually, and they can become an unproductive force when they are not made explicit.

Despite all the good reasons for shifting the balance of responsibility, expertise, and power, it is never easy. It is always hard for the "haves" and "have nots" to agree to stand on a more equal footing. In working on this exchange, you might try a role-playing exercise.[2] Discuss the leadership dilemma in self-directed learning with each

---

[2] For a fuller discussion of role-playing, see the exercise "Which Role Is You? Which Is Me?" pp. 93–102.

other. In the discussion, have a student assume the role of the teacher and the teacher the role of a student. You can begin to experience the difficult process of modifying your role. This can also help to clarify what each side must give up in order to become partners in learning. As you proceed collaboratively, what you all gain will become apparent.

I have some specific suggestions about the group in which the experiential exercises are done. I don't think it needs a leader as we usually conceive of him. An exception *might* be if there is someone who has *extensive* experience and talent in the area of group processes, who's led groups which focused on self-examination and interpersonal issues.[3] I distinguish this from leading the more typical seminar or discussion group. And I emphatically distinguish this from participating in several encounter or sensitivity groups.

Unless you are clearly a skilled leader of group processes, don't take on a formal leadership role and don't find yourself in that role. A teacher who is distant or silent or nondirecting can remain a very powerful leader. Attitude is the key, not style of interaction. Also, if you have a "hidden agenda"—an idea of what the group should do which you don't make explicit—you'll tug and pull, usually covertly, to make the group move in a certain direction. Unless you divest yourself of this agenda or, more practically, make it explicit (as should all group participants), you're again a traditional leader.

The teacher too easily assumes he should lead his students regardless of the situation they are in. But it's always risky to lead someone to a place you have not been, especially when that place deals with personal experience rather than academic information. If you are a good teacher, teach well—don't lead a sensitivity group.

I feel strongly about this question of leadership. A leader, either formally designated or informally recognized, exerts a great influence on his group. And he influences at times *regardless* of his talent or experience. A group too often looks to the leader to establish limits, to tell them when they are going too fast or too deeply into an issue. If the leader is not experienced and sensitive, he cannot fulfill this responsibility and a group can get into trouble.

A good leader is good, a not-so-good one is awful. Since many people with varied experience and sensitivity will be using this book, the risks of traditional leadership are too great. I would instead put my trust in each of you to lead yourselves, to direct your own learning. We could call this model the self-directed group.

---

[3] For example, someone who has led groups for National Training Laboratories (N.T.L.) of Washington, D.C.

Self-directed Groups

I like the term *self-directed group* better than, for example, *leader-less group*. In fact, the group should have as many leaders as there are members—but leaders of themselves. A self-directed group has no one person who continues as a leader, whether formally designated or informally recognized. If the group is to be effective, each member must assume responsibility for directing his own learning and develop his own commitment to the group. Members cannot fall back on one person whose role is always to keep the group going or keep it out of trouble.

I've come to this particular group format for running the exercises because I'm convinced that people can direct their own learning *if* they choose to, and that this process of self-direction stimulates personal growth.[4] Moreover, self-directed groups seem to be as effective as leader-led groups.[5]

There are also practical reasons for using this model: many persons want to participate in experiential groups and few persons are qualified to lead them. Self-directed groups represent a way of creatively educating large numbers of persons.

In this self-directed model, the book and in particular the exercises become resources that the group draws upon. The exercises can function as a leader. And certainly individuals make strong contributions to others, to the group. They initiate a direction, change an emphasis. They lead. But there is no office of leadership they permanently occupy. One likely time for such contributions is in the group's discussion of an exercise. Someone may realize the discussion is getting very abstract, and he may remind the group to be more simple and specific. Someone else may remember something from the book's discussion and add a new perspective on the group's discussion.

There are also certain practical, administrative matters which must be accomplished. These can be performed by any one of you, and I would suggest that the responsibility rotate. For example, someone might explain the ground rules of a particular exercise; and, with certain exercises, (re)read the instructions. Persons should also consider

---

[4] Betty Berzon and Lawrence N. Solomon, "The Self-directed Therapeutic Group: Three Studies," *Journal of Counseling Psychology*, Vol. 13, pp. 491–497, 1966.

[5] See evidence presented in Ralph Schwitzgabel and David Kolb, "Self-Directed Behavior Change," *Behavior Change*, McGraw-Hill Book Company, New York, 1972; also evidence in Richard Katz, *The Self-Assessment Workshop: Research Report*, Human Development Foundation, Cambridge, Mass., 1970. My research report, and a training manual for a self-assessment workshop are available from me.

possible sequences in which exercises can be used. Someone must also consider the spaces needed for particular exercises and other preparations which may be necessary.

The way self-directed groups often proceed creates additional leadership dilemmas. They appear to move more slowly than groups with leaders. Their direction can be more confused and their progress more sporadic. Self-directed groups can have more ups and downs, low points following high points. They can get more involuted in their own self-analysis. When they try to live up to a certain image of what a group should be, they begin to lose their self-directed quality. They are now "led" by this image. Often these self-directed groups have less continuity from week to week, and are more likely to dissolve completely. At times their members will wait to see what happens; and that's *all* that happens.

So the temptation to intercede is great. It seems so easy to step right in and lead the self-directed group into a "productive" direction. But if you're traditionally the leader, be patient. Because when something *is* happening in these groups, it can be quite substantial, at times more so than with a leader-led group. This can be true even when what is happening is apparently inefficient or confused. It is much harder but more valid for someone to forge his own identity than to be told who he is to be; the same holds for a self-directed group as it gropes towards some group identity. Only when it seems a group is about to end should a traditional leader consider active intervention. Then he might use his understanding and traditional power to support a group, giving it a lift so that it could continue.

Here are some practical suggestions for some of the problems in self-directed groups. They often sputter and stall. By doing an engaging exercise, especially in one of its earlier meetings, a group can generate enough energy to get off the ground and continue. Examples of such an exercise would be "Force toward Encounter" or "Who Can See?" Each is both psychologically and physically engaging.

Commitment to the exercises and the group is another problem. At times it may seem as if the group has to start from scratch each meeting. This is very much the natural phenomenon of inertia as it occurs in interpersonal relations. To overcome this force, people could work on an exercise, especially its application, in between meetings. With a break in meetings, e.g., with a vacation, pay special attention to this continuous work with the exercises. In the meeting before the break, prepare to do something with the exercises during the break. Again, applications are very appropriate here. And set up specific things to do on the return, which can build on what was done during the break.

Groups often spend considerable time trying to figure out their own identity. "What kind of a group are we?" "We're not doing what we did in my other group." "We're not as good (or bad) as the encounter group I was in." Discussing these questions can be valuable, particularly when the group realizes that in forging its own identity, it is not a good (or bad) imitation of other groups. Obsessing over these questions becomes valueless. When the discussion is going faster and faster in circles, when the atmosphere is of immobilizing introspection, do an exercise. Then, instead of merely thinking about what to do, you've done something to think about. Doing something can make an overly introspective group work.

CARING ATTITUDE. If you are accustomed to being the teacher, you may wonder: "Now where does all this leave me?" One thing may not be clear. Nobody is losing a job. Jobs are being redefined, becoming more fluid, maybe to the point of becoming less jobs and more attitudes toward learning. You can be released from job stereotypes like the "powerful expert," which may give satisfaction but will, in the long run, impede learning.

There is something that must be stressed here. It is terribly important. In my experience there is a function which needs to be fulfilled for self-directed groups. I would call it the "caring attitude." Participants must care about what is happening in the group and try to be sure it is an educational experience. They must continue to be concerned that nothing destructive happens, that nobody is forced into a situation against his will, that a discussion does not become more personal than people want. In short, that each person always chooses whether and how he wants to become involved in the exercises and their applications.

There is a responsibility to encourage others to be caring and honest and not to manipulate themselves or others. This is not a responsibility to lead or run the exercises. One who has this caring attitude could be the teacher—and should be. And I expect others would also have this attitude; again, they should. More persons than the teacher must care.

THE CARING ATTITUDE IN AN INSTITUTIONAL SETTING. Consider two types of self-directed groups: one, the women's liberation consciousness-raising group, and the other a group which meets officially as a course or part of a course in a university. In the case of the women's group, different members at different times have a caring attitude. But the women join voluntarily and meet voluntarily to discuss what they wish. Also, the group is not part of any hierarchy or institution. Therefore no one need be *legally* responsible for the group. With the self-directed group functioning as part of a university course or any other formal institution, the situation is usually different. Again, it is essential that members at different times have a caring attitude. But also, legal responsibility now becomes an issue.

In my experience with self-directed groups within an institution, such as the university, a particular way has emerged of meeting the need for both the caring attitude and legal responsibility. This is *only one possible alternative*—its strength is in facing the legal issue, its weakness is in terms of group dynamics and collaborative learning.

First, I've stressed that each member of the group must have a caring attitude. Secondly, someone on the teaching faculty also becomes a "caring observer" of a particular group and is legally responsible for its conduct. This caring observer is not a *regular* member of the group nor an *active* participant. But it's *never* so simple or so clear-cut.

The caring observer might try to clarify a discussion point or enhance a discussion by suggesting persons talk more simply, specifically, and concretely about themselves. These kinds of inputs should decrease as the group develops over time. And what is most difficult, he tries to encourage a caring, honest atmosphere. This is most subtle because the quality of self-direction is easily overwhelmed. Even giving someone only legal responsibility can impart too much authority to him. The caring observer must continually back off from being a traditional leader. It is really when someone threatens another's right to privacy, when someone is unwillingly overwhelmed, when honesty is under attack, that the observer can step in. And if the group is working well, he will not have to, because a member of the group will rise to the occasion.

But there are fundamental paradoxes in this caring observer function. Logically one cannot be both "in" and "out" of the group, perhaps not even sequentially. Psychologically, one could rise above that paradox, but that is very difficult. Observers find it difficult being in a situation where everyone is doing something. It's hard to stay out of the way. They usually feel a desire to participate more in the group. Taking on logistical tasks can help, a little; at least you're doing something.

Observers prefer to be definitely "in"—in some cases definitely "out." The group usually feels the same way. Both find it hard to keep the observer's role flexible. Theoretically, the observer is in enough to offer comments but out enough so as not to be too involved. At times the group feels that since the observer is not a member of the group, he shouldn't see what goes on in the group. "We give of ourselves, and you don't reciprocate." A group can suddenly become impersonal and reticent when the observer comes in. When the observer becomes a participant, the group often relaxes and accelerates its movement.

Being an observer also presents obstacles to the collaborative approach to learning stressed throughout the book. You're on the outside, and it's too easy to become an authority figure or the clinician judging "those persons" you're observing. And how about experiential education? Can anyone know what's happening in a group without being a member of it? Isn't the outsider always limited to "looking in"?

In the midst of these difficulties there are some sources of strength to draw upon. The observer himself should be engaged in self-development. Though he may not do the specific exercise the group does, he should at least do exercises on his own. A bond is created between him and the group; they are travelers on the same journey. Being a caring observer is not a passive function. It requires intense and sensitive attention to what's happening in the group. There is more than enough to do. Finally an observer—a good observer—can provide the group with perspectives that the members may lack.

Who could be such an observer? Interpersonal sensitivity is needed; common-sense sensitivity, which is not dependent on special training in running groups. The observer must continually question his motives, consider his inputs, and ponder the paradoxes of his function, for they will not disappear. With the guidelines of the exercises, especially the discussion sections, such an observer can be helpful.

Again, this model of the caring observer was developed to meet certain institutional and legal constraints. The model is a compromise. It is not even that practical; observers cannot really be "in" and "out" —they usually become participants. And I would say that if you feel it is right and important to participate more, then follow your judgment.

If institutional considerations are not so restricting, there are other alternatives which better facilitate group development and collaborative learning. My first choice is completely self-directed groups. Such groups, using the book as resource material, are a much simpler model with striking implications for personal and social change. The teacher or teaching assistant could be a participant in these groups. It is, of course, very hard to give up authority and be an equal, even if you want to. Students are slow to allow a teacher to be a participant.

When there is someone especially qualified in group process and leading groups, he can be available to the self-directed groups for occasional advice or consultation. But in meeting any issue or crisis, the group must rely first on itself, and only when its exhausted its own internal resources should it turn to the consultant. And the "consultant" can't be one who is always telling you what to do and "helping" you implement it—no matter how gently or implicitly. We don't need a "leader" in still another disguise.

Self-directed groups are only one model for doing the exercises. As you work with this book, what model will you develop? Let me know of your attempts and discoveries. The challenge seems clear to me. Can each of you be a student in that you become aware of something; can each of you be a teacher in that you let someone become aware? Can you direct your own learning? Can you be open about the paradoxes in this approach to education and work on them together? Reflecting upon my own experience, I believe that if you want to, you can.

Developing a University-type Course

Note: In this part of the manual, I will at times be talking more directly to the teacher or leader.

I believe this book is relevant to the social sciences and education taught at either the introductory or advanced level. The book brings a humanistic approach to these fields of study, emphasizing human growth and potential. Through the exercises in particular, the book brings an experiential approach to these fields, emphasizing involvement and the personal significance of the subject matter. And since these two emphases are on the frontier of educational innovation, the book invites you to be more experimental with your teachings. I find more and more educators agreeing that a humanistic and experiential approach, used by innovating teachers and students, enhances learning and self-discovery. And so in terms of learning-teaching, I think the book can make a special contribution. It can help bring life to a course.

The book also has characteristics which make it especially suited for specific courses. I hesitate to divide learning into courses, because I think an inter- or trans-disciplinary attitude respects the process of learning more. But let me suggest some of these more specific tie-ins:

EDUCATION (TEACHER TRAINING, EDUCATIONAL PSYCHOLOGY). The book is a course in self-directed learning. As we are more and more overwhelmed by the number of persons seeking quality education, this self-directed approach becomes invaluable. This approach is also an essential component of any learning situation. As a prospective teacher works with this book, developing his own capacity for self-direction, he learns how to teach others to direct their own learning. The book can also be used in this teaching effort. Throughout it, there is an emphasis on communication and helping. And I think that is what the teaching-learning process is about. Finally the case studies describe programs in humanistic education and discuss how they can be established and improved.

PSYCHOLOGY (SOCIAL, PERSONALITY, CLINICAL, COUNSELING). The book focuses on the process of personal growth. Psychology is shifting away from considering man as only a reactive being with bad intentions. There are certainly these aspects to every man, but we must now seriously consider his potential for growth. The approaches of humanistic and transpersonal psychology are seeking to sharpen this new focus. The book views the processes of human development, such as interpersonal perception, from the perspective of personal growth. It discusses, for example, how perception erects barriers between people, or maintains a relationship, or leads to a communication breakthrough. The book, and especially the exercises, is also an actual experience in learning about oneself and working with others and trying to help them. This is especially important training for those involved in field- or clinically-oriented courses.

INPUTS FOR A SOCIAL SCIENCE COURSE. *Sociology emphasis:* The book explores the relationship between individual and society. For example, it considers how other persons encourage or impede one's own learning and growth. Also, it examines the effects of larger and more complex social situations. The emphasis here is on everyday situations in one's daily life. There is an effort to delineate situations which are especially growth-fostering, both for the society and for the individual. The book has a specific emphasis on themes such as group processes, interaction patterns, roles, presentation of self, interpersonal perception, and encounter.

Cultural anthropology emphasis: The book tries to develop the concept of an environment which facilitates human growth. The self-directed groups are treated as microcultures which develop their own special norms about relationships and contact. And so each person studies a culture by living in it. As groups relate to each other, cross-cultural issues become highlighted. When the history of a group is relatively unique, problems in the transmission of values become apparent. There is a focus on how the individual relates to his environment, how he is socialized, when he becomes alienated, and whether he can grow beyond his immediate setting. Throughout the book there is an emphasis on working in field settings. By developing skills such as listening and the reading of nonverbal cues, the book can help one understand what is happening in the field, so he doesn't barge in, turning people off. The case studies are written from an ethnographic point of view.

39

Manual

39

COMMUNITY WORKSHOPS, INDIVIDUAL USE. The book also can be used in training programs and workshops dealing with a variety of issues. I've used it effectively in adult education groups, cross-cultural workshops, communication sessions, and drug programs.

For community groups, the book can suggest a format or provide inputs for ongoing groups. For individuals, it can suggest ways of beginning the process of personal growth.

Setting Up a Course

I want to consider some ways this book can be used in a university-type course. I'll be brief because I respect the challenge involved in creating your own course.

The book could be the basis of an entire experienced-based course. There are fourteen different experiential exercises. Elsewhere I've suggested various sequences in which they can be used (see pp. 5–6). Each of these exercises takes at least one fifty-minute class session, and many of them can take two or more class sessions. Though all the exercises are now written up for one fifty-minute session, let me describe other ways they can be used. With some exercises, the experiential part and some discussion could occur in one session, the discussion continuing in the next session (e.g., "Eye to Eye," "Hand Contacts Hand," "Presenting"). With other exercises, the experiential part could take at least one whole session, with the discussion occurring in a second session (e.g., "Listening," "Which Role Is You? Which Is Me?," "Human Sculpture," and "Line Up and Away"). With still others, the experiential part could occur over two or more sessions, with the discussion again taking at least one session (e.g., "Force toward Encounter," "Who Can See?" "Group Collage," and "Space Exchange"). These experiential sessions would not have to occur during one two- or three-hour period. Finally, there are exercises which can be done at home or in the field and which could be discussed for at least a session (e.g., "I Am Me," "Mirror Talk"). And so there is more than enough material for an experiential course. Also, as the course proceeds, participants should begin developing their own exercises and having more discussions on topics of special interest.

There are other course structures possible. You could use the book as an aspect of your course. For example, you can have it as the basis of an ongoing experiential section, discussion group, or field component. You could also supplement lectures with particular exercises. For example, a discussion on role theory could become uniquely alive when accompanied by the exercise "Which Role Is You? Which Is Me?" Then the lecture can relate directly to something in each persons' recent experience. Or supplement your discussion of social space and territories with the "Space Exchange" exercise. Or supplement your discussion of therapy and counseling with the exercise "Who Can See?" or your discussion of creativity with the "Group Collage" exercise. I could go on, but I want to leave for you the excitement of making these educational combinations. In the introduction to each exercise, I suggest themes which it touches upon.

When you use the book as a source of inputs into a larger academic course, the introduction of experiential exercises requires sensitive timing. Don't just throw in an exercise. Consider why you are using it and what you hope to accomplish with it. For example, with the introduction of new material, certain exercises can help persons be more relaxed and open, which may allow them to approach the new material more effectively. Other exercises can work to eliminate distracting influences, such as daydreaming, boredom, restlessness, and tension. In a general sense, motivation can be deepened since the exercises increase involvement with and personal relevance of material. And through the exercises, feelings can become part of the learning process rather than being ignored or denied.

Self-directed Groups

Whatever way you use the book in your course, you'll probably be using groups for running some of the exercises. I've already described the value of self-directed groups. Now let me deal with the mechanics of getting these groups started, and keeping them going as educational environments.

Before the class divides up into groups, I would suggest that everyone read the manual, especially the section on leadership and self-directed groups (pp. 29–37), and look over some of the exercises. Then set up groups of approximately fifteen persons. I usually do this randomly, though I try to have a balance between males and females and try to avoid small cliques of friends within the larger group. You'll need a room for each group, preferably with movable chairs. Often you'll need a clear space in which the group can work or room for them to sit around in a circle. A larger room is appropriate for several groups provided they do not interfere with each other's talking or movements. Any special space requirements are discussed for each exercise.

Make clear at the start what the manual stresses—these are self-directed groups, they are not a substitute for therapy, participation at any time must remain voluntary, etc. You could be the "caring observer" for one or more groups. I've already described the nature and function—and difficulties—of that role (see pp. 34–37). You can go from group to group, being responsible for two or three groups, or you may remain in one. Moving physically from group to group may make the difficult role of caring observer somewhat easier. A teaching assistant could also be a caring observer, as could one of the students in the group. Whenever full members of the group assume the role, it should rotate from member to member to avoid the informal investing of leadership in one person.

The groups, of course, have the book and its exercises as a guide. Nevertheless, you should consider any hesitancies you have about self-directed groups. I hope that my description of why I choose them as the model for using this book will be helpful.

UNIVERSITY CONTEXT

Certainly there are many uses for this book in a university-type course. But don't be too eager or too idealistic. Consider for a moment the setting into which you will plunge.

Schools focus on content, the learning of information; with this book, you'll also be emphasizing process learning and personal relevance. Furthermore, in contrast to the school's focus on intellectual learning and the verbal mode, you'll be stressing education for the whole man, including his psychological, emotional, and physical development, as well as his intellectual development. Also, you'll be working with nonverbal experience and communication. You may be greeted with surprise and dismay when your class doesn't sit in chairs in rows.

Traditionally, you can describe an academic course to someone— we meet in this room, hear lectures about these topics, read these books, and get examined on these questions. But this book encourages you to expand the definition of a course by considering what each of us experiences and what we seek to learn. More than that, it encourages you to go beyond the classroom and course—into daily life. As students work on exercises in their everyday lives, the course is transformed into an attitude, a way of approaching things. And that is what education really tries to do.

The use of self-directed groups will not make it easier to write a neat little catalog description of your course. "Self-directed groups? But without a leader how can we tell what's happening? When the teacher lectures, the students take notes, and then, when they take an exam and pass, they've learned something. Right?" Even if that's a correct assumption, I would question the depth or significance of that learning. With self-directed learning, it seems less clear who learns what, *except* to the person himself. Each person knows what he's done.

As long as a teacher clearly states his aims, he can encourage self-discipline in his students. This self-discipline can make a flexible structure a source of freedom.

If you do emphasize experiential learning and groups, how can you handle the large number of students who would want to take your course? Large numbers of students often seek courses which emphasize experiential learning—whether it be fieldwork or groups. The model of self-directed groups is one answer to this dilemma. Research suggests they are not only effective but also reliable. What holds us back is our prejudice that groups must be led and individuals must be taught.

But how will you grade these experiential inputs? The university registrar may want to know, and so may the graduate schools. I think we must move away from being evaluated by others on a linear scale and toward a process of self-assessment, where each of us can truly take stock of himself as an individual. Can you evaluate accurately someone else's self-development? We all have opinions about how others are doing, but often they are just that, opinions.

There are many sources of information about work done with this book: self-assessment, peer comments, teacher-student conferences. Certainly there is much to consider. I have asked students to write papers describing what an exercise meant to them and in particular how they applied it. In reading these papers, I look to see if the person makes a serious effort to understand his experience and to apply it. I don't rank persons along some absolute scale of understanding or effectiveness. I look for a willingness to examine issues and explore their consequences rather than some absolute degree of growth or openness. And I hope that each person can increase his understanding of himself and his environment. Having people in the group read each other's papers and comment on them can be quite helpful for both the individual and the group. Also, it is very informative for persons in the "outside world" who were involved in a student's application of an exercise to comment on his writeup of that application. I have also asked students to write more reflective and theoretical papers on topics stimulated by their experiences.

But much of what happens in working with this book happens some time after the course is over. Many times, students tell me that the effect of the course increases later—as they begin to understand what before confused or frustrated them. How do you consider this "delayed" learning? How do you grade that?

All this discussion of how inadequacies in schools can be transformed into opportunities for real learning could make you feel like Don Quixote. It's easy to overstate the differences between the approach of this book and the approach of the typical school. And if you're a defender of the faith—whether the faith be "experiential education" or "education for personal growth"—I'd be more than leery. Try to bring the life released by this book into your course, if you want to or hope to. But above all, teach and learn honestly. That's all I can expect of myself and, of course, only rarely can I be that way.

Section One:

Photograph by the author

Experiential Exercises

*Y*OU may discover that this is not a book. I hope so. I hope you transform this book into your own experience. If you must expect something, try to expect the unexpected. The book assumes that you can direct your own learning and growth; that your experience is at the core of your understanding. Watch a three-year-old in action; it's startling! It's hard to believe that we all once had the vitality to venture into life and to live deeply. If we could begin again to learn and live that way, it would be enlivening. Then this book could become your invitation to truly experience yourself and your world. The understanding which could result is real.

Now this probably sounds idealistic, perhaps presumptuous. And you may be wondering what you're getting into. But I hope that, in working with this book, you go beyond it and come to yourself. I hope the book encourages moments when you experience yourself, others, and your world more directly and more openly. At times such moments can lead to increased understanding and wise actions. I hope you can experience such moments in your everyday life, and, by building on them over time, move toward a process of personal growth.

But these are *my* hopes. And what matters is *you*. Your own experience is the touchstone for your development; so is it also the core of this book. And *you*, in the final analysis, must interpret its lessons. One of the first ways in which you can begin to work with this book is by participating in the experiential exercises. You may not be sure what to do or why; at first, you may be confused. But real learning never follows an easy formula. It grows from inside you and you must work, removing many obstacles, to release it. Confusion can become challenge. As you develop more clarity about what you're doing, you can begin to express your own hopes more clearly.

By reflecting upon your experiences and considering them, you can generate understanding. Other sections in the book, such as the exercise discussions and the essays, can help in this process of reflection. You may find yourself going continually back and forth between experience and reflection. I hope so. You may also find that it is not always clear what belongs where in this book, how the parts relate to each other. Again, I hope so. I have tried to present the book in a way which leaves it open for your recreation.

STOP! BEFORE WE TALK TOO MUCH, LET'S DO WHAT WE SAY!

Try the experiential exercises in the first chapter.

Prepare yourself for the exercises. Be open to them, willing to accept the experiences they stimulate, because the experiences are you. Have an experimental attitude; try things out, be willing to learn something new. Get involved in the exercise. Participate without analysis, and especially without evaluating what you or others are doing, how you or others may appear. An experience is so easily analyzed away.

Try to keep your motivations clear and pure. Use the exercises to learn about—not to manipulate—yourself, others, and the world. If you seek in the exercises opportunities for growth, then you give the exercises a better chance to work.

And most important, let us agree that you have freedom in regard to these exercises. Just as you are free to do them, you must remain free not to do them. You must decide the level and quality of your participation in the exercises: how open you will be, how much you will accept.

Now to Begin

NOW to begin. . . . Begin what? This chapter reintroduces us to the *experience* of creating our own education.

Beginning to grow. We are always growing, both creating and destroying. But I am now talking about growth in certain directions and at a more accelerated pace. To grow in this new way, we must overcome inertia toward change, and chart new directions. The exercises in this chapter encourage us to in *fact* start. But if we are to try out new directions, we must become less ego-involved in that process. Only if we lessen our fear of personally failing and our pride in personally succeeding can we really grow.

The exercises focus on our initial interactions with others, on what we do when we first meet, our "introductory" and "starting-up" gestures. They challenge us to transform stereotypic, superficial behaviors into exchanges of meaning and depth. It may seem difficult to transform a handshake into a significant interaction, but in the exercise it becomes possible.

The exercises work with eye contact and hand contact, basic media of social interaction. We work with these simple interaction symbols and are amazed at the wealth of meaning they *can* release but usually conceal. As we move from the eye contact to hand contact, from a less to a more immediate and direct interaction medium, we explore ourselves and others further. It is, of course, only an opening.

Eye to Eye

This is an exercise for the early stages—maybe the first. When we enter a room, we like to look around, see who's there. Now we have the opportunity to really look—no need for furtive glances—and to really see, to make contact with another. The exercise is simple, yet it can be a fruitful introduction to many themes.

LABORATORY PHASE

Structure

This exercise can be done with any number of people and in a variety of spaces. No special equipment is necessary. The exercise consists of a series of eye-to-eye communications and takes approximately fifteen minutes. Try to allow 2 or 3 minutes for the more extended contacts. If done in combination with "Hand Contacts Hand," fifty minutes should be allowed for both exercises.

Instructions

Look around the room or the space you are in—at all the faces. Do not talk. Try to get a sense of who is there. Now look at those closer to you, then those immediately next to you—on your right or left, maybe in front or in back of you. Where are you looking? At faces or eyes? Are you glancing? Or looking? Or contacting? (This initial phase may take several minutes.) And now, still from where you sit or stand, look across the room and establish eye contact with another. Create a pair. When you find this mutual contact, hold it for a while—for as long as you want to. . . . Then take leave of your partner. How did your pair form? Did you look at someone who was already looking at you? Did you seek to attract someone's attention? How deep or prolonged was your contact? How did it end? Why? Contact another person who is some distance from you. Try a different form of contact. Deepen and intensify your contact. Don't rush it; don't merely wait for it to be over. This time encounter another . . . Do you begin and end the same way? Now establish contact with someone near you. Does distance make a difference?

Discussion

This exercise starts in a very familiar way: looking around the room to see who is there. It's what we usually do when we enter a new space or group. Getting our bearings. And from this situation, the challenges emerge.

How can you achieve the state where you really don't think about what's happening but just allow it to happen?

A familiar piece of behavior. Do you transform it into something with unfamiliar, extraordinary meaning? Is the casual looking around the room less than casual? Do you actually see anything? Does this unfocused scanning evolve into true encounters? Does the unilateral glancing give way to a mutual engagement?

I noticed that many of the students, including myself, were too embarrassed to maintain eye contact for more than a few seconds. Why?

"Eye to Eye" helps set the course of a group. People can start to examine how far they could go, how far they do go. How involved do you get in an interaction? How much of yourself do you express? The potential intensity of the exercise becomes evident when people maintain contact for more prolonged periods. Breakthroughs in communication can help to overcome the inertia to change.

I managed to look into other people's eyes (I do that a great deal). But this time the people looked back at me the same way. Usually I would grin. There would be a moment of a sort of flash—a quick surge of warmth. It was hard to keep from laughing, mainly because I became so surprised and happy as my negative preconceptions about the people in the group melted away, leaving a warm feeling of possibility. As the exercise ended, I left feeling very much *alive* and warm and smiley in a way I don't usually feel.

The prolonged visual interaction is critical. Buber sees in the mutual gaze the opportunity for communion; Sartre, the opportunity for exerting power, one over the other. The simple behavior can have a complex of meanings. Do you open your eyes to someone, or do you stare him down?

Why are some people afraid to confront each other with naked eyes? Why is it that the most fundamental of human experiences are the most difficult to share? Why are people most afraid to share a look which may say everything because it says nothing?

It is time to establish prolonged visual contact with another. Immediately, the space between people is transformed. You may be looking at someone way across the room, but you and he are right next to each other. What do you look at? What do you see? The casual atmosphere has been altered. You may find yourself in the midst of an intense exchange. And, of course, you still may be as casual as when you first looked around the room. What do you want to make of all this? People come with defenses and barriers. It is not easy to look someone in the eye for more than a few seconds while he looks directly at you. It is not easy to use this time to learn about the other and let him learn about you.

Each person puts his own kind of energy into the contact. Some turn it into an encounter, looking intensely, sharing knowledge. They may communicate warmth or hostility, but it is directly expressed. Others seek to keep the contact casual. They find it hard to exchange glances. They avoid looking back when they realize they're being looked at. In such interactions the exchange of knowledge and emotion is minimal.

It seems that the main problem in this exercise was to remove yourself from your own concerns in order to really contact and communicate. The question arises how to do this without "self-consciousness" or "embarrassment."

The development of the contact can be fascinating. How does it start? How is it maintained? How does it end? Were you sought out, or did you seek someone? How do you intuit someone is looking at or for you? Did you find yourself "waiting in line" to look at someone? Did you seek others in a random or systematic fashion? How many "false starts" did you have? How do you tell whether the contact is mutual? When you look into another's eyes, do you see him?

The contact is mutual because two people are acting on and with each other. Did you feel "locked into" the mutual gaze, uncomfortably suspended in time and space? Did you search for cues that the contact should end? Some persons will stare, then ease up by breaking into a smile or laugh; then they are ready to leave. But what if your partner does not reciprocate and prefers to stay in visual contact? Who decides? Is *decision* the appropriate term? Did you leave first, or did you wait until your partner left, watching for his "leaving" cues? Can you just "say" goodbye and dismiss your partner? If the contact is a true encounter, you will not want to leave until you have learned and communicated enough. But what is enough? How long can you stay? These ambiguities can intensify the impact of the exercise.

Time and space are transformed in this exercise. Time can seem interminably long or surprisingly short, depending on the quality of the contact. Those far away physically can be brought closer, and those physically close can become too close. Persons often find that contact with those who are physically distant can be intense or not depending on the nature of the contact.

The exercise revealed the need and possibility of some common warmth . . . individuals communing with individuals.

The exercise is still just an opening. Opportunities for experience will be remembered, barriers will become more explicit. As a first experience, the exercise can introduce people to themselves and others.

APPLICATIONS

How can we apply what we have learned in this exercise to our everyday activities? Can we enhance communication merely by changing the way in which we look at another person? That seems unlikely. More importantly, we have to change why we look at others, what we are trying to communicate. If it works in the "laboratory" setting, will it necessarily work on the streets? Try it out. First in a completely public, open space. Try to make eye contact. Are you staring? Glancing? Or contacting, encountering, relating? See if an impersonal space like a street or a park can be transformed into a more personal one. What are the difficulties involved? The risks? The implication of making contact with a stranger? Will he misinterpret my attempt?

Whenever you work with these exercises in your daily life, you risk something. By changing the usual pattern of interaction, you can be ignored or rejected. But you can also begin to communicate more directly and deeply. Breaking patterns can lead to a breakthrough in communication. To be engaged in growth, you have to risk much more than being ignored by others or thought of as foolish. You have to begin risking the security of your old familiar self.

Another place to work with eye contact is in a store. Generally, people are more interested in making commercial transactions as quickly as possible. If one stopped to make eye contact, what effect would it have on the efficiency of the situation? Is it a worthwhile sacrifice?

Now attempt to make eye contact in a confining space—such as an elevator, bus, or subway—perhaps while waiting on a line. How does it compare with your efforts in the open space? At what point do closed quarters become just too close for comfort? How do people retreat from making contact in such confined quarters? How do you feel initiating such interactions? How would you feel if someone in one of these situations tried to make contact with you? Challenged? Overpowered? Or invited to relate? If communication is to occur, someone must be ready to receive.

Finally, try this exercise with a good friend or members of your family. It is sometimes easier to establish contact with a stranger. But the communication can be very deep during contact with someone close to you. Do you find that trying to make something of eye contact allows you to express more intimacy and directness than you usually do? What does this tell you about how you usually relate to this person you know?

All these applications are suggestions for creating a link between what we learn in group sessions and how we relate to ourselves and others every day.

Hand Contacts Hand

This exercise can be a beginning, or a natural way to continue the work started in "Eye to Eye." It moves us further from the conventional introduction, closer to real encounters. All we have to do is transform the ordinary into the extraordinary. Instead of merely shaking hands, make contact with another.

LABORATORY PHASE

Structure

There are no limits as to the number of people involved or spaces used. No special equipment is necessary. As with the "Eye to Eye," the exercise is a series of communications. This time the medium is touch. Allow about three to five minutes for each contact. The exercise can take between thirty and fifty minutes. If done with "Eye to Eye," fifty minutes should be allowed for both.

Instructions

(This initial phase may take up to five minutes.)

Move about the room or space; get a sense of its shape. Throughout this exercise, do not talk. Concentrate on the people in this room. As you move by someone, look at him—all over, up and down—and try to get a good picture of him in your mind. You look at people and sense what they are like in some way. Already it is time to move on, to work with a different form of introduction, a new point of encounter. Hand contacts hand.

As you move around the room, contact those you pass, right hand to right hand. Try to establish a contact in this brief touching. But keep circulating throughout the space. Don't remain caught in a traffic jam; seek new paths.

(In this next phase of more extended contacts, three to five minutes should be left for each contact, with their length increasing as the exercise progresses. People find it usually takes about five contacts to start exploring different aspects of the exercise.)

You are contacting those you pass, your right hand contacts their right hand. Now stop and stay for a while with the hand you are contacting or about to contact. Now, close your eyes and try to get to know your partner's hand in whatever way you can think of. See how much of this person you can meet and learn about. Contact his hand, don't merely shake it. . . . And now open your eyes and once more look at your partner. What do you see now? Without talking, take leave of this person, and move on, around the room, contacting hands, right hand to right hand.

And now, stop with the person whose hand you hold and, once again, close your eyes and get to know his hand. Focus on your hand and only your hand; put your energy there. Don't let your mind wonder about the "meaning" of this contact; don't let it go off into sexual fantasies. Keep it simple. Hand is contacting hand. . . . Open your eyes, look at your partner, really look, and move on.

And now, with the person whose hand you hold, once again, close your eyes and get to know his hand. Try out new ways of contacting and exploring. Be more passive, more active, more tender, stronger. Contact in a way which is "unlike" you. Is your "usual" way of contacting effective or appropriate? Is this new partner encouraging you to experiment? Are you letting him explore your hand? And as your hands continue to contact, open your eyes and see your partner. Look at this person whose hands you still hold. A new experience. Experience! . . . And when you feel it is time, move on, around the room. When are you "ready" to move on? How do you take leave of your partner? Was it your usual goodbye?

A great discovery: We all have left hands too. And as you move about, left hand contacts left hand. Life returns to that part of your body. Left hands reach out and contact left hands. Stop with a new partner. Again with your eyes closed, try to get to know the hand. It's now left hand to left hand; see what you can do, what new ways there are. Do you know this person? Are you getting there? . . . Once more open your eyes, eye to eye, take leave and move on.

For the last time now, move around, right hand contacting right hand, and stop with your final partner. This will be the last encounter, so really try to be there. If you are yourself and you let your partner be himself, the interaction must be different from all the rest, for each of us is unique. Try to reach the other, make contact. Strive for some kind of harmony with him. . . . And for the last time, open your eyes and look at your partner. Is this the same person? Take leave for the last time.

Discussion

What are certain people trying to tell me through the contact, or weren't they trying to tell me anything?

Are people afraid to let another person really touch them?

The hand-to-hand exercise moves us one step further. No longer can you just look from a safe distance. We are now in the realm of physical contact. Much springs from the American taboos on public touching and the sexual implications of almost everything we do.

When does tactile become sensual, become sexual?

Can't we get beyond that? We are not a tactile culture, though tactile communication is standard for many cultures. This American upbringing undoubtedly affects the intensity of the exercise.

As in the eye-to-eye exercise, we are not sure how far we can go, how actively we can explore part of another's body. The eye contact may have been demanding. The hand contact is even more so.

I found myself able to be either passive or aggressive, but always taking my cues from the other person. When I consciously tried to stop following so much, very often the other person would start taking cues from me sometimes. It was only then that I was able to feel that we were two people trying to contact each other through our hands. It became like one long question, "Who are you? Who are you? Who are you?" It wasn't answered, just silently asked. But it was important to ask that question, one I don't usually ask people.

How do you get to know another person's hand? Maybe you feel the texture and sense what each part is like—the palm, knuckles, nails, and the rest. Then maybe you feel its strength, and, at the same time, you are also being explored. Are you willing? Can you explore and be touched at the same time? How much can you learn about your partner by the way he gets to know your hand? What does he "tell" you? How aggressive is he? How original are his techniques? When you join hands, how powerful is your partner? Does he give you a chance? Or maybe he does nothing and waits for you to take the initiative. A person's style of relating can be expressed in the exercise: the way he interacts with others, how easy he is to get to know, how open and receptive he is.

Think back on the exercise. Which contacts do you remember? Which can you reexperience? Certain contacts stand out. Certain people interact in very special ways.

I think this exercise is easier when you do it with someone you don't know at all. For some reason I felt embarrassed having physical contact with people I knew. Why is this?

The simple behavior of hand contacting hand expresses so much of a person. This becomes more striking once you meet your second partner. You see how different and unique each person is. Or do you? You learn his style and methods and try to go beyond, to create new ones. Maybe you now lightly touch fingertips and feel energy flowing from one hand to the other, or you start exploring with the back of your hand rather than the palm or the fingers. With time come new ways. You see that the "old" ones have told you only a little. There are other areas to be met and understood.

Do you think this was genuine, sincere on the part of the participants? How much do you learn of a hand by merely grasping it, not touching it or moving over its many parts?

But often the old and comfortable ways persist. Maybe you wanted to explore but your new partner resisted. Collaborative exploration is very important.

Did any of the structures toward innovation help? For example, when you were explicitly encouraged to try different ways, or when you switched to your left hand, or when you looked at the other while your hands were contacting? Did it help you go beyond handshaking a "hello" and handshaking a "goodbye"?

Being encouraged to innovate by someone outside of the interaction can be very helpful. Partners are encouraged simultaneously, and can respond without too much ego-involvement. They do not have to feel that they personally are risking new types of involvement.

The realm of encounter can expand when you contact with the left hand. New and refreshing experiences complement the more familiar and stereotyped right-hand contacts. There is a natural force toward transforming the ordinary handshake into an extraordinary hand contact. We are usually not as comfortable or agile shaking left hands. Sometimes there are conflicts, trying to do something you might have done with the right hand and not being sure of your movements.

Looking at your partner while contacting his hand again can expand your experience. In darkness, with eyes closed, there is a certain license to explore. It is more difficult to continue exploring with your hands while you are looking at the other, but it is more meaningful. Particularly if you are also exploring and sharing visually.

Differences between individuals can become more important than *apparent* differences between males and females, especially as the exercise proceeds. One girl seemed as if she didn't want to be touched and might hold back. A boy noted that when he contacted her, she held her hand totally limp. She let the boy explore but did not move herself. As a result, he held back too, feeling that the girl did not want him to do anything. A man who says that he is "strong and quite masculine" tells how he became engaged in a very tender and soft meeting with a woman who set the tone for the encounter. Confrontations vary, depending greatly on how your partner receives you, how assertive he or she is.

Many male-female issues *can* arise. Often they mask preconceived notions about male-female differences which are merely results of social and emotional inequities. You can expand the traditional definitions of masculinity and femininity and begin to transcend male-female issues. Can a male be very gentle when he meets another male? Will a female allow herself to be powerful, particularly with a male? To be open and spontaneous is difficult, and for many justifiable reasons. It is especially difficult now, at the beginning phases of a group. But even during the exercise, spontaneity increases. Soon, as you focus on your *hand* contacting another *hand*, in the darkness of your closed eyes, you no longer remember whether it's a female or male you are contacting. You no longer care. All your energy can become focused in your hand, and it's one *person's hand* contacting, encountering another *person's hand*. And through that, two *persons* encountering.

A forced, prolonged encounter. The fact that it is done nonverbally, and with your eyes closed, means there is almost a vacuum, and the only stimuli that enter are from your partner's hand. Were you able to keep your *thoughts* to a minimum and focus on your *body;* that is, specifically your hand? The opportunity is there. How much can you learn and communicate from just touching? During the last encounter these issues can culminate. You work toward making the contact more meaningful, exploring and sharing more. If there has not been much created between you, it will be easy to say farewell. An ordinary goodbye gesture or a final handshake will do. But if you now feel something more for your partner, you may want to seek some other way. You begin to transform ordinary behavior into something more than ordinary.

The hand-contact exercise moves us to a more immediate level of communication than eye contact. People disagree as to which, however, is more intense and meaningful. A physical communication network is established, and this can break down some of the conventional barriers between people. The exercise tells us dramatically that we can not only touch others, but we can also learn much from it, creating something between ourselves and another. It can be a beginning for more intimate, open, and honest communication.

How can we continue verbally the feeling of closeness we had in the touch exercise?

Does it have to do with real life? What would happen if at every meeting we looked deeply and touched well?

APPLICATIONS

The first step in applying anything we learn in the laboratory sessions is becoming alert to how we behave in our usual, everyday interactions. As you walk around, try to become alert to all the unconscious and unintentional body contact that occurs in public places. What parts of the body are touched? Is there any connection between the amount of clothing a person is wearing, the season of the year, and how he handles himself in public places? Look at people bumping into one another, brushing by others. Notice your reactions, their reactions. Any relationships?

Now, the next several times you shake someone's hand, try to be alert to what you are doing, what you are saying to that person. Really try to communicate something *if* that is your intent. Extend and expand the handshake. If you feel it is desirable, try to extend the exchange, either by holding the hand longer, or softer, or any other way you can think of. If you are saying goodbye to someone, and you feel a regular handshake would be inadequate, try to transform the handshake into something less ordinary. Innovate with your hand contact so you *can* communicate.

In general, explore how creating a physical link can affect the way you talk or interact. How can contact allow you to be more direct in what you are saying? How can it express more of your feelings and intents? Try these things out a number of times in a variety of settings.

FURTHER READING

Erving Goffman, *Presentation of Self in Everyday Life*, Anchor Books, Doubleday & Company, Inc., Garden City, N.Y., 1959.

Is there anything beneath the image we present to others? Is it all a question of wearing a mask or playing a role? Goffman can challenge you to prove that something of the "real you" exists in your daily interactions.

The I Ching (or Book of Changes) translated by Cary F. Barnes from the German translation of Richard Wilhelm, Princeton University Press, Princeton, N.J., 1967.

A key to beginning true self-discovery is learning to ask essential questions. *The I Ching* is here for us to work with. If we can honestly formulate penetrating questions, the book opens up and begins an exchange with us. If you respect yourself and this book, not seeking from it advice on petty matters, then *The I Ching* can be a companion and guide.

Creative Alertness

*W*E seek increased understanding of ourselves, others, and the world. A very large goal. I think the key to attaining this goal is self-understanding. We start with some understanding of ourselves; this can lead to some understanding of others and our world. When I begin to know who I am, *and* begin to accept that, then I can begin to know you and accept you. Only when I start to see myself clearly can I hope to see you without prejudice. And when our understanding of others and the world increases, so does our self-understanding. For we then become more of a microcosm of our world. It comes full circle to self-understanding.

How can we increase our self-understanding? I think we must create the ability to see ourselves more accurately. As this ability to see develops, it ceases to involve our two eyes, and starts to involve a deep, intuitive knowing. We begin to uncover our "inner eyes." For we must be really concerned with our essential nature, not our superficial appearance.

We must be able to see ourselves *as if* from the outside. I'm not suggesting an alienation from ourselves but developing a perspective on our selves. Then we must accept what we see, without necessarily liking or disliking it. For example, if I see that I am outgoing in large groups, I try to be neither proud nor ashamed of that fact; rather, I try to accept it because that's me. As we see ourselves in different situations, at different times, we can see more and more of ourselves. I am convinced that only when we start to accept ourselves do we begin change. It's not a question of wanting to change; it's really a matter of changing. As we accept ourselves we *are* changing.

It's very hard to create the ability to see ourselves. Therefore we should try first in simple situations, for example, when alone. In the exercise "I Am Me" you can try to become more alert to yourself when you are alone. Here the distractions, taking you away from yourself, come only from yourself. Then, in the exercise "Presenting," you have a chance to extend this creative alertness, trying to see yourself as you relate to others. The presence of others complicates the situation. Their wishes and your idea of their wishes can be another distracting influence, clouding your efforts to have a clear view of yourself. But you make an effort when you're with others because that's how we spend most of our day. You then return, continually, to situations when you're alone, to recreate your ability to see yourself.

Try to dedicate yourself to developing this ability to see yourself accurately. Be experimental. Put yourself in situations which are novel so you can become less habitual and more transparent. Be serious. Be honest with yourself. Try to introduce some discipline into your life so you begin to do what you intend. This is not meant to sound somber; it *is* meant to be real. Real growth requires real work on your part.

I Am Me

How can we begin to see ourselves more as we really are? How can we learn to accept ourselves as we are, so we can *be*? In this exercise, try to simplify your day. Try to remove distractions so you can be more in touch with yourself. In simpler settings, you can become more apparent. It can become clearer that your actions, thoughts, and feelings are you. You can see more clearly how mechanical you are, how judgmental, how influenced by others. You can hear your own hopes and aspirations, your own inner voices.

The challenge is equally simple and clear. Can you step aside, for moments, from your usual selves? Can you develop more perspective on your selves? Can you accept what is characteristically you, whether it be so-called good or bad? This acceptance can be a strong foundation for change.

LABORATORY PHASE

Structure

Structurally, all you'll need is time and space. The remaining and most important ingredient is up to you. You should decide in advance when you'll do this exercise since it requires extra preparation: it calls for setting aside a twenty-four-hour period in which you suspend in some way your usual routine, perhaps arranging to travel to a particular place. The space used is an entirely individual matter.

Instructions

It is not easy to see ourselves clearly; it is even harder to accept what we see. When we simplify our conditions we can become more simple. In the context of simplicity, our characteristic selves are highlighted.

The direction in which you simplify is not as important as the simplicity itself. One direction, however, is especially productive: spending time alone, preferably without talking. For a long period, twenty-four hours if possible, try to be alone without talking to anyone, not even yourself. You may want to be physically alone, for example in a wilderness retreat, or psychologically alone, a stranger in a crowd. You'll probably find your experience in some combination of these physical and psychological elements.

In being alone, you can begin to see yourself more clearly. The ways in which you structure your space, order your time, what you think and feel, what you do—all this will be a more direct expression of you. If you keep outside distractions to a minimum, you keep the directness of this self-expression to a maximum. We can be very distracted by others—we often pretend to be something we are not when we're with others. We can be very distracted by ourselves—we often hide from ourselves by talking so much.

If you can't be alone for twenty-four hours or you can't stop talking for twenty-four hours, be alone and silent for as long as possible; but during that time *be* silent and *be* alone. And do try to extend those periods. Taking the twenty-four hours from your "busy life" may add to your real life. You may even see yourself for a moment.

And that should be the only purpose of the exercise—to see yourself more clearly. Free from distractions, let your selves emerge and express themselves. Let the distractions which persist—and there will be many—come from you, your own idle, restless mind. Treat the fluctuating moods, the boredom, exhilaration, loneliness, calm, as your own moods, as parts of you. Try to focus on the present, on what you are doing, thinking, and feeling right now. Avoid extensive diversionary trips into the past and future.

Prepare yourself for this time alone. Self-discipline will be necessary if understanding is to develop. Prepare by strengthening your ability to be still, to reflect, to meditate. Set aside times in your time alone for these vital functions.

Keep a journal during this alone period. Note your thoughts and feelings, your insights and confusions, your hopes and aspirations. But exercise self-discipline. Write when you realize something important, though it may be obvious; not when you're bored, so as to fill up time. Getting these thoughts out on paper can help to empty your mind and reprepare you for meeting yourself. You can also rework material in the journal as you reread it at some later time.

Letting your selves emerge is only the beginning. Being able to accept what emerges is another step. Try to see yourself as if from the outside; have perspective on your selves without being alienated or withdrawn from yourself. Try not to judge what you see as being good or bad, something you like or dislike. Accept what is presented to yourself by yourself.

Throughout your time alone, try to be honest with yourself. Look into yourself as much as you can. But don't fool yourself into thinking you are seeing more than you are. Have respect for yourself.

Discussion

How much did you see of your selves? Did you begin to accept yourself as you are? Each person who does this exercise will have a different experience. But the same question remains: Did you emerge more clearly in the process?

How did you prepare for the exercise? Perhaps you selected certain ideas to consider during the alone period, certain questions to ponder? Or maybe you set as a goal learning more about your emotions, or how you behave in unfamiliar places? Did you try to be spontaneous and just let it happen? Did it *just* happen, or did you find yourself planning what to do? The quality of your preparation influences the quality of your time alone. Not only do topics considered in your preparation appear during the time alone, but the energy spent in preparation can deepen your subsequent experience.

How did you structure your experience? Some decide to be physically alone—that is, to go camping, to go to the woods or the waterside, or otherwise to isolate themselves from all contact with people. Others decide to be psychologically alone—to spend the time among strangers, in the city, in their dormitory rooms, or on a fourteen-hour bus ride. Some try to be alone among friends, telling them beforehand,

"Ignore me completely for a day," and simply suspend interaction. Did you give yourself time to "unwind," to get out of the habit of not listening to what you hear? Did you have time to contact yourself? Were there many distractions, pulling you constantly away, away from the obvious facts of your thinking, feeling, and behaving? The goal is to highlight yourself. You try to simplify conditions so your own behavior emerges more clearly.

Sometimes trying to be alone among friends can provide one distraction after another. We are so skillful in distracting ourselves from ourselves that "outside" distractions seem gratuitous. You soon realize you are not alone when among people, even though you are avoiding interactions.

Two guys walked in, talking in an affected sort of speech which I too have affected. At this point I realized that I could not really be alone among people. I had to recognize their presence. They were there. . . . I can only be alone when I'm alone. When those two guys walked in talking like that I couldn't restrain myself. "I can say something to you two because you're automatons, not humans." And the jig was up. "She's talking," they all said. And I guess I was. I couldn't go back to silence, though I tried for a while.

I entered the room and sat down in one of the desk chairs. At first I was a little on edge. I felt as if I were waiting for something to happen, like any moment someone was going to walk through the door. It also occurred to me that there might be a 12 o'clock class coming into the room and I thought a little about what I'd do then, but didn't come to any decision. I also thought I'd feel a little silly if a class were to come into the room and I was just sitting there by myself, thinking. I thought a little about making excuses for myself. Then it seemed to me I was wasting my time getting hung up on what I'd do if someone were to come into the room. I decided that I could handle that if it happened and that it wasn't worth any more thought. The anxious feeling eventually went away. I started to think about what was said about being alert to what was happening at the moment.

Getting to be alone can take a long time. There are many avenues to explore, each of which keeps you from focusing on yourself. Will someone disturb me? Is it quiet enough? What's over there? The place is never perfect. Your commitment to exploring yourself makes the place just right.

Attention to the outer world shifts to the inner—

I went down a road and over a chain with a sign "No Trespassing." . . . Why don't they want me inside? Am I invading their privacy? Whose privacy? My own, for I am alone.

I took my sleeping bag and walked deep into the woods, pretending to look at the trees, the shapes of the branches, and the beautiful evening. But I was really very far from such selfless thoughts.

I kept thinking, without trying, about my course work. My mind would slip into a guilt-ridden confusion.

This shift could be in the right direction. But can you look honestly at these inner workings? If not, you're merely involved in reverie, introspection, or daydreams. And you certainly don't have to be alone for twenty-four hours to have a good daydream. We're trying to collect facts about ourselves, not manufacture fantasies.

The moods and states which emerge during your time alone can be endless. But were they now clearer? Were your characteristic moods more obvious? Too often moods emerge as they do on an ordinary day—chaotically and little understood.

Loneliness. Those who try to be psychologically alone often experience loneliness. Frequently they can see friends or hear them talking. They are greeted by people and force themselves not to respond. For some, there is a feeling of estrangement. A few reported that they began to see their own and others' behavior as mechanical. Many were unable to complete the full twenty-four-hour period. Others expressed great relief at the termination of the time alone and immediately sought out friends to talk with. Some were discouraged to find that this psychological aloneness was no different from the loneliness they had often experienced, which was simply a problem to cope with and not an interesting source of insight. Did you turn your time alone into *just* another chance to feel sorry for yourself, lonely and "unloved"? Or were you able to avoid your usual retreat into loneliness?:

I felt moods of depression when people ignored me, and I felt very neglected . . . and then, almost like it was for the first time, I realized I have a fundamental need to be paid attention to . . . this realization made me feel lighter, not heavier; it gave me a sense of more options, not fewer. . . .

Sensory enhancement. Those who are physically alone and moving around often report a richness of sensory detail. The attention first turns outward, to the surroundings, then to physical sensations.

I discovered what my body is like and how it performs physically. I found that it is a fluid organism, capable of tremendous exertion. I further realized that I had been suffering from beauty starvation. . . . I let my "inferior" senses—hearing, touching and smelling take over. I became attuned to my own body, alert to how it can respond to all kinds of emotional factors.

Boredom.

Upon entering the room, I began to look around for sources of amusement
or diversion. The room, however, was a barren, vacated office and I felt
constrained in the sense that I wasn't able to touch anything or visibly
rearrange the setting to suit myself. I devoted a great deal of thought, at
the outset, to my discomfort and boredom. I attributed my apparent lack
of progress in the exercise to this uneasiness, caused by a setting which was
so confined and structured. Perhaps, a second handicap was the fact that I
was wearing a watch and was acutely conscious of how I was wasting the
allotted time.

Fantasizing.

My mind began to concoct interesting situations and thus creating a new
world inside me. The fantasies were part reminiscences, part speculation,
but part totally improbable contrived circumstances.

Involvement.

I became engrossed first in the activities of a pigeon, studiously pecking
away at his feathers, and then in studying a painting, the texture of which
was particularly involving. These more passive activities, while not satisfying, permitted me to dispel some of the tension which had before con-
stricted me. As I became less preoccupied with the fact that I was participating in an exercise, per se, I was able to spend some reflective moments
considering myself, my habits. I became less concerned with how I fit into
the structure of the exercise.

Restlessness. While some exploration is deliberate, there is also a
general feeling of restlessness. "Being alone makes me so fidgety." One
explores the surroundings, and then reexplores. Perhaps this is another
expression of the need to preoccupy oneself, to avoid confronting the
obvious, yourself. One becomes more alert to shifting moods. Most
people who go into the woods report feeling excited—at first. This can
be overturned by feeling the discomforts of boredom, insects, weather,
and impassable undergrowth.

Each of these moods and states is no better or worse than the other;
each is only a manifestation of you. Most often they distract you—you
become fascinated with your fantasy, anxious about your own fear.
The difference is in how you approach these moods and states. When
you begin to see them clearly, you can begin to see yourself.

More than moods and states emerge. Many persons consider their goals and ambitions, their tensions and conflicts. Some focus on their professional lives, others on their personal lives.

Did you notice any difference between attempts to see your thoughts, feelings, or actions? It is invariably easier to see your body in action, doing things, stopping here, bending over there. Again, remember we're not talking about seeing with our two physical eyes, but with our inner "eyes." We are generally less personally identified with our body and therefore are more able to have some perspective on it. But your body is very much you. By becoming alert to it, you can become alert to yourself.

Your time alone is probably not quite what you expected, not what you planned for. Sometimes, as if by surprise, you come face-to-face with yourself. One man, who built a camp in his wilderness site, met himself:

The camp was a reflection of my own mind—a reflection of the way I had approached the whole project—there it was, well laid out, a perfect supporting environment which would help delay the time when I would eventually have to be with no one but myself.

Did you take advantage of the unexpected? Did you turn these unfamiliar situations into opportunities to see yourself in a new light, highlighted? We can express ourselves directly when we no longer rely on a habitual response.

But after these characteristics of you and characteristic "yous" emerge, what then? Unless you can accept them as a part of you, the growth circuit is shorted. You've got to be honest with yourself. You have to receive what is given, whether it pleases you or not. You may not like to be fidgety, but you must accept that characteristic if that is what you are. Change occurs as you accept who you are.

When I noticed that I was hurrying along as I always do, as if I had to get this over with and go on with something else, I stopped myself, sat down and tried to slow down.

You have to make your time alone productive. You can easily let it run away with you, leading you into endless "thinking about thinking," fruitless acting from habit. One person realizes it takes time and relaxes the urge to take a walk for yet a fourth time. Another struggles with his reactions to others, which seem magnified by solitude:

There was always the temptation to slip into fantasies about others. I find that my mind will want to comment . . . it refuses to see if it can't comment. . . .

I realized that my outlook was at fault; that in order to proceed, it would become necessary to isolate myself from the concept of an exercise and to devote myself to nothing more than recognizing my feelings and thoughts in a state of aloneness; and that this would not require any effort to prove something, either to myself or to the group, at a later point.

In their own particular form, people pose the fundamental question: "Who am I?" One person asked herself, "What has happened to me in the past four years? Where am I going? What do I really want?" You can't really answer these questions in any final sense. You can begin to understand them. One student, whose experience involved a fourteen-hour bus trip, writes:

. . . I started thinking about how each of these people, each had a life, a home or a place they were coming from, and some place to which they were all going. Millions of lives and here we all were, sitting in this rectangular box on wheels and none of us knew anything about anyone else except what they looked like, what perfume they wore, etc. It's hard to explain but suddenly it all was so overwhelming and I felt a part of the whole thing. As people we were so complex and unique, but for these fourteen hours we were a group. . . .

Another person reflects:

Something that had been bothering me about myself became more apparent; I saw it in myself throughout the day. Now will I be able to change? In the time that I was alone, I got to know myself a little better.

Was your time alone a period of renewal before a reengaging in your daily life? Next time, try to make it even more so.

The return from your time alone is a significant aspect of the experience. Some people have spoken of a feeling of detachment on returning. For a while, one looks with a stranger's eye on familiar scenes and takes a kind of surprised pleasure in commonplace events. Gradually, one slips back onto the old level of attention. Others report a need to talk and make contact with people. They are very glad to be done with the experiment; it seemed to be "the extension of an awkward pause in a conversation." Still others describe feeling more "together," more present to themselves. If "Who am I?" is not answered, "I am" is somehow affirmed.

With all this focus on seeing yourself clearly, you many wonder if you can still go about your everyday affairs. But it is just your everyday functioning which you try to see. If you find yourself becoming so introspective that you no longer want to act, then you know you're on the wrong road. Creating perspective is not an empty process. You

keep trying to meet your everyday responsibilities with more understanding and care. You then try to catch a view of yourself—you, behaving, on a day-to-day basis.

APPLICATIONS

Our lives tend to be so overcomplicated that we rarely see what we
are doing, let alone who we are. Simplifying our environment can help
to highlight ourselves, making what we do and are more apparent.

You can always simplify your environment. Withdraw some of the
resources you've become dependent on. Change your diet: eat less;
eat more slowly; eat less of the overdone, overprepared foods; make
your own bread. Change your sleeping patterns: sleep to rest your
mind and body, not to escape from being awake; arise early so you
have time to contact yourself before you start your day, rather than
being immediately engulfed by your day. Change your financial picture: consume less; make more things for yourself; buy fewer "top of
the line" gadget-ridden things. Be an explorer, changing your habits
so that you might uncover more information about yourself.

But don't forget the purpose of such simplifications. It's not to
appear more self-reliant than others, nor more hip, nor more of a
pioneer, nor even "earthier." The purpose is more essential and straightforward. You simplify your environment in the hope that you might
see yourself as if for the first time.

Another tack is to enter unusual situations, unfamiliar cultures. You
go to a nightclub for the first time, or to a convention, or to the Kalahari Desert. You rely heavily on certain habits because they provide
some measure of familiarity in the unusual situation. The habits become exaggerated; you become more obvious.

There are several other things you might try which are more intellectual, but which can provide some helpful perspective. Do you
keep a diary? Try to reconceive of the diary as a record of your states
of consciousness, your moods, your goals, your wishes. Write down
accurate and comprehensive pictures of yourself on various days, at
various times. And work with your diary. Don't keep it in the secret
drawer, rereading it in a state of reverie or nostalgia. If your diary
reports a particular mood reappearing in certain situations, try to see
that mood more clearly the next time it appears, and accept it. If your
diary describes a tendency to set unrealistic goals and then feel guilty
about not meeting them, catch yourself the next time you set goals and
confront yourself with your own tendency. If your diary describes a
person without a spiritual center, reflect on that; if you can realize you
are in that condition, you have some chance of changing it.

The diary can become a continuous opportunity to view yourself. Periodically, you can try two other techniques to get views of yourself at particular stages or times. The first technique is more immediate and process-oriented.[1] Take about thirty minutes and follow these instructions:

You are going to write an "essay," the title of which will be "Me." First write a series of the letter *I* to begin the body of the essay. Write them in succession and, at the same time, think about yourself. As soon as a thought concerning yourself comes to mind, write it down, right after the *I*s. Keep writing down your thoughts. If you run into a momentary lag in your thinking, if your mind goes blank, keep writing the letter *I* until another thought about yourself comes and again write this down immediately.

Feel free to write down whatever comes to your mind, whether it is about problems you have, or dreams, or just any random thoughts. Don't censor your thoughts, and don't worry about spelling or grammar. Try to get down as much of what you are thinking as you can.

Your thoughts form on the page and, again, you begin to emerge. One girl writes:

. . . III'm mixed up I can't do anything I want definite action II . . . I'm so preoccupied I can't see you IIII want to stop IIII'm too stupid to do what I want . . .

Another writes:

I I I I I I Jane I I I am skinny I I I feel silly I I I . . . I I I EGO I I I . . . I I I I I am in my room, I am wearing a pink suit with brown shoes I I I I I have brown eyes I I I didn't do my work III . . .

A boy writes:

I remember the time in Kindergarten when we had to copy the picture of a house and I couldn't draw the chimney—I cried I I I I I I I

In the second technique, you write down six or so ways in which you would describe yourself, your life goals, or your characteristic moods, etc. Basically, the idea is to put on paper what you want to explore about yourself. This writing down can help clarify an area of concern. It can also represent an explicit promise you make with yourself to explore that area. But beware of the drawback of writing things down. Writing about your intentions is not a substitute for

---

[1] Bonnie Geller, a student in one of my courses, suggested it.

doing what you intend. The essential thing remains your experience, what you *do* about your goals, your moods. Use the written material to catalyze your experience and highlight your behavior.

Each of these three techniques—the diary and the two written self-portraits—are by you and for you. The purer your motivation, the more you can learn. Since no one else need see them, you can be honest with yourself. Tell yourself what you want to know, not what you would like to hear.

In all these applications, you must be honest with yourself. What's important is who you are and what you do in your everyday life. You can't afford to indulge in "idle-ing" introspection. You have to look into yourself as you are in daily life, face what you see, and try to accept as much as you can. It is only you.

Presenting

It is hard to see ourselves for what we are. It is even harder to accept what we see and start from there. Anyone who says that it's easy is either uninformed or talking of only accidental momentary glimpses of yourself, not a process of growth whereby these moments deepen and cumulate. It requires effort, hard work, and dedication to let yourself be and become. It requires effort to screen out all that distracts you from your own center.

In the previous exercise, "I Am Me," I hope you had opportunities to see yourself. Try doing something like "I Am Me" before you do "Presenting." In "I Am Me," you try to minimize the distractions from seeing yourself, and still, I'm sure, the distractions persisted. Now, in "Presenting," you can work more purposively with a major source of distraction, our tendency to create an image of ourselves for the benefit of others.

Though we are very involved in projecting an image, we usually don't realize how we appear to others. With people we don't know very well, we often concentrate on eliciting some kind of response or creating some kind of impression. With good friends, we often work from expectations. We know what pleases or disturbs them, and this, plus the way we feel about the person at a particular time, influences much of our behavior.

Can you increase the harmony between your inner state and your physical self? Can you look the way you feel, expressing yourself directly? Can you be yourself, without cleaning up your image to appear certain ways for others?

We do spend most of our day in the presence of others. Perhaps, by considering our tendency to create images for others, we can understand this tendency a little better.

In "Presenting," we focus on your physical self, and specifically on its manifestations, e.g., your posture. We tend to be less personally identified with our bodies than with our feelings or thoughts. Therefore you have a better chance of seeing these physical manifestations accurately—of really seeing them, with your inner "eyes."

And don't be discouraged at such an apparently small goal. Your physical self is a facet of yourself. Your body exists; it behaves; it can express the life inside you. As you see your physical manifestations, you can see yourself beneath them.

Structure

This exercise can take an entire session. No special equipment is necessary. Choose an open area or a room that has as little furniture as possible, moving what is there to the sides. You'll need space for an individual to walk in front of the group. This exercise is good to do after you've done "I Am Me."

Instructions

Try to establish some contact with yourself. Try to realize where you are now, what state you're in, what your thoughts and feelings are. When you have some sense of yourself, walk up to the front of the group in a way which expresses yourself now. Then assume a posture which expresses yourself, and tell the group your name. Then go back to your place. You should walk up, say your name, and sit back down one at a time—each person getting up when he feels ready, when he has some sense of himself.

Before you get up, still your mind. Try to see some manifestation of your physical self—your gestures, or your posture, or your facial expression, or your body tension. Remember, try to really see, to see with your "inner eyes." Don't remain locked into the surface views of your physical eyes. As you get up, try to see beneath this behavior; try as you walk toward the front, again, to contact the life within you. Try to see it. As you say your name, try to see another manifestation— your tone of voice. As you walk back to your place, try to see your body behaving, as an expression of life. And as you sit down, again try. Keep it simple. Still your mind. Calm your feelings.

Remember that seeing your physical self is not a moment of alienation. You don't see a "dead" body or a detached limb. Can you see your body expressing the life that is you? Can you realize you exist— at that moment?

When another person is getting up and going to the front, look at

him without judging. Rather, try to be unbiased, and to get beneath
the surface. Later, you share with him what you saw, sharing with
care and concern.

Supplement

As a supplement to this attempt to see your body in motion, you
can utilize visual and aural images of yourself. Make photos or a film
or tape of yourself doing what your normally do, being yourself. Either
you or someone else can make them. Then, as you view the photographs or hear the tape, talk about your physical manifestations as
they appear in the photographs or on the tape. Be as specific, descriptive, and nonevaluative as possible, almost as if you were describing
a machine. Use the third person in your description. For example,
"Now there John lifts his hand to cover his face," instead of, "Now
there I lift my hand to cover my face." Or, "Now, when talking about
a feeling, the voice gets softer." You can view these recorded images
and describe them when alone or with the group.

As you are describing your physical manifestation in the third person, try to come back to your real self. Use the recorded images of
yourself as a spotlight, pointing out things you can then try to see in
yourself without external recording devices. You might work with
these recorded images both before and after you do the "Presenting"
exercise. But remember, *these photographs and tapes are both too
literal and one step removed.* The essential issue is for *you* to contact
yourself as you exist at the moment.

Discussion

We've tried to approach ourselves more simply and directly, focusing on manifestations of our physical selves. Since we are less identified with these manifestations than, for example, our thoughts and
feelings, we are more likely to see them without prejudice. Yet seeing
our physical selves is *not* easy. Invariably our focus shifts away from
our bodies toward presenting ourselves as we would like to appear to
others. Invariably, thoughts and feelings, conjectures and conclusions,
hopes and wishes crowd into our consciousness.

I knew my turn would come soon. . . . I felt a tightness in my throat, and
a nervous quivering in my stomach. Then, I was overtaken with this image
of myself walking calmly up to the front and confidently saying my name
. . . and then I realized that was what I had done, and I *still* felt the tightness and the quivering.

If we could only be what we are inside, then perhaps we could see our bodies in action and, in that, see ourselves. Did you express your-self directly? Did you look the way you felt?

We specifically added a distracting ingredient—something which takes us away from seeing ourselves. You were not merely with others; you were in front of others in a potentially embarrassing and stressful situation. And this made the situation that much more charged, and allowed the distraction to emerge that much more clearly. But the distraction is not people. We live in context, with others. That is our reality. The distraction is our trying to present an image to others, usually so as to please them, sometimes to overpower them, sometimes to put them down, etc. Can you accept the tension in your body which signals you're about to put on an image, and you're not sure whether it's going to "succeed" or "fail"? Often you can see this image dilemma more sharply when you purposely place yourself in front of others.

I felt I would be awkward; so to overcome this, I assumed the role of play-acting. My mood on this day was very good, receptive, open. I felt alive and was looking forward to the session. I expressed this by almost marching to the designated spot and when on stage I said in a positive and deliberate fashion, "I am Margaret Steiner."

Sometimes it's easier to see yourself after you've presented yourself to others or before you stand up. Could you retain something of your-self when you rose up? Did you walk and speak as you wanted to or expected to? Invariably we lose ourselves on the way.

It is important to remain as much in the present as possible. Were you able to express your present state?

My reactions to this exercise are simple. I wanted to express how I felt about myself that moment. I felt perplexed and tried to express it.

Sometimes we assume an image which we feel will be helpful to others, perhaps relieving others of some burden. But is that really helpful? How much play-acting can you handle before you really lose touch with yourself? When you're out of touch with yourself, you can't really help another. You can be manipulating another even when you're trying to make him "feel good." If you are there being yourself, this can inspire another to be himself. Help must come from your own center of strength.

This tendency toward creating a certain impression can also be seen in your photographic or film self-portraits. Were you trying to impress another with your film or tell him about yourself? Would your film be easily recognized as yours if it were shown with others' films? How much of your private self was portrayed, or did you keep to your public image? How would another's film of you be different from your self-portrait? How does this film description relate to your verbal self-description?

Trying to understand these film and photographic self-descriptions can be helpful. They can provide a little distance from yourself, give you some breathing space. But they are secondhand, once removed. Eventually you have to return to the heart of the matter—seeing yourself as you now exist.

Hearing others' descriptions of your physical self can also be helpful if they are objective and nonevaluative. But they too are secondhand. In discussing this exercise, create spotlights from what others say about you. Turn these spotlights back toward yourself. They can motivate *you* to see yourself more clearly.

. . . I hated the thought of doing it because then I would be exposed in all my fatness.

Why can't we simply look at the facts about ourselves as they emerge? Why can't we see what's happening without wasting all our energy trying for a particular effect? Instead of trying to be somebody or wishing you were not somebody, why not accept your own givens? Can you start with what you are, and leave aside image building? It is difficult, but the facts about you are right there.

Were you able to keep your attempts simple? Could you, for a moment, see your body manifesting itself, and not evaluate it? More importantly, could you experience (your) life existing within that body? Build a strong foundation. First, focusing on your body, develop some ability to see with less prejudice. Then branch out and try to apply this ability to seeing your thoughts and feelings more clearly. For each of these facets of the self leads into the heart of the self.

One woman, seeking to keep simple, reports:

As I rose to walk toward the front, I saw my knees unbend, and my back straighten up. Then I saw myself standing there, straight up, taking a first step. It wasn't seeing in any literal sense, I didn't use my eyes. Yet I knew that I was there, at that moment, as my body was standing and taking its first step.

When we see our physical manifestations, it isn't a dry process. Nor is it literal, like taking a static photograph of our body. Rather, it is a way we can contact the life inside us.

But for most people, much of this exercise concerns thoughts and feelings. And the views of thoughts and feelings which emerge are less clear and more elusive. Too often these views fail to reach the substance of yourself.

Perhaps you can get some idea about your tendency to assert your individuality:

I consciously and deliberately chose the words "I am" rather than "My name is" because I wanted to say I am "me," not a label someone gave me.

My first thought after hearing the instructions was "Frances Kane," my maiden name, at which point I laughed out loud.

Or maybe you begin to realize the influence of your physical self on yourself:

I began to think of my image of my physical self. At 29 years old and after having been a very late maturer physically, I finally had decided that I like what I look like—I see myself as more attractive than pretty, but interesting looking; sexy, not in a buxom way, but rather like a sophisticate; I wear clothes well and enjoy dressing myself. I use this image of myself oftentimes to bolster a sometimes shaky ego and certainly to assure myself of making an impression on people. I see myself walking up to the front rather confidently, hands in pockets, eyes direct and saying quite clearly and with a degree of pride "I am Frances Murphy."

We must keep trying to be simple. In really seeing our active body without evaluating it, we can realize that, at that moment, we exist. This experience is a key to growth.

Applications

The application of this exercise is simple yet unusually difficult. You'll never run out of opportunities in which to apply the *point* of this exercise. No need to seek out special situations; for example those in which you feel the stress of having to do something in front of a group of people. We continually interact with others and invariably present images: how I want to appear, what I want others to think of me. We *also* continually present ourselves to ourselves, being less than honest with ourselves. But instead of presenting yourself, try to be where you are at the time. Then try to see yourself clearly and honestly.

Start with the physical self and its manifestations; then perhaps experiment with your thoughts and feelings as objects of study. Pick situations at first which are not too distracting or stressful. Return again and again to times when you are alone. Prepare yourself. Relax. Still your mind. Give yourself all the help you can!

Incidentally, do you know how much control you can have over your physical manifestations? Deliberately change your facial expression: when you smile, does it make you feel happy? When you are happy, can you generate a frown? Explore these manifestations. Realize they are only the form which can express your life.

If your views of self seem empty, or if you are becoming overly introspective at the expense of fulfilling everyday responsibilities, then you know you are on the wrong road. You are seeking to contact what is alive inside you. That aliveness cannot be empty; that aliveness exists fully through your everyday functioning.

FURTHER READING

Abraham Maslow, *The Farther Reaches of Human Nature*, Viking Compass Edition, Viking Press, New York, 1971.

> What has been called humanistic or third-force psychology tries to focus on man's potential for growth. Maslow was a pioneer in this field. I think you'll sense unfinished aspects in this book, aspects which Maslow himself was always trying to deal with. For example, how do peak experiences relate to ordinary everyday life? Are peak experiences similar to spiritual experiences coming from intentional efforts in a spiritual discipline? And how does humanistic psychology deal with transpersonal or transcendent issues? Maslow's work always has an open-ended quality— he encourages you to go on from where he was.

William James, *Varieties of Religious Experience*, Mentor Books, New American Library, Inc., New York, 1958.

> James discusses psychology and religion, consciousness and growth. His case material is alive. This book was published a while ago, but it is very contemporary. I think it will remain contemporary because men's consciousness remains essentially the same. What fluctuates is our attempts to understand consciousness and allow it to exist fully. James's attempt at understanding can be helpful.

Encountering

*W*E continually remain superficial, moving with all possible skill over the surfaces of situations and experiences. Yet we seek encounter; not because it is easy or comfortable, but because it is alive and enlivening. Encountering can become an expression of the growth process.

Encountering is first and continually a matter of encountering yourself—seeing yourself as if for the first time. If you have lost touch with yourself, how can you reach another? When you demand that someone else be more open and give you more freedom, and you *yourself* are not trying to *live* freely, then the demand is empty. If you are in contact with something deep inside yourself, then you can let another reach inside himself. Your own example can be a challenge, even an inspiration for another to meet himself. Each of us must grow in our own terms, but others can catalyze our growth.

In the first exercise, "Force toward Encounter," you can experience the simple dynamics of encounter, its building blocks, its basic qualities. You will probably re-realize how rare true encounter is. The next three exercises may give you some more clues as to why encounter is so rare; each focuses on how we usually behave.

In "Which Role Is You, Which Is Me?" the costs of playing roles can become clearer. Roles are supposed to increase our efficiency. But if they also deny our aliveness and sacrifice our growth, how important can efficiency be? Can you expand some roles, drop others? Is the real you another role?

The "Listening" exercise raises other considerations. How can we experience encounter if we don't really listen to ourselves, let alone to others? We stay on the surface, merely hearing words in the air— my words, your words. We don't pause to listen deeply.

Finally, in "Who Can See?" a basic dilemma becomes more apparent. We each live in our own special worlds, populated by our own way of thinking and feeling, our own hopes and wishes. This individual world can be a source of strength, enabling us to meet others. But too often it is a place to be comfortable in and to protect. During "Who Can See?" you can explore the helping relationship as a possible bridge across worlds. Can you learn from another instead of merely helping him? Can you have your help received instead of merely giving it? Can you go beyond the helper and helped dichotomy, beyond the superior-inferior distinction? Perhaps then you enter another's world.

Clearly experiencing obstacles to encounter can help you increase encounter in your everyday life. Also, while experiencing the obstacles, you can experience encounter.

The Force toward Encounter

The *possibility* of encounter happens every day, all the time, every way, everywhere. Meeting and exchanging, face-to-face, eye-to-eye; maybe for the first time, maybe the hundredth; with another, in groups of three, in groups of all sizes; at home, in school and stores, on the street. But we keep it as only a *possibility*. We don't want to risk really meeting another; we keep our interactions superficial and safe. We go to a store to buy something from a salesman; we don't relate to him as a person—that would be too inefficient, take too much time. We go to class to hear the teacher; we don't relate to the teacher as a person—that would be too irrelevant, we wouldn't learn enough material, enough facts. I disagree! If all our interactions are merely safe and functional, we give up too much. I think we can be *both* effective and alive—it just takes more care and energy.

Let's take time to approach encounters more simply, to get inside them. In this exercise you can explore the structure and building blocks of encounter. First you must contact yourself, then you can work with another, then with others in larger groups. We will also focus on qualities of interaction, such as tension and collaboration. All these qualities can facilitate encounter if they are first expressed openly; most of them impede encounter because they are not made explicit. The interaction medium will be immediate and direct—physical contact. This can highlight issues. We can work toward transforming tension into collaboration, physical proximity into encounter. Instead of being forced into encounter, we can move with the force toward encounter.

LABORATORY PHASE

Structure

There are four principal phases to this exercise. In the first phase, all persons participate together for approximately twenty minutes. Then, for the several minutes of the second phase, each person tries to get in touch with himself. Then, during the approximately ten minutes of the third phase, pairs work together; and finally, in the fourth phase, for another ten minutes, groups of three or more work together. The basic exercise takes about an hour.

For each phase, I've described extensions which can be tried if time permits. They allow you to consider issues from a new perspective and to consider new issues. Incorporating these extensions into the basic exercise, you can work for up to two hours.

You'll need a fairly small space with physical boundaries for the first phase—a fenced-in area if it's an outdoor space. The space should be open, with furniture moved to the side. In the subsequent phases of the exercise, you'll need a large, open space; it need not have physical boundaries.

In phase one you'll need a blindfold for each person.

Instructions

PHASE ONE: APPROXIMATELY TWENTY MINUTES. Put on your blindfold and explore the space in whatever way you like. Please do not talk. This is very important. Explore. (Allow about ten minutes to pass.) Now stop where you are and take off your blindfolds. Will all of you who are grouped together form a very tight, close circle in the center of the room. One by one, each of you on the outside, try to become part of the circle, physically breaking in if necessary. Those who are in the circle, you can either resist his entrance or invite him in. But once he has entered the circle, welcome him; invite him to take his place in the circle. Repeat this until everyone is in one circle.

Now that we are all together in the circle, look around at everyone. Try to establish contact with someone you don't know well; try to contact the group.

PHASE TWO: AT LEAST SEVERAL MINUTES. Take leave of the group and, for the next several minutes, try and come to yourself. Keep it simple. Start by loosening up, stretching, breathing deeply. Increase your circulation. Begin to feel yourself being alive, lungs breathing, heart beating. Then try to establish a calm quiet in your body and heart and mind. Within this vital quiet, try to contact a more essential you. Again and again, try to reach a place of substance within so you might honestly realize you are alive.

PHASE THREE: APPROXIMATELY TEN MINUTES. Keep in touch with yourself as much as possible. And from a point of strength inside you, seek out another. Find another without talking and together select a space to work in. Join hands with your partner, and briefly loosen up together. Now explore together three qualities of interaction: relaxation, tension, and collaboration. Spend several minutes on each quality, develop it, experience it, try to express it purely. Don't rush through any of the qualities. Use different kinds of physical contact to help express the qualities. Don't talk. Don't ask when you should move from one quality to next; just move. Are you clear about when you moved from relaxation to tension, from tension to collaboration? Can you make these qualities feel different? Do they begin to merge?

PHASE FOUR: APPROXIMATELY TEN MINUTES. Now, choose two or more people to work with, and again explore the same three qualities: relaxation, tension, and collaboration. You and your partner can remain together in this larger group if you wish. Is it easier or harder to express these qualities in the larger group? Less direct? Less intimate? Can you intensify interaction in this larger group so it functions *as if* it were a dyad *without* breaking into dyads? Try increasing physical contact. Try expressing the qualities more purely.

Extensions

In the *first phase* of the exercise, after everyone has opened his eyes, you can try several other things. The cluster of people stands and forms a very close circle. One person who was not in the cluster moves to the center of the circle and closes his eyes. Then he is physically passed around from person to person, while trying to remain as loose as possible. Is he pushed around or treated gently? After going around the circle several times, the person in the center assumes a position in the circumference of the circle. Then someone else from the outside comes into the center. This is repeated until everyone in the room is in one large circle.

Once the entire group is together, it can do things together. For example, the group can move as if it were an amoeba. It becomes very flexible, moving irregularly, but it somehow always sticks together. Perhaps the group can try to ingest something, or grow large or small. Or it can be a snake, moving in waves, expanding and contracting. Whatever it becomes, the group should function as a single unit.

You can always use more time in the effort to contact yourself. You need time so you can direct your energy to a deep, substantial level within. *If you make but one extension in the basic exercise, lengthen and deepen this second phase. It is both the most difficult and most fundamental phase.* Unless you first have contact with yourself, you can't contact another.

In the *third phase*, there are many other ways you can work with your partner. Keep the interaction physical. Explore other interaction qualities: balance, centrifugal and centripetal force. Focus on physical rather than interpersonal qualities; focus on the body rather than personality. Keep it simple and direct.

Here are some other things you can do with your partner. They are especially good for "warming up," loosening up so you can interact more directly. You might start by putting your hands on your partner's shoulders and, together, try to rock back and forth, side to side. If you like, close your eyes. See how far you can rock in different directions while maintaining your balance and physical contact with your partner.

While still standing now, begin to stretch your partner. First take his arm and stretch it. Don't be too tentative. Stretch enough so he can feel it: his shoulder, above his elbow, below it, his head and fingers. Stretch, don't pull or tug. Now try the other arm, and then both arms together. Stretch them above his head, high into the air, so you are both standing on your toes. The person who is being stretched should try to relax and be open to what he is feeling. When you feel you have finished, change roles. The person who was just stretched now stretches the arms of his partner. Now, sitting on the floor, continue stretching— your partner's legs, his neck. Don't rush. Stretch so he can feel stretched. Stretch parts—the calf, the foot.

See how many ways you can bend and stretch together. Explore the limits of the body, explore the limits of the space.

Here is an extension of the basic exercise appropriate for the *fourth phase* if you are working with five or more people. It emphasizes trust within a group; it is called lifting. Lifting can also be done in the first phase. One person lies on the floor, flat on his back. He should close his eyes. The others in the group slowly lift him in the air, supporting his limbs and his head. Try lifting him over your own head; carry him around the room if you can. Now lower him very slowly, very gently until he touches down on the ground. All who want to can be lifted.

Discussion

We've tried to simplify encounters so we can experience them more fully and understand them more completely. Could you experience the basis of encounter, the coming to oneself in order to go toward another? Could you experience the different qualities of encounter, the tension, the collaboration? By concentrating on the physical aspects of inter-action, did these generalized qualities become even more apparent? And could you experience the rhythms of relationship—inside a close-knit circle, outside and separate, working with another, with others, with yourself?

It is almost ironic that, as an introduction to encounter, people are asked to explore in the dark, with their eyes closed, and on their own. It is even more so that they generally wind up with each other. If nothing else, it tells us that people are interesting to each other. There seems to be almost a magnetic attraction. Is there a force toward en-counter? Or merely comfort in company? The key lies in whether you build relations with others upon a solid foundation, a simple fact—being in touch with yourself.

Throughout the exercises, people were very conscious of group participa-tion and cooperation, but the idea of simplicity seemed to be disregarded.

The idea of exploring the room itself soon boils down to contracting the others in it. You can feel walls and floors for only so long without being distracted by others, constantly bumping into them and being bumped. Do you try to identify persons or to get your bearings? If you are willing, you can transform bumping into an exchange. Instead of wondering where you are, you can meet who you're with. People may start to explore each other—feel another's face or hands. Maybe you will begin to explore the room with another. Those who shy away from this contact might remain on the sides or in a corner. What were your contacts like? Satisfying? Superficial? Exciting?

When the blindfolds come off, there is an obvious split—those who are together and those who are alone on the outside. We then work to repair the split in the group. Those who are together are not necessarily more successful in the exercise. Perhaps they are more casual about relating to others; perhaps they seek to lose themselves in a crowd. Only you know why you are where you are. We take the situation as it exists and work with it. Having people on the outside join the inner circle is a good way to form a single group. Did you want to join that group? Did you force your way in? Where was the force toward encounter?

> We held hands in a cir
> cle and I felt
> my spirit flow
> quietly
> through the chain of hands
> and back to me
> enriched

We are using our bodies, making physical contact. This medium helps remind us that encounter is not an abstract notion; it is a direct, immediate happening. By using our bodies we can be more direct and down-to-earth. The way we relate physically can highlight the way we usually relate, which is on the less tangible level of personality. Being physical also helps people put energy into the exercise. You struggle to get into the circle, and then you are accepted, overwhelmingly. You trust others to protect you and prevent you from being hurt.

Center . . . circle . . . pushing and pulling . . . joined around . . . holding hands . . . feet joined in the center . . . stretching up and down, up and down . . . in and out, out and in . . . the human circle.

I felt like I was slipping from one person to another rather than actually being tossed back and forth. As the constant rhythm and pattern continued I lost all idea of what was around me and slipped into myself . . .

If you tried moving each other around the circle, passing each person from one to another, you could explore trust further. At the core, once again, is you—can you trust yourself to relax, to let go?

Once a certain rhythm was established, I began to feel like I was floating. . . .

Finally, I closed my eyes and it was as though I were wandering in the air.

How are you relating to others? Can you rely upon others to catch you? Do people push you, or do they move you with care? Are you loose or stiff? Again, an abstract notion, trust or acceptance, is expressed and tested in the physical dimension. No longer can you just think about trusting other people. You must do it if you can.

Could you reach a substantial point in yourself? Did you go to the source of encounter before you began working with your partner?

. . . and I'm standing motionless in my corner thinking about going back to sleep in my room . . . but this girl is standing in front of me, hands held out looking at me so closely that I start to wondering if I look as bad as I feel. . . .

. . . I was very scared and apprehensive. It was like a microcosm of social interaction in general, and I was surprised to find that I was really nervous when suddenly asked to "make friends." There was no escape route, no possibility of solitude. We were called upon to commit ourselves, to go up to another person and nonverbally say, "I want to be your friend. Please accept me." And if that person did not accept you, there was no possibility of saying, "I was just kidding, anyway." There was no way to pretend, except by pretending totally, by simply not becoming involved in the experience. . . .

. . . my fears no doubt originated in the fear of being rejected by someone who I chose as a partner, or in fear of not being chosen. I remember having the same feeling in Junior High when. . . .

I experienced a strange fear that he (partner) would find me to be somehow insensitive, link me with all the "straight" people (a feeling which strikes me on reflection as potentially leading to some kind of hippy fascism). . . .

. . . My choices were mostly based on proximity . . . I followed this method because of two reasons: (1) I did not want to insult people by passing them without choosing them, and (2) I wanted to find a partner as soon as possible to avoid the tension of having to look for a partner. . . .

. . . I had a very strong wish to be chosen by one of the people I was attracted to but was afraid to approach. . . .

. . . At this point . . . I could not find a partner. Each time we were supposed to choose, I would have preferred to be chosen, but was at the same time afraid of being "stuck" with someone I didn't want to know. This time, when I realized that there was an odd number of students, and that I was the odd one out, I moved to a corner where I could get a view of everyone. . . .

Well now I have been chosen and the initial anxiety of remaining alone is gone. . . .

I think I was too influenced by outward appearance and used it as a criterion for choosing a partner. This indicates the presence of a type of snobbery in me which I strongly dislike but nevertheless played a part in my choices. . . .

Then I knew that everyone was at least as scared as I was, and there would be times when I would have to step out of the passive role I often choose for myself, as a defense, revelation, coming in the form it did.

It's all familiar, painfully familiar. And it remains like "being asked to dance" until each of us can contact ourselves. The encounter evolves.

The entire encounter experience could too easily become a series of "hello-goodbyes." And nothing more. I know now that I must discover the middle.

Unless we put something into the exercise nothing comes out; it's all "hello" and "goodbye." You can put in only what *you* have; you put in yourself, to varying degrees, in the desire to reach another. And the interactions reflect you in relationship.

How did you approach these situations? How much energy did you call forth? Were you timid? Were you afraid to really stretch his arm—perhaps tense, reluctant to be stretched? People often feel awkward, not sure of themselves, not knowing whether or how to touch another.

Feet, legs, head and other parts of the body were largely neglected in favor of the more familiar tactile instruments of hands and arms. The touch of arms and hands also seemed to be considered less personal and less involving—perhaps because of the commonness of such modes as a part of everyday communication.

Is the body relaxed? Does it move and stretch easily? Is it *willing* to be moved and stretched? Did you let it be?

I feel the trust of others in me, that I will not let them fall, that I will not pull too hard, listening to the messages from others, the strain of their muscles, their calmness or not, their gentleness or not, their trust or not; and they both listen and do not to the others in the group; they learn to listen to their silence, to hear what the body says . . . the boy does not, he drops me and the other boy, he does not bother to listen to the tension of the arms . . . but he learned some and eventually listened more. . . .

The entire question of leadership maintained an air of spontaneity about it. In almost every instance, the member who would be the first to think of the exercise for the particular quality assumed the position of temporary leader . . . we had created a situation characterized by equal status as opposed to the unequal status of a normal teacher-student relationship. There were definite "leaders" who traveled from group to group or tyranically stayed with one group base with various new followers. These leaders brought with them their particular conception of how the various attitudes could best be expressed. Upon the given command, they immediately set off to impose their ideas on the whole. Thus they stifled any ideas the others may have merely slowly manifested.

Who is the leader? Who the follower? Who is active, who passive? Who initiates the action? When two people lock arms, who is to determine in what direction to move? Who will change the movement? Suppose you sit back to back. You can't talk, and you can't see each other. How do you decide what to do?

What is it that binds two people together like this? You can sense the other person's strength—his willingness to take action. Then you want to move in different directions; there is conflict. There must be agreement, and communication to reach that agreement. How to communicate becomes the question. Each person must be open and receptive. He must try to sense what his partner is like. Feel his grip, his body. Look at his face. Notice how he responds when you want to do a particular thing. Testing limits before you can relax with each other. Giving and receiving.

Not only relaxation but tension might hold people together. They may confront each other on different terms—each wanting to do his own thing. And the conflict and tension will keep the two together. And psychological tension too. You are both nervous. Your uneasiness leads you to act in certain ways, and you sense the uneasiness of your partner; and this might become the basis of interaction.

You can learn about yourself.

I found myself taking the role of leader in both the cooperative and the non-cooperative movement exercises and realized that I was annoyed when a partner I did not choose "forced himself or herself" on me, or when a partner attempted to dominate the relationship.

You can learn about yourself and others and relationship.

My partner was my boyfriend. To be with him was like to come to security, someone you know very well, someone with whom there are no fears and no distrust. There was also the added anticipation of perhaps getting to know him even better than before. After talking with him about this interaction, I found that I had discovered more about myself than about him. He said he felt that I was always taking the initiative and that he was just following. The more I think about it, the more I decided that his feeling was very significant. However, the question is not one of leading and following. In general, in the exercise, I did not take the initiative of finding a person (except for once or twice) i.e., I tend to be a follower. The important issue here is the issue of "getting one's own way." I think the exercise brought out the fact that it is more important for me to get my own way than for him. This has very important significance for such a relationship.

With this kind of knowledge about leading and following, you have a chance to go beyond the overly simple dichotomy of leader and follower into collaborating both actively *and* passively.

We're speaking of self-knowledge, and how that can lead to true encounters with another. Let's hear what one person said of this exercise; and *listen:*

. . . the session can become a source of invidious comparison, of competition, of smug pride instead of openness and exploration. A kind of "how-creatively-alert-are-*you?*" feeling. I hope that creative alertness means necessarily a self-sufficiency that allows you to free yourself from this. . . .

Moving on to a larger group can be both a more and less intense experience. There are more people to get to know, more to come to terms with. Issues of leadership and direction are complicated. The chance for conflict is greater. But the possibilities for creative activity and communication are also increased.

There was a great sense of intimacy and responsibility among the three of us. I really felt as if I were receiving "vibrations" from the other two. . . . I was not involved with anything beyond our group. . . . It was as if this mutual confidence was a bond holding our group more closely together. . . . We were all very careful of each other. . . . I feel that this exercise was real . . . it reflected the behavior of people in everyday experience.

The intense, intimate atmosphere of the dyad is easily lost. There is less pressure to act. It is easier to follow.

With three people there is usually one outsider . . . and the chances to let up and draw back increase.

The level of communication can become more superficial.

The group of three relieved me of the direct person-to-person relationship.

It is sometimes harder to share with more than one person at a time; it is usually easier to fall back into stereotyped behavior.
You've moved outside yourself, you've met another. Can you move beyond that dyad to the larger group? Do groups of four resolve into two dyads? Is encounter the relationship, the "in between"? Where does it begin, or end? Where does what you and your partner have built together go? Can you let go, let it go all the way?

So, to begin. You and I, should we create a nucleus, a tootsie roll pop center, of doings, with spun filaments, cotton candy strands, correlations and derivatives, shooting off from the center to God knows where? O.K. that's fine. To show, recreate, project the center and the strands is simple. BUT: where do the strands finally go? And how hard are they glued to the center?

I kept going in and out . . . when my partner and I were engaged in something, it seemed beautiful; when there seemed nothing to do, I was nervous and wished the exercise was over. It soon became very clear that I was not relating from a point of strength within, and what I thought was "beautiful" was more a fortunate coincidence where two persons' behaviors meshed to help delay my coming to grips with myself.

What was the quality of your interactions? Where you able to express relaxation, tension, and collaboration purely? Tension can be difficult. We are reluctant to express something which is usually so divisive or hostile. Yet when it is expressed openly it can lead to encounter—you accept the tension in yourself and the other accepts you. This holds for each of the qualities. Express them openly, accept them; then there is a chance for encounter.

In exploring tension, often the group creates ways of pushing and pulling each other. One fascinating technique is to create tension by *not* touching: perhaps by exerting pressure on a blank space between yourself and another, making sure not to come in actual physical contact. The growing temptation and desire to touch becomes intense. Psychological tension is important here.

Collaboration can also be explored in many ways. Some groups actually had each person supporting and supported by another. Almost a human pyramid. In another group, each person lay on his back on the floor, with his head on another's stomach. The group was completely connected stomach to head to stomach to head, etc. People tried to breathe together and achieved such a harmony that they naturally breathed together. At one point, the entire group got up and swayed and moved about the room in perfect unity. Each person could feel the presence of each other, and the group itself became the focal point of everyone's energy. Each person devoted himself to the group.

It is interesting to note just how far each group explores the limits of the situation. In how many ways and directions can you stretch a limb or bend your body? What are the limits of tension? How far can collaboration be extended? And then too, the transition periods are important—between tension and relaxation, touch and nontouch. Each quality can be expressed physically, emotionally, psychologically. You can establish collaboration with eye contact, and you can have psychological collaboration. As you continue to explore, the specific qualities may merge; relaxation is collaboration is tension.

Another fascinating area to explore is the differences between males and females. Our culture has so forcefully set up the models for male and female—for example, the active, assertive male and the passive, weak female. These models are hard to challenge:

There were two people I had considered meeting, but I felt it inappropriate for a girl to be the first one out of the circle, especially since I would have had to walk over to a boy.

I was unable to choose a boy for a partner in an encounter. The reason probably lies in my own doubts as to my masculinity and a fear of tension which I would have felt having close contact with another boy. . . .

In dyads, males and females tend to handle themselves differently. Some males may be anxious about having to be more "powerful" than the female, but still might enjoy displaying their strength. Some females can be unsure to what extent it is appropriate to lead or direct a male to do certain things. But these are not clear-cut differences; we can't say "all females are . . . ," or "all males are. . . ."

And what happens when there are larger groups of all males or all females? One male describes his all-male triad:

We had an attitude of athletic and inventive fun . . . but the playfully uninhibited mood that developed was also responsible for the lack of true creative, cooperation and experience. . . .

A woman notes of her group:

More often a follower than a leader, I felt a bit more powerful when the other two members of the group (both girls) followed my cues and my actions. . . .

What we're "taught" to be so often restricts our own development.

The challenge is clear. How can we respect the *essential* differences between men and women and break through the dehumanizing stereotypes? How important is sheer physical strength? "brute force"? Where is the place of the gentle touch? Strength is physical *and* psychological; it has nothing to do with muscles. How can we change existing differences which are repressive and discriminatory, regardless of their origin.

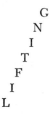

I first had my eyes open and when I neared the ceiling I touched it and laughed in exultation. I did not feel self-conscious. I lost any sense of where I was. . . . I felt light.

I had only a sense that I was floating . . . how high? who was touching me? . . . I could not tell. . . . It was sheer bliss.

In a moment I had no feeling of height or of people supporting me. . . . I no longer realized where I was or what was happening to me, but I was more intensely alert to what I was feeling.

The lifting exercise highlights issues. You relax, let yourself be; you can then trust in the group which can give you intense satisfactions and can encourage you to go beyond yourself. But growth is more than "sheer bliss"; it is hard work. And we are not talking about giving up responsibility and succumbing to a group psychology.

You start simply, with yourself. You build toward encounter on this firm base. You relate from strength, not weakness. Then you experience how we are all the same; we are all one.

In the discussions, some of the most self-contained people began to tell personal feelings about the exercise. A real feeling of camaraderie developed. I found out other people have reactions and feelings like my own. I also found out about different reactions. By mere introspection you only know a small part of yourself, but by sharing experiences with others, you have a basis for comparison with other parts of humanity and you know yourself as a part of humanity.

APPLICATIONS

Try to experience encounters in a variety of settings. What are your limits? What are the limits of encounter? Does group size affect you? Do you withdraw in large groups or do you "perform for an audience"? Can you really communicate with more than one person at a time? Is encounter possible in large crowds? Crowds with a high density? With pushing and shoving? What can happen in a crowded elevator? What are your density limits beyond which you can't encounter anyone, especially yourself? When are you forced toward encounter, and when do you go with the force toward encounter? And when you are alone, can you meet yourself? Have you tried? Study encounter by experiencing it.

Begin to experiment with the form of encounter. You might work with triads or quartets. Are triangles necessarily unstable? Try building an enduring relationship with two other people. Or perhaps you and your partner can explore encounter with one or two other couples.

Try bringing encounter to all your empty relationships, the power-saturated political relationships, the money-motivated commercial ones. Don't you have something to say to another person, as one human being to another, regardless of the function he performs? You can be efficient *and* remain a person. When you begin to change the quality of your encounters, previously difficult forms of encounter become possible. And they can be especially rewarding.

One way of changing the quality of your relationships is to make it more explicit. Select a tension-filled relationship, perhaps in your family or with someone else you know well. Express the tension, openly, physically. We often have to "stretch," air out feelings. You can transform the tension into collaboration—not by denying the tension, but by accepting it and going on from there. Tell the person who is always so political to be himself; if you *and* he can accept his political style of relating, he can become himself. He may even decide to change his way of relating. The salesman may decide to sell you only what you need, really need, after you and he talk about his tendency to create needs for you. Rather than chaos resulting, we could have honest tradesmen entering necessary transactions. We might begin consuming less . . . but what more could we want!

In trying to be more direct and explicit about the quality of your relationships, you might repeat parts of the exercise with people in the "real world"—with those you care about, with those you work near, with those you dislike. This will not be easy. Can you invite another to relate to you directly, perhaps physically, without scaring him, "freaking him out," appearing foolish or crazy? Can you work with such sensitivity to *his* state that you encourage him to be open, not defensive; to meet you, not withdraw? If growth is your goal, it might work. If power and manipulation is your goal, it won't.

Which Role Is You? Which Is Me?

You need very little preparation for this exercise. In contrast to the previous exercise, where we tried to explore encounter, we can now examine the way we usually relate to ourselves and others—not directly, but filtered through and diffused by roles. Though it's not a simple case of cause and effect, playing roles is often a chief obstacle to encounter.

The effect of roles is not simple, because we each assume a series of roles during the course of a day. It's not even as obvious as the man who acts like a husband, father, son, or boss depending on the situation he is in and what is expected of him. The series of roles we assume is both more complex and more subtle. Also, roles are not easily dismissed as "evil"; at times they are necessary and useful.

But, too often, we act and react according to our roles unnecessarily, or use roles as vehicles of oppression. Even when we want to, we cannot contact ourselves and relate to another, person to person. The goal of this exercise is to become more alert to our different roles and perhaps to learn how to function more humanly within these roles, or to drop them or substitute them when appropriate. You have to face the question: Is the "real" me just another role? By working with your roles, you can get some leads toward finding yourself.

LABORATORY PHASE

Structure

Decide who should take responsibility for developing the materials for this exercise. This person would then run but not participate in the exercise, though he should join the discussion. The person selected develops and writes up roles for each member of the group before the exercise begins. PARTICIPANTS SHOULD KNOW ONLY ABOUT THE PARTICULAR ROLE THEY WILL ASSUME. Twelve should be a maximum group size. It's all right if several of the roles are shared by two members. Some of the roles should be arbitrarily chosen: for instance, to support those people wearing eyeglasses, or to disagree with the person sitting to your left. Some roles should be inherently conflicting with others. For example, a role "to act as a leader" might be given to several people and a role "to prevent anyone from assuming leadership" to several others. Another possibility for conflicting roles is the mediator versus the devil's advocate. Other roles might capture archetypal images, such as the unrecognized "holy man" or the unpredictable, irrational adventurer. Still others should allow for shared, collaborative activity, as when one person is given the role of being helpful and another of seeking help. Of course, collaboration may not result; instead, it may become a contest as to who is helping whom. Try to have some of the roles subtle, complex, and even ambiguous. Avoid too simplistic a situation where you have only role polarities.

(You might work with actual masks. Participants might wear, for example, a blank face or a smiling or angry one. Then you will make explicit the usual conflict between a person's feelings and his expression.)

If there are more than twelve people, you may want to divide into two smaller groups, having one of them participating while the other observes. Then switch.

The person who develops the roles should also develop a verbal task for the group to do. Each person in the group will play out his given role while trying to do the group's task.

Here is one example of an appropriate group task:[1]

Task Description
AN EXERCISE IN RATING THE GRADING SYSTEM

You are to work as a group, to discuss and to rate eight statements given below which refer to the grading system. The group will have fifteen minutes for this task. It is possible you may not finish in the allotted time.

Place a "one" in front of the statement the group decides is the most valid way of characterizing your position, a "two" in front of the statement the group decides is the next most important, etc., until the eight statements have been rated.

You must work as a group. Record the rating as the group decides upon it.

Read through the statements carefully before beginning your discussion.

_____ It is impossible to summarize what a person has learned with a letter.

_____ Grades cannot be assigned reliably (a given letter may mean something very different to two different professors).

_____ Grades tend to obstruct continuous learning (they raise artificial end points rather than making for an even flow of the education process).

_____ Grades create undue competitiveness.

_____ Grades don't provide a basis for equitable interschool comparisons.

_____ The grading system places constraints on what should be a free and open student-faculty learning relationship.

_____ The grading system places the emphasis of education on performance level rather than on understanding and growth.

_____ Grades do not reflect individual differences.

And here are samples of seven roles you might give to a group:

1. Your goal is to have the group make their decisions during the task by consensus. In order to achieve consensus a group must first have information on how each member feels. The actual decision can't be made until each member is heard from. Each member must end up feeling that his feelings were at least heard by the group, even though the group may decide to do

---

[1] The following sample group task and role descriptions are adapted from material prepared by Dr. William McKelvey.

something else. You feel one good decision by consensus is better than just trying to finish the task.

2. Your goal in the group is to be friendly and helpful. Your role is to carry out behavior such as the following: attempt to reconcile disagreements; reduce conflict and tension; be cooperative; help keep communication channels open; get people to explore their differences; be friendly, warm, and responsive to others' needs; show acceptance of others' contributions; offer compromise solutions. Try to develop a friendly, cohesive group. Work at the feeling level, trying to get all the good feelings out. Group cohesion is more important than getting the task done.

3. Your goal is to get the task done. The role you should play is one of "full speed ahead." Do anything you have to to speed things up. Develop the most efficient and quickest decision process. Get impatient with people who slow things down. Convey the impression that this task is a ridiculous waste of time; that the group would be better off if it just got through the task as quickly as possible and got on to more important things.

4. Your goal is to be an autocrat. Your role should be to initiate activity, propose tasks or goals, define problems, and then try and get your ideas accepted by the group. The main thing is to get the group to do things your way. Convince the group that your way is best. Things to avoid at all costs are group influences. You should develop formal procedures for the group. Take control.

5. Your goal is to be a sturdy battler. Your role is to pick out the people in your group who are wearing glasses and express the following behavior toward them: disagree with them; make humorous undercuts; debate and argue with them; quibble over semantics; deliberately withhold support; give "yes-but" reactions to what they say. Generally ignore or be neutral toward people not wearing glasses. If nobody is wearing glasses, fight with members having shorter haircuts.

6. Your goal is to be an analytical, logical thinker. Your role is to behave in the following general manner: place most emphasis on cognitive abilities and develop ways to get the most correct and rational decisions. Stress factual data, past experience, and logical arguments. Define terms, clarify peoples' thinking, get relevant information, criticize comments that are not well thought out and supported by data. Put a stop to expressions of emotion which detract from a logical, rational decision process.

7. Your goal is to rise above the task *and* influence other people in that direction. Your role is a meditative one but it should not lead to withdrawing from the task and the group. Transcend the task by doing it well and in a special way, not by ignoring it. Affect others in the group more by your example, your presence, than by direct urgings. Try to raise the level of the group so it has a broader perspective and deeper understanding. Above all, be calm within yourself.

The role-playing exercise should take up an entire session. No special space is needed, just a place for people to sit in a circle and talk with each other.

Instructions

These instructions may sound formal and constricting. Much of the exercise may feel formal and constricting. Try to work under these conditions.

Each one of you will be given a slip of paper with a description of the role you will play. Do not show or discuss your role with anyone else. A few minutes will be allowed for you to read the roles and to become familiar with them. Now gather together in a circle and begin to work on the task which has been given you. Your goal is to stay in your role while, as a group, you finish the task. Try to be realistic in your given role *without overacting.*

Discussion

My immediate reaction was one of relaxation because the way I was to act was not going to be "me" and, therefore, I felt I couldn't be blamed for my actions. This feeling was almost immediately displaced with a feeling of tension precisely because my actions weren't "me" . . . then I slowly realized that there was something of that role I was given inside "me."

At first, the role-playing exercise can evoke an uncomfortable feeling of being split between your (real) self and your (new) role:

I was unable to get outside of myself and into my role . . . I was too worried and self-conscious.

I felt unwilling to confuse my "real" self with my "role" self.

Usual problems were intensified because the roles were rigid and in some cases completely alien to the person forced to play them . . . they resulted in a tension, a feeling of suffocation. The *true me* had to be eliminated.

During the discussion, however, people can warm up to their roles, the fit becomes less strained.

It was frightening to see how little control I had over my role, how easy it was to be the role and have it run away with me. . . . The self was being eaten by the role.

Where you surprised when, for a moment, you had assimilated a performance that had once appeared so exterior to your self? Or did you remain continuously uncomfortable in your role, outside of it?

I'm not really like that! . . . but, of course, the role always fits, more or less comfortably.

The ease with which we can assimilate new behavior, and even attitudes, gives us some clue to the difficulty we all have in distinguishing our "true" self from the accretion of roles:

Was he being himself or playing a role? And if he was himself, then would he think I was being myself?

How did you play your role?

Can I be myself? Must I exaggerate certain of my own traits?

When you are yourself, is that also a role?

With each person playing his role, the discussion can become frustrating, fragmented, divisive, tense, and unproductive. Each person seems more intent on achieving his own particular goals, protecting his own interests, than in relating to others and working with the group to finish the job. Many find themselves trying to excel in a role which they do not feel to be themselves.

Instead of being able to lose myself to fully grasp what another was expressing, the exercise forced a continuous assertation of self (in the form of the role) . . . my ideas had to be injected.

I was so concentrated on playing the role that I could not relate or see others. My emphasis was placed first on getting across my own role, then discovering who everyone else is, and finally (and remotely) on what was being said for its intrinsic value.

Doesn't this sound familiar? It could be a description of much of our everyday interaction.

The dynamics of the discussion can be patently clear. When you sense similar or identical roles in another, there is a tendency to work together; when you sense an opposing role in another, there is usually a continuous attack. Again, it all sounds familiar. A bit exaggerated and obvious, but basically realistic.

My first impression of the persons I saw "going at each other's throats" was that this was only a contrived game, but as the people in the group seemed to "become" their roles and fully *became* conflicted . . . I felt a tremendous amount of tension as if someone had wound up a group of persons and told them to attack and counterattack.

It isn't only role-playing. Our feelings are aroused, our motivation intensified; we become involved. The exercise is more than role-*playing*. It's a mirror of who we are and how we act everyday.

. . . one player said he felt compelled to break his role for an instant and smile, so as to counteract the antagonism he felt rising between himself and another player within the context of the exercise.

I reacted with a good deal of tension and a desire to yell either "no," or "this isn't it at all!"

Could you turn off your roles? Can you begin to experiment with mastering your roles rather than being mastered by them? In the exercise, you left your roles when the discussion ended, or did you?

Although the actual dropping of my role was fairly easy, it took quite a while for me to get rid of the taste of playing a role.

The conflict of roles can test the bonds developing between persons.

Since many people were only beginning to become acquainted (outside of roles, that is) the interpersonal encounters had been fairly delicate up until then. . . . This sudden antagonism was startling, even though the roles are only enforced ones. . . . People started to be not so sure that the roles weren't real.

Players expressed frustration at having to "be" something they didn't want (or like) to be and a fear that their fellow players would now indelibly type-cast them into their exercise roles.

And did you feel the fragile nature of the contacts you had built up? Concerns can extend beyond the exercise. Will you hold my playing that role against me?

How can anybody hold playing that role against me? It was all so arbitrary; it was only a game.

My first reaction to my role was one of amusement at the arbitrary nature of the prejudice . . . but all prejudice is, in reality, fairly arbitrary and just as unfounded. People are considered bigoted if they can't tolerate others but not if they are logical thinkers.

In this exercise, we intentionally developed arbitrary and constricting roles. Also, roles were chosen which would intrinsically conflict with each other. The resulting discussion was probably quite self-centered, fragmented, frustrating, and divisive. We exaggerated the costs of role-playing. In everyday living, it is all usually more subtle. Roles are less obviously arbitrary; there is less obvious intrinsic conflict and inefficiency, and discussions are less obviously self-centered and divisive. But we still all continually play roles. The subtle quality makes it that much more difficult to understand.

It was amazing how well people "grow into" their roles. In daily life, there is no one to call the game off. The game begins.

Perhaps, by highlighting the self-centered quality of most roles, you can begin to sense more clearly some of the dilemmas in your usual mode of relating. Perhaps you can become more alert to your role-playing in everyday life.

During the exercise each participant was alert to the limitations of role, whereas the limitations within our habitual daily activities are usually unnoticed.

Perhaps, after experiencing the joy of not having to play a role, for just a moment, you can begin to experiment more with your everyday roles.

Everyone experienced tremendous relief at being able to drop their roles . . . it was expressed through changes in physical attitude, relaxation, facial expression, breathing (sighs).

Apply what you've learned here. Try expanding your roles, making them more human; try dropping roles which are unsatisfying and unproductive. Consider dropping roles which, though efficient, seem counter to your own growth—you may lose a particular job, but you can't afford to lose yourself.

APPLICATION

The preceding exercise exaggerated the costs of role-playing. Hopefully, it gave you some ideas about your role-playing in daily life. Since your everyday role-playing is more subtle, it may be harder to become alert to your roles; more than likely, it will be even harder to change or drop a role. In daily life you have more at stake; you are more committed to protecting your image and position. But now, instead of defending your particular role as you probably did in the exercise, try to expand your concerns and become less self-centered.

You should have no problem in locating a place to start applying what you've learned—we're playing a role nearly all the time.

Consider again this idea:

It is amazing to realize that there is something of that role we were given inside each of us.

Here is something you can try in the interest of gaining some mastery over your roles rather than being dominated by them. It may also suggest that you can extend yourself; that your self-image is probably exceedingly narrow, based primarily on what you would like to be. We can call this application "Be the obverse."

First, consider your characteristic ways of behaving and relating. List three phrases or adjectives descriptive of yourself. Select specific but essential characteristics. You might be outgoing by nature, or moody, or hostile when talking to your boss, or generous with your family, or reflective in the early morning, or emotional when talking with your son.

Now take the opposites of these characteristics and assume them as your new character. Create characteristics that are distinctly not you yet are at the same time realistic.

Remember, you are not going to *become* destructive. Unfortunately we already have too many destructive exchanges. But, for example, being stingy or unfriendly for a brief period need not be destructive. After you have tried being the obverse, tell the person you interacted with what you were doing and why. Tell him you tried to be stingy because, being usually generous, you wanted to explore other aspects of yourself, parts you may tend to avoid or deny. If possible, share some of your feelings about the way you were with him. What are his ideas about the characteristic you worked on?

Try being the obverse of your usual self by working on one characteristic at a time. Prepare yourself; consider what you will do. Get ready to experiment and explore. At the start be the obverse of your more generalized characteristics (e.g., if you are outgoing, try to be shy). Also, at the start, be the obverse in situations which are "safe." A situation is safe when there are no strong expectations about who you *should* be; when there is no great risk in trying out this new behavior (e.g., don't try to be loud at work if you would be penalized for it); and when your intentions will not be misunderstood. Pick a situation where you aren't known. Perhaps in a store you've never been to before. There, people won't make personal demands of you. They react to you usually in terms of your role and no more. Thus it might be easier to play your new role. It won't be an obvious performance. You can get comfortable behaving in a way that is "unlike" you. You can be shy, for example, where you might normally be outgoing.

Then try being the obverse with friends; here expectations will pull you back toward being your usual self. We all like to know where each of us stands, and we like to count on your being in the same place each time.

Also, try working with the obverse of your more specific characteristics; for example, if you're usually hostile to your boss, try being friendly. Again, the pressures will be toward maintaining your old, familiar behavior, even though it is mutually deadening.

It shouldn't matter whether being the obverse means you are trying for the moment to be hostile or kind. As I mentioned, you will not become destructive. Rather, you will be expressing a characteristic on a temporary basis. For the purpose of trying out roles, kindness and hostility are the same. For the moment, you are trying to develop mastery over roles. Can you put them on; can you take them off? How does it feel being other than your usual self? Can you now see a little more of yourself—aspects which you would rather not see, aspects which don't fit your self-image? When you have some degree of mastery over a role, you can understand it better. Then you can *effectively* work toward the values you believe in. Wanting to be kind to another when you are still trapped in a selfish role remains a wanting, not a being.

There are countless roles you can explore and experiment with. Develop the hidden aspects of yourself, those aspects about which you say, "if they only knew what a _____ I really am!" Or try to understand how you use roles to oppress yourself and others. Start with one of the classic role-relationships: male-female, parent-child, husband-wife, teacher-student, employer-employee. Break into the role; break out of it into yourself.

Study the question of efficiency and effectiveness. Which of your roles increase efficiency? Which decrease it? What are the personal and psychic costs of such efficiency? How efficient can certain roles be if they cost too much? Prove for yourself the difference between effectiveness and efficiency.

Consider the way we celebrate the passage from one role to another, or better, the way we deny these transitions or make them empty. Can you reenter the myths about passing from one stage to another? Why have births, graduations, marriages, deaths became so empty? Make them once again celebrations of life. A good start would be to bring your own life into these events when you meet them.

The most central but elusive goal is to be yourself. Is the "real" me another role—perhaps a richer, more complex role, but a role nonetheless? When you believe you are being yourself, are you in fact acting closer to your *ideal* self? Isn't the real you realistic? Isn't it all of you; the "good" and "bad" in such simplicity that there is no more good and bad?

Listening?

So much of human interchange is patterned and familiar that we become quite cut off from what is actually happening. We can select an "adequate" response to any situation by attending to only a minimal set of cues. We don't need a lengthy exchange with someone before we can "tell" that he's angry or cautious or curious—because we've come to expect consistent patterns of behavior in those we know.

But don't you sometimes wonder what is actually happening? Too often, we answer someone on the basis of what we expect him to say or what we think he said, without questioning the accuracy of our understanding. We hear but don't listen. We talk without caring about what we are saying. And naturally, others hear us without listening.

In this "Listening" exercise, you can examine the communication process more closely. You can try listening to another. You can start by listening to yourself. You may even establish moments when there is mutual understanding. And that is communication.

LABORATORY PHASE

Structure[2]

All you need is a space for one or more groups of approximately seven people to sit in a circle and talk with each other. Groups shouldn't exceed that number because interaction in this exercise will be slower. It will take more time for members to participate. The space should be large enough so the groups can't overhear each other.

This exercise can take approximately an hour. It can occur during its own session or can start in the middle of a discussion the group is having.

Instructions

We will establish a specific ground rule for our group today. The ground rule is as follows:

Before you say anything to anyone, or before you answer anyone, you must first restate what the person being addressed has said. Try not to merely repeat what he has said in a sterile, literal manner. Try to restate the sense of what he has said, including the emotional quality. But don't overinterpret. You can speak only after the person being addressed is satisfied you have restated what he said.

This ground rule may seem arbitrary, and your interaction will certainly not go as smoothly as it usually does. But that is exactly the point. Though it may be more difficult to carry on a "conversation," stay with the ground rule. Hopefully, you can then begin to communicate.

---

[2] The idea for this exercise came from Carl Rogers. You might want to read his discussion of listening in Chapter 17 of *On Becoming a Person*, Houghton Mifflin Company, Boston, 1961.

When you discuss this exercise after completing it, don't use the ground rule explicitly. But try to apply some of the exercise experience. During the discussion, pause for a brief moment: Are you listening? To yourself? To others?

Now begin or continue your group following the ground rule. Anyone can start. You can talk about anything. Why not talk about something which is important to some, if not most of you? But don't waste time selecting a topic. Begin trying to listen.

Discussion

We hear but we don't listen. Sometimes we don't even hear. We go about our business without listening to our own inner voices, without listening to others. We fail to communicate, to reach ourselves or others. The exercise can make this all too apparent.

How do you deal with these conditions? Do you seek to increase communication?

When others interpreted what I said, I wanted desperately to "urge them on" or even change what I said so that they'd understand me. How infrequently we react with anything other than automatically conditioned nods of the head . . . "yups" or the like. Such an enormous effort is involved in *really* listening and being listened to . . . nothing can be assumed.

Or are you tired of trying, are you at times resigned to comfortable "miscommunication," ships passing by silently, unnoticed in the night?

He very easily quoted her as saying the opposite of what she actually said. . . . yet she accepted his statement. . . . It was all very sad and yet very familiar.

We must first accept the situation as given, but in becoming more alert to that situation we can change it.

First, did I fully understand what the person had said? Second, did the person actually say what he had thought? Third, if I had understood and the person did verbalize his thoughts well, could I express in words my response to his utterance—clearly and precisely?

By working with the ground rule for this exercise, you can highlight this situation as given, this state of miscommunication. "Understanding" becomes more than merely a value; it becomes a problem.

The conversation does not flow smoothly.

The artificial barriers to a smooth flow (of conversation) seemed to isolate one idea from the next. The dialogue was impeded by the circular effect of "about what you said about what I said about what you. . . ."

The sequence of thoughts seems hard to follow. The conversation becomes nonlinear, moving in spirals or concentric circles.

It is not always clear when you should start, when you've ended. How did you become part of the group? How do you express a new point? Were there rights of entry established, traffic patterns of conversation, "talking" rights of way?

It was quite easy for the conversation to be confined to two or at the most three people . . . after this triangular motion continued for a while, someone would finally break in, repeating the last person's thoughts then dropping the subject, invariably saying, "Well, let's go on to something new."

Invariably, there is a feeling the conversation isn't going well, it's not very "smooth." Nor is much being accomplished. Points are not being made or "scored." You might feel you're not convincing others, or that this is a very inefficient way of talking with others.

But it would be a mistake to think the interaction was meaningless. The very fact that nothing seemed to have been accomplished could signal that something was being said and that people were listening.

Or did you keep the conversation superficial, being civil and polite? You might have missed an opportunity to exchange rather than merely converse.

Staying with ground rule is hard. When someone spoke in his usual manner, without first trying to restate what the other person said, how did you react to this? Did you, by your own example, show him how to work within the ground rule? Or did you step outside the rule by telling him he had broken it, and then realize you were in the process of doing so yourself? The apparent dichotomy between talking and listening seems arbitrary. And it is. We put ourselves in unusual situations and accept demanding conditions *in order to* see ourselves more clearly.

As the exercise unfolds, you can begin to see the dynamics of miscommunication. It seems that I focus on what I will say in response to you, rather than on what you're saying:

The exercise demanded a unidirectionally focused mind over a fairly long period of time. I'm thinking of my response before he's completed his statement. . . . I have to focus . . . focus . . . at which point I am attending to focusing rather than to the speech.

I would rather immediately interpret what you say than ever actually listen to you. No wonder we can't remember what another says.

The difficulty people had in remembering what had been said seemed to indicate people tend to decide for themselves, often wrongly, about what's been said.

We want to say "our own thing" first *and* last.

People's enthusiasm for saying their own thing is a powerful force. People will take their thoughts and rephrase them in their own frame of reference.

We end up not even speaking honestly with ourselves.

We all tend to speak to anyone, in partial vacuums, more for our own edification than for communication.

And we are the ones who make it so hard for others to listen. Did you try speaking briefly and simply, encouraging another to listen, helping him to restate what you said by rephrasing it even more simply? By the word *simple* I mean straightforward, clear, and honest; not simplistic.

How did you use your right to have the other restate what you said? To encourage the other toward more understanding of you and of himself? Or for your own personal power, manipulating the other, preventing him from talking until he more than satisfied you?

Were there moments of understanding? Could you listen to yourself and to others? Did restatement expand into understanding or contract down to dry, sterile repetition? Did you find yourself *merely* restating, so as to follow the ground rule and give yourself a chance to speak as soon as possible? This quick and dry repetition can inhibit the interaction; listening can spark it.

What was said after the repetition didn't seem to have been sparked by what had been said by others.

Sometimes it's not clear what happened:

Once A agreed with B's interpretation, one which I thought contained more than what A had actually said. Perhaps it was what A was thinking but hadn't been able to express well; perhaps it sounded good; or A forgot what he (A) said; or it was easier to agree. Perhaps I heard or interpreted incorrectly.

You can't always remember what you said—often it was not important enough to remember. Some image of you was doing the talking. Then it is always hard to determine what changes the restatement involves. Within a network of communication, however, you don't hassle over small changes and total accuracy. Rather, you listen to the meaning behind the words, accepting the other person in a more general sense.

The moments of understanding may have been few, but the dynamics of misunderstanding probably became clearer. In everyday life it isn't so easy to see ourselves not listening.

There is a tendency for us to make our discussions sound smooth even if in reality they are senseless.

I was impatient with the breakdown in communication. . . . later I realized my impatience shouldn't have been with the people in the group but with a whole way of life and of thinking which takes the discipline out of the act of communicating.

But it's not discipline in any rigid sense that impedes listening. Rather, it's not taking the time and making the effort to come to yourself first and become ready to receive.

APPLICATIONS

In different situations, at different times, prove to yourself that listening is more than hearing. Begin at the beginning. Do you listen to yourself? Do you listen to your own inner voices; do you trust your own intuitions? Does being able to listen to yourself help *you* listen to others? Does it help you say something and not merely converse? Find out for yourself. Test out this general principle. Live it before you decide to live by it.

Be more alert to yourself when you are supposedly listening. The next time you are in a group discussion, on the side, jot down all the ideas that come to your head, regardless of whether they are directly related to the conversation or not. Later, look at those ideas. How many were actually related to the discussion going on? Of these, how many were related to what the other person was saying, and how many are strictly your own "points"?

Work in situations which place particular emphasis on talking and listening, which usually means "nonlistening." For example, a classroom situation. The student role is usually an especially verbal one, with this idiosyncrasy: the author of an utterance, rather than a listener, is expected to understand the utterance. Traditionally, the teacher's job is to make sure the student "knows what he's talking about." The teacher himself isn't particularly interested in the student's view per se, it being, after all, elementary or naïve. Similarly, the job of the student's peers in a classroom is not to listen to a point of view but to gain entrée for their own conceptions. Can you really listen in the classroom? Would it remain a classroom if several persons did?

Another situation is where leadership is emphasized, and as usually happens, where leadership is equated with talking. Can you really listen and avoid being relegated to a mere passive follower? Will you be type-cast as quiet, or strong but silent (and without authority)? Work toward transforming individualistic displays of verbal agility into moments of communication. With verbal peacocks, you can only hear; it soon becomes impossible to listen. But by listening you may encourage the peacock to *be* for a brief moment, before he shows off. And such moments are precious.

Also, try the exercise we just did. Work within the exercise groundrule. At times, make it an open agreement with others. At other times, introduce the technique spontaneously. Can you do it for the sake of understanding and not power? Do you have an exchange or do you force another to speak on your own special terms? When you start listening spontaneously, do you encourage others to also start?

There are always opportunities to listen. Keep little notes to yourself in places like your wallet, your table, your pocket. When you reach one of your places, you see a simple message: LISTEN! You remember you haven't even heard very much recently. Then you try to listen. Try to be as if you are the only one being spoken to, even if you're in a group. When responding, try to carry on from where the *other* left off, and sensitively create a continuing exchange.

Who Can See?

This exercise confronts a basic fact of our everyday life. Each of us lives very much in his own "world." To be interested in another's world is one thing. To understand that world is something else. To enter each other's worlds, giving and receiving, being truly helpful to oneself and another, that is still another thing.

In this exercise, we will start in two different worlds—one populated by the sighted, one by the blindfolded. Quickly there are many more than two worlds, and it is unclear who "sees" what. But the challenge remains. Can we trust another to help us? Can we trust ourselves to help another? Do we care to help? Can we help with care? Can we enter into another's world? Do we dare?

The nonvisual world assumes particular importance in this exercise.

It becomes the medium through which we can enter another's world, through which we can help and be helped. But it is just that medium which we in the West are most unsure of. We live in a basically visual culture, often to the neglect of our other senses. We depend heavily on our sight and take it for granted. This can easily be "seen" when there is a loss of sight, as simulated in this exercise. Through this exercise, we can begin to appreciate the expanding world where we are engaging all our senses.

LABORATORY PHASE

Structure[3]

Blindfolds for approximately half the group will be needed. They can easily be made from an old sheet. Both blindfolded and sighted people will be instructed to move about in an open-field situation. Therefore a large area is necessary; an out-of-doors area is preferable. Be sure that the environment in which people move is safe for the blindfolded person (e.g., no heavy traffic, dangerous stairs, or sharp objects). This does not mean that an empty, clear, soft meadow is necessary or desirable. You will rely on the group, both sighted and blindfolded, to avoid difficult spots for themselves. Members of the group will be responsible for each other.

During part of the exercise, it is good to have people involved in some task. Working on something can be an informative contrast to the merely aimless wandering which occurs. Eating together is very good—it gives people an opportunity to break and share bread, to bridge "worlds." If you decide to eat together, have people bring food to the exercise.

Any number of persons can participate in this exercise—limits come from the size and nature of the area you work in. You don't want to have your space too densely populated. You'll want room enough to enable people to move and discover and to be alone when they want. Consider how much contact you may want with the "outside world," how isolated your space must be. Having blindfolded persons interact with "normal" people can be very informative; it can also raise delicate issues (e.g., in interfering with the desire of those not connected with the exercise to go about their usual routines).

The exercise can take anywhere from approximately one to several hours or longer.

---

[3] I first heard of this exercise from Dave Kolb and Irv Rubin. Their writeup stimulated my thinking about the potential richness of the exercise.

Instructions

For the next _____ minutes, you will be free to move about in an open-field situation. Approximately half the group will be wearing blindfolds at any one time. We will meet back here at _____ o'clock. (We can then eat together.)

There are no restrictions as to how you proceed in this exercise: you can travel in pairs or larger groupings; blindfolded or sighted persons can work together or separately. There are no particular things you must do. Try to explore. Don't *just* sit around. "See" as much as you can.

One very important thing to remember: During this exercise, the group is a group, and as such is responsible for *each* of its members. No one should be allowed to wander into situations in which he could hurt himself. The area has been selected so that such risks are minimized.

Most questions you still have before you begin, you can answer yourself—just think about it. For example, you can figure how to get back here by _____ o'clock. If you meet someone from the "outside" world, try to learn something from him, and teach him about your world. Be sensitive to him rather than playing with him or manipulating him. If you want to switch during the exercise from sighted to blindfolded, exchange with someone. But don't switch more than once. Stay with your blindfolded or sighted condition if you hope to learn from it.

When everyone has returned, we can talk about the exercise. If you want you can leave your blindfolds on during the discussion.

Now, take a blindfold if you wish. Balance your group so approximately half of you are blindfolded.

Discussion

When my sight was suddenly taken away, I felt almost completely removed from the world around me. . . .

When you suddenly become blindfolded, your world changes dramatically. It becomes a new world within the old world.

Persons chose to be blindfolded for many reasons—some intentional, some accidental; some substantial, some vapid.

I choose to be blindfolded—so as to be "in." . . . It was pretty scary, but certainly being blind is the thing—so I will—so I did. . . . I alternated between being a brave man in search of experience and a little boy very much afraid. . . .

But once the blindfold is on, your world changes, and this changes everybody's situation in the exercise.

Many blindfolded persons find that before they begin to experience the world of darkness, they must first deal with those who remain sighted. How did you relate to those inhabitants of the other world, the world of sight?

Some blindfolded persons leave little room for working out a relationship, even less room for being helped. Refusing help, they strike out on their own, sometimes boldly, sometimes impulsively, sometimes carelessly.

Others are more dependent, standing there, waiting to be led:

I became alert to myself, and saw an image of myself standing alone in this tremendous emptiness. I called out to a sighted person, but I heard none around me. I realized that the dependency I had felt myself losing before, now became extreme. . . .

Don't dwell on "dependency." Realize that it's a part of your personality, shared in some degree by us all. Accept yourself more.

Still others work toward independence on the basis of help from others:

. . . When we came to the stairs, she warned us of them and guided us individually up the first two. From then on I was on my own. I proceeded very cautiously into the unknown—sliding my feet and groping for a railing. It occurred to me that this time and the only other times that I had been cautious and concerned were when I was out on my own, when I had no one to watch over me, when I didn't have confidence that I could do everything myself. . . .

Did you experience different reactions to your helplessness? Did you try different styles of receiving aid? How aid is offered to you can determine your ability to make these changes. An effective helper can encourage you toward independence. An ineffective one can force you into unrealistic and exaggerated independence or seduce you into dependence. Too often this is the case.

How did you as a sighted person offer help? Did you try to enter the blind world? How empathic could you become? Did you try closing your eyes for a time? Or ask a blindfolded person to describe his experience and then try to listen? Or ask him to lead you through his world, taking your hand over surfaces as he explored them?

Too often sighted persons resort to less challenging paths. Some retreat from much of the exercise, avoiding responsibility for relating and helping—and possibly learning. You can physically leave, avoiding any contact, or withdraw psychologically, performing in only a cursory manner. In either case, loneliness, isolation, and alienation usually result. Could you see something of yourself under such gloomy conditions?

I felt terribly lonely, even useless. It seemed that the only real experience to be had was to be blindfolded—there was a negative value in being sighted.

Other sighted persons assume a rigid role, constantly leading, continually overprotecting. There is often real concern ("Will the blindfolded person hurt himself?") and good intentions ("I wanted to help"); but little imagination and exploration. In this relationship the person being helped remains helpless; he doesn't grow. Since you risk very little—on either end of the relationship—there is almost no chance you will see yourself from a slightly different viewpoint.

But perhaps you do try; you try offering help to the blindfolded persons, you try to be sensitive to their needs.

I tried guiding, not leading the group. I kept from talking. I tried more to communicate my presence, sometimes by the scraping of my feet along the ground. . . .

And you realize what a challenge it is to guide well, how subtle and fluid is the guiding process.

His steps were sure; he trusted me, I suppose, yet his expression changed from one of intense concentration, through awe and wonder, to a very childlike hesitation, even fear. . . .

Sensitive guidance is often accepted. Careless or manipulative or rigid leading may be tolerated but not sought after. And yet many of the sighted, regardless of how they approach the blindfolded person, can't get into his blinded world.

. . . I felt slightly the possibility that I might not get back to the room, but the surroundings were familiar enough to give me faith in my ability to fend for myself. (Not until right now did I realize that I could have taken off the blindfold.)

There seem to be several factors at work. The world of the blindfolded person is becoming richer, more involving, more separated off from usual events. And then, the blindfolded are not particularly interested in inviting the sighted to enter their world, *even* if the latter could. They are more interested in the varied and new lights emerging from their assumed darkness.

For many blindfolded persons, the beginnings of darkness were less attractive though still involving. There is considerable disorientation, often physical in nature:

We spun in circles in a fear of darkness, disoriented with all the sounds.

The disorientation can be more generalized, leading some to try placing others to get their own bearings:

"GRAB OTHER BLINDED MEMBERS. . . ." "Are you blindfolded? . . ." "Will you show me who you are when we take our blindfolds off? . . ." "We DON'T WANT YOU." "Tony. Are you here? Tony . . .TONY. . . ." "Who are you? I'm Ginny. Who are you? . . ." "Can you see? . . ."

Then the lights begin to filter through the darkness:

I actually pictured in my mind a gray fog and someone approaching me bathed in light. My isolation ended with this discovery of others outside the initial bunch. . . .

Instead of grasping onto the nearest person, blind or sighted, blind-folded persons may begin to relate to another or to their world.

You might begin to explore your nonvisual space:

It was interesting to *give* and *take* food from people—merely for the spatial enhancement involved: Where is your hand? Where is your mouth? Ah, yes, there it is. . . .

Are you blind too? Only the other blind person understands this; that the importance of textures and echoes has grown. The sighted person says the building is brick but we who are blind explore together the nature of brick. Rough, not red; and cold and a bit damp, and high beyond reach. Not a building but a surface to be explored.

The blindfolded ones begin to play, becoming perhaps more uninhibited:

We *pretended* to be like seven-year-olds exploring the woods. . . . NOVELTY . . . they're not just white rags, they're magical, they're BLIND-FOLDS!

Gooey cake, smell of mustard . . . (uh, oh—must be all over my face). . . . Quick! Napkin someone! Dummy, nobody can see it anyway.

. . . I totally lost myself in the "space" of my mind and was only returned to earth when Lynn's hand plunged through the picture and knocked me in its direction. . . .

The blind are exploring an inside world. They feel as if their eyes have turned inward. They explore the world inside their heads. Colors disappear from mind. The world is turned into objects, sound, and touch without appearance. They are learning to exist within themselves.

. . . I became progressively less concerned with the reactions of others toward myself and more concerned with my own reactions toward them. In this sense my singular reality loomed larger and more significantly than ever before, whereas the outside world was diminished to a shadow of its former pompous self. . . .

Then out of this self-contained reverie, they move toward other like-minded blindfolded persons. Hearing hands clapping over there, they go together. The nervous laughter and the excitement identify the group as blind. Together they cross the unknown space, filled with trees and bumps and rocks. And when they arrive, they bump into one of the group, hands go out searching; finally two hands are touching tightly to one.

Who are you? Are you blind? What are you doing? Hey, we have two new members, he says, holding them with one hand and the group with another.

The sighted are quietly watching.
The community of blindfolded ones takes on a form. The common experience of living in the same world works as a cement. The blinded trust each other more—they don't lead each other into blind alleys; they appreciate each other's special talents—they *can* "see" more than the sighted. A blindfolded man "sought for an 'honest' hand or an 'honest' voice"—he found both among his fellow countrymen. The blind lead each other more honestly if not more efficiently. Something more than individuals begins to exist.

By collectively confronting a similar plight, we were able to diminish the power it held over each of us individually.

The blindfolded enter their own worlds, forming their own community. Where did that leave you if you were sighted? Most sighted persons simply feel left out.

. . . the notion that "in the land of the blind, the one-eyed man is king" was not so . . . the sighted ones were ignored. . . .

Though you want to help, your offers are either spurned or strictly limited. There is little you can do.

. . . our cries are answered by Judy. . . . sighted, she reunites us. . . . yet I do not feel dependent on her nor do I feel gratitude. . . . This is her function as a sighted person . . . it's to be expected of her. . . .

At times you seem more able to help, leading a blindfolded person through a difficult psychological or physical passage. Then he reestablishes his blind identity, and you're once again on the sidelines.

The blind person grabbed hold of me, firmly, and asked me to guide him around the parking lot. At the time, I was filled with self-importance and gratitude; I felt necessary and indispensable. That my services and not my "being" had been in demand became quite clear as soon as my blindfolded companion became reconciled to his loss of sight. . . .

It is not unusual to begin feeling resentment toward the blindfolded group. You may feel unwilling to remain responsible for keeping these ungrateful people from hurting themselves. Sighted persons begin to manipulate, fool, and take advantage of the blindfolded ones: guiding a blind male into the ladies room or warning another of an impending crisis like a stairwell when there is none.

. . . I found my main objective to be to return to the room with as little assistance as possible. When a sighted person led a group of us into a cul-de-sac, I felt frustrated and betrayed, and hesitant about trusting them further. . . .

But as a sighted person, did you explore other possibilities? Granted, the blindfolded were usually more into their own thing than into relating. But did you explore your own world? Instead of merely sinking into feelings of being unwanted and left out, did you try to see something about yourself when in that state? Is being left out especially hard on you? Or did you develop other things to do? Were you able to participate, even for brief periods, in the blindfolded world? Were you willing to function on their terms when in their world?

It has to be a mutual process. The blindfolded sometimes keep maintaining distinctions. During the discussion, a person may keep his blindfold on. Perhaps he still enjoys experiencing without sight, or maybe he feels he can then participate more freely in the discussion. Perhaps he wants to keep a we-they distinction, or perhaps he wants to show up the sighted for their prior insensitivities. It continues to be hard to harmonize the two worlds; again, for both substantial and insubstantial reasons.

Where were the harmonizing influences, the forces transcending the dichotomy between helped and helper, sighted and blindfolded? There are basic similarities between the two camps, some obvious.

Someone who was watching the exercise from the outside asked: Why are they eating with blindfolds on? His companion answered: I guess because they're hungry.

As a helper, did you try guiding sensitively, perhaps by your presence, emphasizing intuition? Did you realize where your guided person wanted to go when he was exploring on his own, and how he was guiding you? As one being helped, did you make clear when you needed assistance, when you had something to teach and when you wanted to learn, on you own? Could you empathize with the helper, and facilitate his functioning?

The issue is not whether we are sighted or blindfolded. That is more the vehicle for raising the issues. Can we enter another's world? Could we first learn about our own world so we can learn about another's? Can we help without assuming a superior attitude? Can we realize that "help" isn't helpful merely by being given; it must also be received.

APPLICATIONS

In the blindfold exercise we examined our condition—living in separate worlds—and explored a way of bridging these worlds—helping and being helped. You probably experienced how helping is so much a matter of learning and receiving. Before you can aid another, you must be able to aid yourself. You become helpful only when you seek to learn from the other as well as to guide him, when you know something about how he lives, and when he asks for and receives your aid. Helping is give *and* take for both parties.

Experience the helping relationship in more depth, over more extended periods. Begin by working within one of the classic helping relationships, where someone is "obviously" more "helpless." Work with an older person or a young child or a blind person. Tutor someone. Seek aid in some area where you are weak; for example, find someone to teach you to swim. Keep the relationships simple, focusing at first on some specific area or skill where aid is needed.

Certainly you've been in such relationships before. But now, try to experience the relationship as if for the first time. Experience the helping relationship from both ends. Transform the assumption that one of you is helpless into the fact that we all can learn from each other in different ways, at different times. Confront your own areas of ignorance. Instead of improving the other's skill, try to exchange, person to person, through working together on that skill. Begin to transcend the dichotomy that originally separated you.

Explore other worlds. Go to another "country," where another language is spoken. Put yourself in unfamiliar situations. Seek out the "foreign countries" immediately around you. If you are a college student, spend time in the surrounding "other part of town." If you are more inclined to be sedentary, spend time doing some manual labor or factory work. Try to enter a closely-knit, closed circle of friends. But remember, you're not visiting a zoo, where you may stare at the strange and unhappy creatures; in fact, you're not even visiting. Stay for a long period of time; be there. If possible, make it an open-ended stay. Don't give yourself too much comfort in knowing "it's only for a summer."

Keep regenerating your motivation to experience and learn. Can you begin to understand this other culture? Try describing this culture, which is new to you, to one of its older members. Does he agree with your perception of his cultural norms, norms you have *experienced*, not read about? What about your own worlds? How are they affected? Can you see something more of your worlds after being away from them, and into something else? Do you try to become part of this other world? Can you ever, really? You can, through this other world, come into closer contact with your own worlds.

Create different worlds to explore for yourself. Try to function without sight. How does it affect your other senses? How does it affect the way you feel about your world and the people in it? You can try to focus on your other senses in your own room. Close your eyes and try to sense the room: how it feels, smells, sounds, etc. How about the feeling you get being in that room? Do something very similar the next time you walk down a street or road. You don't have to close your eyes; just try to focus on what your other senses are telling you. Instead of functioning without sight, function with all your senses.

If you decide to use blindfolds to create this different world, be sensitive to those who are going about their "normal" business while you are in your new nonvisual world. You can function with blindfolds in such a way as to freak people out or bother them or merely let them be. Unless you are prepared to work with those unconnected with your exercise, let them be—they will then let you be.

Certainly you should try working with others outside your exercise; integrating your own discoveries into daily life and learning from it.

But bumping into another while wearing your blindfold may not create the possibility for an exchange.

I left the room for the joy of getting a drink alone and blind. Groping along the wall to the fountain I bumped into another drinker. "What the Hell? Are you blind?" "No, I'm a Professor of History." And then he left.

You have to be prepared to see where the other is, to work with him, not work him over.

FURTHER READING

Joseph Campbell, *Hero with a Thousand Faces*, Meridian Books, World Publishing Company, Cleveland, 1956.

> People have always reflected on the question "Who am I?" Today there are few situations where our culture actively supports confronting this question. Campbell, with a broad sweep across culture and history, demonstrates that this lack is not a universal condition. He describes many structures of self-discover: initiation rites, adventures, journeys. We see how often individuals have been supportively confronted until they recognize their own identity. Don't be carried away by the romance of Campbell's historical examples and references to "primitive" groups. Dig into the book for yourself; for today!

Martin Buber, *I and Thou*, Charles Scribner's Sons, New York, 1958 (second edition).

> "All real living is meeting." Buber says this and expands on it. He moves back and forth between specifics of encounter, like glances and gestures, and the ground of encounter, which is man's relation to God. When man can relate to God in himself and another, he is encountering. Buber offers us a picture of man with potentialities far beyond our superficial interactions. If at times Buber seems abstract, bring him down to earth. See if he makes sense for your everyday life.

Carlos Castaneda, *A Separate Reality*, Simon and Schuster, New York, 1971.

> Castaneda wanted to learn from Don Juan, an Indian sorcerer. He wanted to learn about becoming a man. He goes to study with him. Or does he? What kind of a student was Castaneda? What kind of a teacher was Don Juan? Did Castaneda trust enough so he could really learn? Could he truly be affected by Don Juan's approach, which evolved from a culture so alien to his own? Did they really meet? How do you judge for yourself whether Don Juan's approach is knowledge? Might some of it be illusory for you? Do drugs really help you to see, or is it the harmonious and supportive culture in which they are taken which is the key? How do *you* deal with this man, Don Juan?

Creating

*W*HO is an artist? What is art? How do we create? I am convinced that we create growth, that growth is creation. Since we all can grow and do grow unless we subvert that process, we all can be creators, "life artists." We can be creative in approaching ourselves and others; creative in performing everyday tasks. It seems absurd to restrict such an enlivening quality to persons labeled artists and the media labeled art. That quality flows beneath and beyond art products. Don't you know housewives and repairmen who are life artists, and painters who are dead inside?

It seems equally absurd to view creation as the outcome of one person's ego fulfillment. More and more we see the need to collaborate if we are to be truly creative—the world is just too small to support each of us in his little garret being an artist. Collaboration of individuals—coming to ourselves first, then trying to transcend ourselves in the effort to communicate with others. Communication as creation as communication. And at the base of this collaboration is a realization that we are all part of a larger process of cosmological creation. In going beyond our individual egos, we can both express ourselves more freely and accept others' expressions of their selves. In approaching creativity as a process occurring throughout the universe rather than as a product of one person's efforts, we can *each* be truly creative. We can give birth for life rather than pride, fame, or individualistic expression—which in the end destroys.

In the "Group Collage," the format seems familiar, but the approach is challenging. Can you allow everyday materials to express the creative process? Can you be creative and simultaneously allow others to be creative? Can you become part of a whole and remain alive? Again, in the "Human Sculpture," the format is familiar, the approach challenging. There is only one material to work with, which appears simple. But the material is ourselves and the implications are many. Then, in the "Space Exchange," the format becomes less familiar yet the exercise appears to be the simplest to do. I think a better word would be *simplified*. By simplifying conditions, the "Space Exchange" intensifies issues: you can form "something" from "nothing" *as* you *let* yourself create; you can enter another's space and welcome him into yours *as* you get beyond your own private concerns. Only when we experience and accept the transpersonal basis of creativity can we all become life artists.

Group Collage

Will you let yourself be creative? Must you produce a piece of "art," meeting certain aesthetic criteria? Can you transform everyday objects and tasks into expressions of the creative process? This might be relatively easy if you were working alone. But what happens when others are also trying to be creative? Can you allow them "room"? Even when they seem to be covering over your own efforts? With mutual respect you can create together, becoming living parts of a larger whole.

Laboratory Phase

Structure

Allow a one- or two-hour period for the collage. At least several days before the exercise, participants are asked to bring a variety of materials. Use your imagination: found objects, spray paints, leaves, magazine pictures, etc. Be sure certain materials will be brought: several pairs of scissors; several containers of glue or paste; materials which can span distances, such as toilet paper or recording tape; paints and brushes; a large surface to work on, like brown wrapping paper or cardboard; and provide for a way of making it easy to clean up the space afterwards (e.g., using a large drop cloth). If people know beforehand the approximate size of the surface to be worked on, they can decide about the size of the objects they bring. This exercise can occur in any space, indoors or outdoors. The surface to be worked on is more critical; e.g., the smaller the surface, the more likely are interactions between creators.

Variation
You might focus on three or four specific media: e.g., construction toys, clay, wood, several nails, and perhaps a hammer. Try to have diversity in your media, such as the pliable clay and the rigid wood. Subdivide the group and give each small group one medium.

Instructions
Put the materials you brought in one section. We will pool our resources. Take several minutes to see what we've all brought; examine the resources; begin to share them. When you feel ready, spread out your working surface and continue by making your collage. Remember this is a *group* collage, made by each of you. During the exercise, you may want to reexamine the pool of resources or use it differently; you may want to reexamine the collage or approach it differently. Try to accept both your own and others' creativity.

When is the exercise over? When the collage is done? Can it be "done"? Finished? It is often easier and more to the point to select a certain time when you will discuss your work and leave open the question of endings.

Discussion
What materials did you bring? Which materials did you use? Were you able to express a different part of yourself by working with another's material?

I brought some very interesting pictures and I wanted to use them to suggest certain themes. . . . Then this can of spray paint appeared, and there I was spraying paint all over—over my picture *too!* It felt right. I don't let the expansive side of me out enough.

We tend to bring materials we are comfortable using: neatly cut out pictures, or messy shaving cream, or all-covering spray paint. We can expand ourselves, express our undeveloped aspects by using others' favorite materials.

How did you create with others? During one collage, a girl was constructing an intricate, lovely Japanese garden in a corner of the paper. Suddenly it was drowned in a blast of red spray paint, and immediately thereafter draped with toilet paper. This particular gardener was not identified with her product; she was more involved in creating. She accepted the new direction in the collage and helped transform careless expressivity into an expression of energy. But many times you remain identified with your own work and others don't respect what you've done. Snags develop; the creative flow sputters. Then there is resentment and a feeling of being ignored and taken over:

I resented those who worked on details . . . they seemed to be so narrow-minded to have no regard for what I was doing with the string going back and forth over the collage. . . . It was only in our discussion after the exercise that I saw how much I was trying to protect *my* thing and how little I had gone beyond my own special concerns.

The relationship between your own creation and the group creation is complex. Often, people begin to define personal areas on the working surface with their personal supplies. At various times, certain persons will break through tenuously defined spatial areas by changing places or moving their bodies onto the surface. At first, others may be annoyed by intrusion on their personal territory. The smaller the working surface, the more interactions there are, and the more one person or one material can dominate the collage. Territorial claims enable persons to control the aesthetic content of some part of the surface and also to avoid involvement with the group. Gradually liaisons develop and people begin to accept the rest of the space as their working space. The collage activity gradually draws people into more communication and cooperative effort. This could be recognized in the conversation of one group which chose to be partly verbal throughout the exercise. At first, talking was limited to "Pass the glue, please," "Scissors, anyone?" etc. But quickly people were relating to their neighbors, making suggestions or requesting that someone "stick this on top of that," "spray this gold," or exclaiming "oh yes! we can make a face. Where's the nose?" As the collage progresses, verbalization often decreases.

People working with connecting-type materials such as paint, glue, toilet paper, or string play a special role in the collage. Do they use the spray paint to build on others' creations or to link these creations together? Someone delicately connected the three highest points in the collage with loosely draped string. Or do they use the spray paint to cover over others' creations, either merely destroying them or converting them into a new kind of material? Do some "hog" the space? It is not easy for a large number of people to allow each other to work together.

The collage can transcend the flat working surface: it can become three-dimensional, and you can become part of the collage. Did you expand the media you worked with? Often people find themselves participating in a way they haven't experienced since childhood, with release and joy and involvement. They can express visually things they don't normally express, protected against criticism by the anonymity of the total effort. Did you work from different perspectives—at ground level, standing up, moving around the collage? Did you consider the collage as a process of collaboration?

After the collage, questions emerge. "What should it look like?" Is that a relevant question? "How did it feel?" Isn't that too simplistic? Shouldn't we ask: How was it to participate in the process of creating the collage? Did you work as an individual who was part of a group? Were you creating with self-discipline, caring for what you did, and in that getting beyond shallow expressivity and moving toward real expression? Were you able to create somewhat beyond your own self-boundaries? These are questions for the quiet of our inner selves—we need a moment of silence to consider them honestly.

People often suggest how the exercise should or could have been structured; for example, deciding on a theme first. Someone suggested that the group stand in a line and one at a time add onto the collage. People who hold to traditional concepts of art are usually dissatisfied with their lack of control over others' aesthetic choices or the failure to complete their own planned efforts. These people often feel disappointment with the result. But those who accept the activity as an experience in collaborative creating can appreciate the evolution of the collage—from the separate and more conventional efforts beginning on the flat surface, to the building up of textures and attempts at composition and unification.

What develops from this organic growth is unpredictable, depending on the freedom of the group and the amount of time allotted. Usually the collage is considered finished when the available materials and/or surface space and/or people are exhausted. It is then important to examine how you feel about what you've created. What do you decide to do with it? One group acted out the making of a collage in mime, using people as materials. Another group decided to display the result and then to destroy it. But what *is* the result? Can you act out a process of collaborative creating? Can you display it or destroy it? Just because we can see and touch the collage, we shouldn't overemphasize its importance. I think it merely makes explicit what happened; it's only a symbol—a way of remembering, perhaps reevoking, a state. If we can again engage in creating beyond ourselves, that's important.

APPLICATIONS

In the group collage, the stress is on creating as a group, a whole, a unit. This means striving for a common goal, but with many individual contributions. While the identity of these individual contributions is often lost in the larger work, they must still be respected. One way to explore these themes in everyday life is to have a communal meal or picnic. Everyone will bring something—some kind of food, plates, utensils, etc.—but *without* that prior planning which insures that there would be a main course, bread, drink, dessert, etc. Also, things will be contributed so that no one can tell who made what or who brought what. As well, no one will know which dishes were intended to be eaten with which. See what happens. Does it matter if you are not recognized or given credit for your contributions? Are people more honest in expressing preferences when they are not sure who made what? Are you offended if someone else does not like what you have brought? The whole meal is likely to be a different experience. Will it be worth something? Will it bring you together, let you relate and create?

The most obvious application of the "Group Collage" is to repeat the exercise itself in different settings, with different people. Have your family do a group collage, or a close group of friends. How about the people in your office, or members of the school community? See how the issues differ depending on the group.

You might apply your ideas about creating to the building of some communal structure. Perhaps a temporary camping structure that you and your friends or family might want to use. In a school, students and teachers might be interested in designing and building a learning dome. The important thing is to design and actually build the structure as a group, with each person contributing his ideas and with each person's needs being cared for.

The idea of group creativity can also be applied on a larger scale, say in your community. Perhaps you know of some vacant lot or space that is not being used for anything. Investigate transforming that space and designing a playground or park. You could work on an existing playground that might be run down and in need of repairs. Get the people in your community together to clean and fix it up. If you live in the woods or by the ocean, you might assume, as a community, responsibility for a common resource, cleaning and maintaining a stream or a beach. This would mean that periodically people would meet, decide what had to be done, and take action together.

Street theater, ecological action, day-care centers, neighborhood radio stations—there are countless opportunities for merging creation and communication.

Human Sculpture

"Human Sculpture" tries to create an explicitly human, organic art. We usually think of art as something to be viewed or heard at a distance. Now, we humans will *become* the creative process. We will explore the idea that anyone can be an artist, anyone can be the substance of art, and together we can create. As the human element enters more directly into our creative efforts, the creative process becomes richer. We can work with each other as materials, as objects—and, unfortunately, we too often do. But when we work with each other as living beings, we can encourage aliveness.

LABORATORY PHASE

Structure
The exercise should take about an hour. Work in an open, large space. No special materials are necessary.

Instructions
Decide whether you want to be a sculptor or be sculpted. (A desirable ratio of sculptors to sculpted material is 1:3 or 1:4; a good-size group would be two sculptors working on six persons who are to be sculpted.) Those who wish to be sculpted go to a corner and sit or lie down. Take a comfortable position and relax. Steady your breathing—in and out, in and out—and as you do so, imagine yourself to be a malleable material, a piece of clay. The sculptors are going to mold you into different forms while you behave as a piece of clay. As you continue to imagine yourself as clay, try to become clay.

Now sculptors, you may talk to each other or remain silent. You may plan out the sculpture or decide to do it spontaneously. Try sculpting in different ways, in any way you want. Try to understand the "materials" you are working with—human clay. Or is it clay humans? Try to be alert to your approach to sculpting. Are you forming? Shaping? Manipulating? Twisting? Allowing? Give the "materials" several minutes to become clay. Then begin to work with them.

Change positions after a sculpture is "finished." Sculptors become material, and material becomes sculptors. How will you know when a sculpture is "finished"?

Extensions

There are no limits to what can be sculpted. You can be a rock, water, marble, oatmeal, machinery, a flower, steel, a tree, etc. You can even be a human, or yourself, provided you are willing to be sculpted. Sculptors can tell each person who is to be sculpted what kind of material he is, or the sculpted can become certain materials without telling the sculptors. The sculptors can ask the sculpture to come alive or to move in whatever way it wants.

Discussion

We were to decide which of us wanted to be material ánd which the artist. I was the material. Material closed its eyes. We were to be a soft and malleable substance. It was a very nice and relaxing feeling to be molded. Be alert to how this feels (I think I and probably most people in the class have conquered the fear that anyone would hurt them. My trust does not yet extend to every area of our encounters but it is quite strong in this one. I did not feel the need to peek in order to be sure that everyone else looked and felt as dumb as I—I already knew it).

The early phases of the sculpture can be unclear, reflecting your indecisions, your confusions. We are unused to working with another's body; we are unused to working *with* another! Did the sculptors move the sculpted persons with consideration for the comfort or feasibility of poses? Did they make any effort to relate the bodies to one another? When does physical contact engaged in and induced by the sculptors become comfortable?

Did you laugh at your work, were you laughed at, did you laugh together? Did you, as material, try to hold a pose with care and attention to details, such as head position, finger positions, weight emphasis, etc.? Did you choose to cooperate with the sculptors? To what extend were you will-less material?

What is the effect of the materials used? Did it make work easier? More challenging? Sculptors seem to function more comfortably when the material is flexible. Inflexible substances such as wood or stone seem harder to work with, especially since they require "tools." The choice of material can unify or separate, depending upon how the human body is able to identify with its texture. Clay is a relatively easy substance to assume; oatmeal can require many difficult adjustments.

As the exercise progresses, is there increased respect for the human material? Humans as material—our mechanical, material aspects. Material as human—the transition between inorganic and organic. The complex bending and breaking points of humans: physical, emotional, psychological. Did you find that the human form holds the most potential, that it is the easiest and most organic form to be? We can begin to develop an understanding of each other's bodies—of just how flexible or versatile they are. We can begin to work *with* each other.

Was there a theme to the sculpture? Was it recognizable? Or is it free-flowing and formless? Who decides this? Usually, the sculptors initiate directions and characteristics for the sculpture. Some sculptors continue to control the form of their work. Others allow the sculpture to start forming itself, to grow from the inside out.

Be clay. Relax. She'll be gentle. Loosen up. Aaaah. That feels good; keep doing it. Remember, you're clay. She can mold you. I wonder how clay feels, I mean inside; what does it think? Cold and damp, I bet. O.K. I'm cold and damp. That's funny. I normally wouldn't lie down on the floor like this—it's dirty and cold and I just washed my hair—but it feels so nice. Yeah, everybody else does look silly. But I bet they feel as good as we do too. It's funny how they never seem to create anything startling—nothing really new. But I guess they're just beginning to explore. . . . Oh Oh. Now I have to be creative. Don't worry; I'll be gentle. Close your eyes. O.K. Now what am I going to do with you? There, I'm molding your fingers. I like details. Why doesn't anyone else seem to notice details? Oh, well. There, you're holding a flower. I know you don't feel it, but it's there.

Being sculpted and sculpting—the two roles mirror each other and can highlight each other's needs and concerns. Usually, however, these two parties to the sculpture fail to appreciate their union.

The "material" often feels "used" by the sculptor. It can feel silly, having to assume an awkward or ridiculous position. Or it can be physically uncomfortable. A common complaint is that the sculptors do not respect the individuality of each body-material, its particular physical flexibility, its special expressive potential. The material seeks its humanity. Sometimes a person objects to being used to support the weight of other parts of the sculpture. Sometimes he fails to see he is important as a part of a larger whole.

A discussion of sex roles ensued when one young man mentioned that he enjoyed being "molded" as if from wax. He said he wished to be "formed" and felt complete trust in the sculptor to form him. Another male member of the group said jokingly, "You'd make a good wife." This later opened up a discussion of roles, since the second young man considered such passive cooperation to be too "wifely" or feminine.

Varying degrees of sensitivity are shown by sculptors. One woman roughly pushed and pulled the materials into place, with no regard to particular position. When the materials were grouped in a general sense, she avoided further contact with them. She left them as material. Some sculptors begin with the desire to make an aesthetic grouping of some sort. Most change the positions of bodies around as the sculpture evolves. Some people show care for details: arranging fingers, facial expressions and subtle angles of limbs; trying to induce eye contact between materials. Some sculptors combine experimentation with discipline, and the materials can come alive.

Communication among sculptors is often diffused by their own separate movement or by their separate intentions for the whole sculpture. Two sculptors who were working together nonverbally discovered, after having grouped and regrouped their materials with care and sensitivity, that neither was satisfied with the result. One sculptor said she had been "working toward a feeling of unity and involvement"; the other said he had been trying to create a feeling of "separateness and aloneness."

How can you become a better sculptor? More of a creator than a controller? One approach is to help develop the creative impulses of the material. Try to keep your ideas flexible. Allow yourself to change your concepts as you explore the potential of the material. Try to communicate your ideas clearly through physical contact with the material, but be open to the material's *own* capability to execute and develop them. Avoid relying exclusively on the omnipotent creator role. Regard the potential in human material that will-less material does not have. Work with it. Respect its humanity. Finally notice your feelings when *you* are material (e.g., feelings when you are manipulated, how it feels to be posed or "frozen" in position). When you "sculpt," try to be sensitive to the material you once were.

This exercise taught me more about myself, about my desire to be in control rather than be controlled, to explore rather than be explored, to be active rather than passive, and to create rather than be molded.

As the sculpture progresses, the relationship between the sculptor and sculpted can become richer and deeper. Sculptors become more sensitive in handling materials, more willing to explore new forms. The sculptor and sculpted begin to change roles, back and forth. Material suggests to the sculptor a new direction for the work, and roles become fluid. As the sculpting becomes more creative, sculptor and sculpted begin to transcend the subject-object relationship and work as one.

Introducing movement or life into the sculpture can bring a sense of unity. One person introduced a moving part into the sculpture by swinging an arm in rhythm and making a sound inspired by this movement. Others joined him and began relating their positions and movements to those materials that were already functioning in the sculpture. The sculpture became a machine with a variety of moving parts. When the invisible barriers of inertia and silence are overcome, the sculpture can take on a will of its own.

Another group decided to become something alive, a growing flower. It was a voluntary sculpture, where the material formed itself without sculptors. The idea of behaving as one organism seemed to open up new possibilities of expression. A feeling of organic relationship between the bodies was expressed in a kind of "dance," where the bodies seem to be unified in their style of movement. Participants said they felt their movements were "organic," seeming to generate spontaneously from within the union of bodies. This particular exercise was done in a dance studio with mirrors on the wall. One girl said that when she looked from within the group to the mirror, she was disoriented and disappointed. For her, the role of the sculptor as an "outside person working on the group" had dissolved into the experience of moving and working as one. Her "disorientation," she said, came from the switch in identity, from her being "part of a whole" to being "one of the people in the mirror."

The emphasis in the exercise can move from concerns about maintaining individuality in the group (and various types of self-conscious behavior) to a "flowing with" or *experiencing* the group effort. How *you* look matters less when you are working as part of a larger community. I'm not talking about mob psychology or group-think, but individuals in unison and union.

Coming as it did (mold; be molded) it was an offering (sing; be sung). I am art form and artist, and my grace is the grace of my creation, as my creation's grace is mine. I am free, captured in the deceptive softness of clay, the delicate resistance, the careful hardness of plaster, yet I am free. I am inside and outside of clay, bronze, plaster. I am molded, bent, chiselled, poured, and I stand with my tools (my hands) in my hands confronted by rawness and purity that I must smooth without denying purity. Purity, too, is an offering.

When is the exercise over? Is a sculpture "finished"? Do you judge its completeness or value according to aesthetic criteria? Expressive criteria? Or is the standard whether persons, with self-discipline and caring workmanship, become part of the creative process?

APPLICATIONS

With the human sculpture, we emphasize creativity and communication; relating creatively, creating communication. First try to realize the difference between working *with* others and manipulating them.

In this exercise, we have been concentrating on working with others. But how often do we see manipulation: the molding and conditioning of the child by parents; conditioning of students by teacher; hypnotizing of workers by the assembly line; manipulation of people at demonstrations and rallies? Try to be alert to the different situations in which people try to manipulate you, and you them. How can manipulation be transformed into collaboration? Once you've come to yourself and developed a sense of self, collaboration becomes possible.

In considering the exercise as one in creating human art, try to apply this to your immediate environments. In the home, try to make space more livable. Are there chairs which are uncomfortable, rooms with harsh or inadequate light? Try to think of rooms as atmospheres, related to what people do in those rooms. How should a kitchen be different from a study in ways other than the obvious? Sit down with your family and discuss your home, and how to change it. Then do it. Try to think of your home as a piece of sculpture.

How are you a piece of sculpture or architecture? How do you express certain emotions by putting yourself in different postures? Using certain gestures? Try different positions for different feelings. Consider certain variables in your daily life: closeness and distance, relaxation and tension, stasis and motion. See how your body as sculpture obscures what's alive inside you. Can you make this form respect more the life within?

Space Exchange

Our entire world is marked off in sections, territories with certain boundaries and limits. There are countries and states; homes with fences around them; offices with desks. And there is a personal space that we carry with us. Depending on where we are and who we are with, people can come only so close. You talk right up to a friend but keep a few feet away from a policeman.

What do these boundaries suggest? What do the territories they mark off signify? At issue is the sense of property; what's yours, what's mine—a possessiveness of the mind and heart. At issue also is the sense of privacy and integrity; having something you work on, and from which you can develop yourself. In different situations, at different times, boundaries and territories serve either or both of these purposes.

Regardless of the character of boundaries, we each create our own spaces—where we live and work, where we feel at home. And we create our physical spaces from our psychological needs and hopes.

At times a mood or state—anger, ecstacy, love—may be our most important space. Internal and external space merge; you create your space and your space is you.

But there are many spaces; each of us lives in several "places," and then there are all those other people, with their own spaces. Do we relate to each other as if from inside our own plastic bubble? Or are our boundaries permeable, inviting? Can we enter another space and experience it on its own terms? Learn to live in it? Do we want to? What is integrity of self? Of selves? Can we build spaces together, transforming our own space or starting from anew? As we begin working with smaller spaces, maybe we are beginning to work with larger worlds.

LABORATORY PHASE

Structure

Choose a large room, with an average amount and variety of furniture, or any outdoor space. Allow at least an hour for the exercise and discussion; it can certainly occur over a two-hour period. A timer, to mark off the different work periods, is helpful.

Instructions

PHASE ONE. Explore the space around you, where you stand or sit now. Try to understand it as best you can. After a few minutes, look around the room and find an area that you like, a place you want to explore and make your own. The place need not have clear physical limits. When you are ready, go to that area and create a space for yourself there. If where you are is too crowded or you're too close to someone else, select another space. Now, for the next fifteen or twenty minutes, create a space. Use whatever materials you have available, external and internal, furniture and your mood. Your space may have physical boundaries, emotional ones, or both. Explore your space— feel its texture, smell it, get to know its limits. Experience your space.

PHASE TWO. When you know your own space, leave it and enter another's space. Are you invited? Do you seek another? Do you wait? And now, for the next fifteen minutes, try to get to know this other space. When someone enters your space, show it to him, make him feel at home. Try to allow him to experience it. Can you share it with him, can you build something with him from your original space? And then, for another fifteen minutes, go back to your own space with your partner, and now see if he can also experience your space, and help you recreate it.

If you feel at an impasse—that there is nothing more to show another about your space, that you are bored or unsure of what to do next—stay with it. Entering another's space and being at ease is hard. But instead of giving up and looking for an "out," relax and be yourself. Then you have a better chance to work with another, experiencing and recreating each other's spaces.

Try exchanging with several other people if time permits. Don't cut short either your stay with him or his with you. Explore both phases of the exchange.

PHASE THREE. At some point, step back from your space and look at it from a distance. How does it feel to look at your space from the outside in? And conversely, how does it feel to look at another's space from the inside out? What can you tell this other person about his space? What can he tell you about yours?

PHASE FOUR. At the end of the exercise, go back alone to your original space. Is it still there? For you? Try to recreate it, experience it again, perhaps be in it for the first time.

Discussion

As we are creating our own space, we can see many things, some very clearly. We begin to understand that the location, dimensions, and quality of the space, and how it is created, tend to be highly individual, reflecting quite a bit of the creator. We can begin to understand more about ourselves when we consider where we chose to build our space. Maybe you worked in a cozy corner, or wanted to be surrounded by chairs and tables, or chose to stretch out in the middle of the room. Did your space have clear physical boundaries, or was it defined by your mood? Was it contained or constantly moving? Were the boundaries permeable or impassable? Did your space begin somewhere but have no definite end?

How did you go about building your home? Was it forced or did it evolve? What techniques did you use? Some start by feeling everything with their hands. Others try to employ all the senses: What does it smell like? Can you hear anything? How does it feel on different parts of the body? What dimensions did you work with? Did you work on one or many planes? Did your space extend up high vertically? And then, how did you explore it? Did you sit or lie in one position or did you move around, viewing it from different perspectives?

We're not trying to be amateur psychoanalysts, analyzing all our little slips. It's really much simpler, more direct. We create our spaces, express ourselves in our spaces; it is hard to draw the line between what's inside and outside. As you reflect on your space, you can consider how you approach the world, what your orientation to others is.

In the process of creating his space, each person is alone. The information you get is dependent on your own action and how novel and effective it can be. Each step in the process leads to more unanswered questions. As you examine the consistency of a surface, you may begin to consider how flexible it is or its capacity for supporting weight. Successively, you learn about the space, its limitations, and its possibilities. The element of time becomes important, for most realize that the repertoire of techniques they possess is quickly exhausted. And if they are to continue and get to know their space better, they must invent new ways of looking at it. As one person reports, "I felt this demand on my creativity throughout the exercise and was constantly straining to come up with something." It can become this self-conscious effort.

. . . the overriding motivation for my "creative" activities was the avoidance of monotony by the provocation of my mind. I somehow felt that if I did nothing, I was wasting an opportunity, and to repeat what I already did was equally useless.

You can feel pressured to "be creative." Relax. Come to yourself. Through this discipline you can let the creative process be. You are creating.

In most cases, the individual becomes part of his space. Identified with it? It's mine; I created it. Attached to it? Possessiveness. Merging with it? In harmony with it? As you get to know your space, you begin to feel for it. Or were you never satisfied with your space, eager to leave it, never putting yourself into it?

As you become comfortable in your space, the question arises as to whether you are willing to leave it. After all, it is your own creation. You feel you know every inch of it. The space has become a reflection of you—your thoughts, moods, emotions, and ideas. In some sense, you *are* the space and the space is you. A girl who is lively and verbal creates her space on a large soft chair and jumps up and down on it joyfully. Another, who is very quiet and introspective, goes into a sheltered space and assumes the full lotus position. Was it the same old you, or did you experiment, expressing usually hidden parts of yourself? We begin to look also at how accessible our spaces are to others. Can the spaces be easily entered? Are they open or closed? Narrow or wide?

The sharing of a space adds new dimension; it can raise the exercise to a new level. Can two people create together, going beyond their individual attachments to their own spaces? It's not easy. The first problem is who will venture out of his space. How can it be done? Perhaps you catch the eye of someone across the room. Immediately you both understand and you venture to his space. Or maybe you go out and look for an interesting-looking space and ask if you may enter. Some always remain in their space and wait to be asked. And still others don't want to impose on another.

How hard was it to enter another's space? Where did it begin? It is usually harder to find another's space when it is intangible, formed from a mood; but once found the experience can be very rewarding. If your space was primarily emotional, it may be harder to enter another's space; first you must change your state. Were there entrance "gates," an admissions "fee," rules for behaving in the space?

We had done everything we could think of—looked, laughed, explored, worked together—and realized we had to do no more. We sat under the table silently, holding hands and smiling, and enjoying the time together. We had built a space of quiet.

Since I felt self-conscious, I do not feel that I communicated with my partner as fully as possible. This created a certain amount of loneliness, or feeling alone with another person; I also sometimes felt the lack of stimuli and was afraid that my partner might become bored and find me and my space inadequate.

While in another's space, issues can arise in much the same way as when you were alone. What happens when you enter another's space? Maybe you are a little apprehensive, and your partner will try to put you at ease by showing you his space. He will relate all he has learned; he will try to have you experience what he has experienced. He will ask you to touch something, or smell a fabric, or sit in a certain position that will reveal something different about the space. The creator offers parts of himself to his guest, who in return may start to explore with him and relate what he perceives. Whereas the initial space expressed the work of one person, there is now a transformation. Two people may work together to form a new creation. They alter the original space. They may move what were previously fixed objects. Perhaps they will enlarge the space to allow for more room. Maybe they will close off their space entirely. To whom does this new space belong? It can no longer be identified with one particular person. It now reflects a collective effort. Neither can say, "This space is mine!" Can each accept it and live in it as a creation of both? Can each acknowledge their fused contributions?

Creating with another is not easy. There is a tendency to get it over with, to leave the other's space as soon as you've exhausted the obvious or comfortable ways of relating. Did your guest reflect your ease or discomfort? Did he also want to leave when you wanted him to? Did you feel pride or embarrassment in your space? Either of these feelings can present an obstacle to another's really experiencing your space, since both feelings show him the space is still *yours*. Sometimes a person will merely perform self-expressive games in his space, rather than letting you into it to experience it.

In a small space, interaction can be more intense; games are more easily exhausted. For some it is too much.

I was not comfortable being with another person in such a small space. The sudden intimacy in closed, limited surroundings. . . . We gradually expanded the space and hence, the space between us.

For others the intimacy is an opportunity that is welcomed:

You as the source of all thoughts and ideas were the space.

Unless something is happening between people, you cannot create together. Accepting another is critical; both accepting what he gives you and accepting where he "is at" before you give him something. Without this acceptance, your "creative" efforts can deny the other's aliveness.

It was an utter violation of anyone's conception of space. . . . others were "doing" me when I didn't care to be "did."

As the exercise ends, where are you? When you stand away from your space, what do we feel? Do you remain identified with it, either pleased with it or displeased? Do you know your space? Did working with another help you go beyond your individual space, beyond yourself? Were you willing to accept his presence in your space, his ideas? Were you sensitive to what he was trying to "say," or were you always trying to think of something to do? Could you enter another's space, see from his point of view, experience his creation? Working in a space which is unusual for you and respecting its unfamiliarity can help you express more sides of yourself. A generally expansive person can be more of himself as he works, respectfully, in a small, closed-in, delicately constructed space.

Can you ever experience another's space, his orientation, his world? Treating your own space possessively, as "private property," cannot help. Only using your own space as a base from which to build individual integrity can. And then being *willing* to enter another's space and letting him enter yours. Putting aside your need to show him *everything* in your space, and especially how one is *supposed* to behave there. Listening *to* him, working *with* him. In creating together, we can go beyond our spaces, a bit beyond ourselves.

APPLICATIONS

A first step is to examine the personal spaces you come in contact with in everyday life. Try to be alert to the nature of your personal space and how it changes with different people and in different situations. How does it feel to have your space violated? How rigid are the boundaries of your space? Observe these things in others too. Perhaps try intentionally to alter your space with another. Suppose you are talking with someone across a desk. Deliberately walk to the other side of the desk and talk standing next to him; or lean over the desk so you are very close. *But* do it in such a way that you can both learn. Talk about your reactions to the space "violation," and about his reactions. Consider together whether you both desire the present boundaries of your relationship. Consider also that we define our spaces, then they define us; and that spaces can be re-created.

Apply the exercise in your own home. Draw a map of your home, defining those spaces reserved primarily for particular individuals who live there, those spaces shared by all persons, those shared by only some, and those where no one goes. Try to understand how much and what kind of interaction takes place in your home and how it is related to the different spaces. Are some spaces more conducive to gatherings than others? What areas are the scenes of the most conflict? Why? What happens when spaces in your home are exchanged?

Do the spaces in your home satisfy all the needs of its residents? If not, discuss this with your family or those you live with, and, together, as a unit, arrange your home so that each person's spatial needs are more nearly met. If you think the quality of interaction in your home is poor, do something about it. If there is not enough space to be alone, do something about this too. Change spaces; they express and influence your relationships. Change spaces to gain a clearer access to your selves.

You might also focus on relationships where there is intense interaction but usually little empathy or collaboration. Start exchanging spaces and building spaces together; begin to relate with some understanding. A teacher sits in his classroom being a student while a student teaches the class. Not the "queen for a day" idea, but with the student actually having responsibility for some teaching over a period of time. Executives and clerks might exchange their offices for a period of time; a more humanistic enterprise might develop. What will offices then become? Judges with some experience living behind bars and prisoners with some experience in "officially" judging others might even develop a more humane system of justice. And not merely play-acting, where the judge spends the night in jail, *in* the very nicest of the cells. Certainly mental hospitals couldn't exist if those psychiatrists in power had an opportunity to inhabit them.

It can be very helpful to enter another's space, particularly if his existence is the reason for yours. The polarity relationships maintained by a struggle for power, the haves and have-nots, the condemned and the blessed. Exchange spaces and begin to transcend polarities.

FURTHER READING

Bernard Rudofsky, *Architecture without Architects*, Doubleday & Company, Inc., Garden City, N.Y., 1969.

It's all there, in the pictures, that is. These creations of man in collaboration with nature are inspiring, and so down-to-earth and simple. Man seems at his best when he is working within his natural environment. The text, by describing the function of the creations, adds another element of respect for these "person-architects." But the text is unnecessary to what is so clear in the pictures—that the process of harmonious creating exists.

Buckminster Fuller, *Ideas and Integrities*, Collier Books, The Macmillan Company, New York, 1963.

Fuller is a strange and wonderful man. Through an apparently mechanical and technological approach, he draws conclusions about human nature and potential. This is one of his most autobiographical books. If you can get inside his language, you can start seeing things in new and challenging ways. World communication becomes a real issue.

Self-assessment

*W*HERE are you now? Why? What have you been doing? How will you work toward your hopes and aspirations? These kinds of questions do not yield easy answers. Sometimes they seem so inclusive that they must be approached slowly, considering different aspects of the larger question. Often you can't verbalize your response. But you keep these questions with you; you work on them, they work on you.

Too often, however, we put these questions aside for a while. We say that we'll consider them when we have more time, when we're less caught up in our series of obligations. And when someone suggests a more conventional evaluation system to measure "where I am now," we agree, but only half-heartedly. Even though the conventional system seems totally inadequate to the task, it does seem more efficient—at least we won't have to go deeply into those questions now. We all know but don't dwell on the fact that the conventional system employs scales which are arbitrary and superficial and which entail competitive comparisons. For they seem efficient: some will be rated "good," some "poor," and many "average"—on all kinds of issues. But they may not even be efficient. Certainly they are not keyed toward growth.

I think these questions—call them life questions—are the heart of the matter. Granted they are not easy to handle; they shouldn't be! It's a long process, with much inner searching, to gain some perspective on yourself. Certainly the person who employs the conventional evaluation system is avoiding the heart of the matter. In putting us all on the same line, he is missing the point. At times, that "person" is you and me.

The "Line Up and Away" exercise emphasizes some of the differences between conventional evaluation and self-assessment. Part of the exercise occurs in a more sociological context, part in the privacy of yourself. In the "Mirror Talk," you can go again to the privacy of your inner self. Alone with yourself, you can experience for yourself the difference between evaluation and self-assessment. Likes and dislikes, praise and condemnation are one and the same—evaluations. They make you feel good or bad. Rarely do they tell you anything real about yourself. Self-assessments can do just that.

Being evaluated by others can be comforting, but it takes you away from yourself. We need to know the facts about ourselves if we hope to change; whether someone likes or dislikes you gives you only a momentary rise or fall in your mood. After being praised, do you change more—or merely repeat your now established success pattern?

If self-assessment can become part of your daily life, you can guide yourself toward growth. As you fool yourself less and less, you begin seeing more of yourself. You waste less energy restlessly looking around to see what the other person is doing.

Line Up and Away

Where are you headed? What are you seeking? What do you value? Most approach these life questions relying too heavily on others' opinions, looking around to find out where others stand before they decide about themselves. Most do not search deeply enough for their own core values, using instead arbitrary and superficial categories as a basis for their judgments. No wonder few people know the direction in which they want to grow, and fewer still know that they are now moving about aimlessly. No wonder the process of taking stock is so lifeless and unpleasant.

During this exercise you can examine more carefully the usual pattern of taking stock, which employs external and arbitrary categories. We can call it "conventional evaluation." And you can explore more fully an alternative way to assess your present state and generate growth goals—the process of self-assessment.

To develop the capacity for self-assessment, you'll need to establish yourself as the final judge, the "court of last resort." In the last analysis, and usually in the first, *you* know yourself best. Also, you must break out of the linear tyranny of our normal grading system. Instead of being compared—here, there, and everywhere—to the next fellow on a single, superficial scale, you'll have to establish your own core values. These values can be your criteria for judgment and your inspiration for growth. You'll have to see yourself in your own terms, others in their own terms. How you assess yourself should not entail an assessment of someone else. Don't settle for zero-sum games where, for example, your feeling positive depends on your evaluating another as negative. Finally, you'll have to make your self-assessment an ongoing part of your everyday life.

Self-assessment is a dynamic process, not a static event. You're finding out where you are so you can realize where you've come from and where you want to go.

LABORATORY PHASE

Structure

There are two phases to this exercise: the first, where each person works alone on assessing himself, occurs several days before the group meets; the second, where the group works on issues of assessment, occurs during a group meeting. Therefore you'll need extra preparation, setting aside time to work on your own before the group meets.

Phase one needs no special equipment or space. You work on your own, where you want to. But you should set aside enough time to reflect upon your situation and consider it thoughtfully. The actual time needed will vary with each person, for example, several hours a night, fifteen minutes on several different days, and so forth.

Phase two calls for no special equipment. You'll need a space which is relatively large and cleared of objects or furniture. Phase two should take a fifty-minute session.

Phase one can exist as a separate exercise.

Instructions

PHASE ONE. Take some time away from your normal routines. Try to get away from your usual concerns. Develop some perspective on what you are doing.

Work at both decompression and creation. Go through a series of "decompression chambers," releasing yourself from your habitual chores, pleasures and worries. Pick a quiet, secluded place; let your mind empty and your feelings drain as much as possible.

When you feel apart from your routinized self, relaxed and in the present, begin creating something. Create a place within yourself from which you can consider yourself realistically.

You can choose any issue or incident in your life. Reflect on it, consider it, and try to clarify it. Select specific issues, especially at the start. If you will be doing this as a prelude to the group meeting (Phase two), there is one condition: among the issues you choose, at least one should be an issue each member of the group will reflect on for himself.

Let one common issue be your work with this book. Reflect on what you have been doing with this book, with the exercises; and how involved you have been in the group. Consider what you are seeking from the book, what you have learned. But if you have really created a place within yourself, be sure to reflect on more than this group issue. There are undoubtedly other issues more central to your life which might become less dense through your reflections. Take full advantage of any opportunity for perspective you may create.

Write down on a piece of paper your conclusions and intentions regarding each of the issues you consider. Be as specific and clear as possible. In writing down your thoughts and feelings, try to clarify them further. Keep these writings; read them at special times.

This process of reflecting, considering, and then writing down takes different amounts and kinds of time depending on who you are. Some people work for a solid block of time late in the evening; others work for briefer periods of time over several days; still others work for a while, then leave it, and come back again fresh, as if for the first time. Whatever your personal approach, leave enough time. The more you put into this effort, the more you will learn from it. By considering your present situation and state honestly, you can generate more realistic guidelines for the future.

Remember, you are trying to develop what may be a new way of approaching yourself. You are trying to realize your wish for self-assessment. Focusing the self-assessment process on your work with the book is only a convenient way to begin developing that capacity. The capacity for self-assessment matures as you apply that process, continually, to issues that matter.

Keep what you've written with you. In particular, consider the group issue again several times before the group meeting and bring it to the meeting.

PHASE TWO. We're going to focus again on some of the issues you already worked on by yourself. Now we will view them in terms of the conventional evaluation system. If you feel frustrated or dissatisfied while working within that system, that is only natural. Stay with it so you'll know about that system's limitations.

Let's focus on the issue of your involvement in the group. This was probably not the most important issue you worked on by yourself, but it is one everybody in the group worked on and it can start us examining the process of self-assessment. Subsequently, more important issues could become the focus. Consider again how involved you've been in the group. We will select two points, one of which will represent the highest or total involvement, the other the lowest or no involvement. (These points can be two walls, two chairs, or anything that can mark a place. They should be far apart with nothing in between, so members of the group can line up between them. If space is severely limited, persons can mark their place on a large sheet of paper. This situation is less desirable. It is important for people to put themselves literally "on the line.")

Form a single line between these two points, placing yourself on a continuum according to how you assess your own involvement. For example, if it has been high, you would place yourself near the high point. Keep to a single line though you may have ties, where you occupy the same place on the line as someone else. When you've placed yourself, consider where you are. How does this lineup compare with your work alone on self-assessment? Can you express your prior self-assessments in this new form? How much do you thereby give up? (This lining up might take about five minutes. It is helpful to have some discussion after each lineup.)

Now let's work with a different scale. Again, considering your involvement in the group, place yourself in one of three groups: high, medium, or low involvement. The high-involvement persons should gather at the high point and the low-involvement persons at the low point. Again, once you've placed yourself, consider where you are. (This procedure might also take five minutes.)

This time, we will assess our involvement without knowing where anyone else places himself. Form a straight line midway between the two points. You are standing side-by-side, facing one of the points. Close your eyes. The point in front of you represents high involvement, the one behind you, low involvement. Move backward or forward closer to one point or the other, according to how you assess yourself. After several minutes, open your eyes. Where are you? Where you belong?

Extensions

There are many things you can do to continue testing the limits of the conventional evaluation system and examining its effects on you.

You can focus on the idea of placement—what's my place, what's your place, what's "place"? Talk to the person who is in front of you, explaining why you chose your spot on the line. Do this with the person behind you as well. Change your place on the line if you think your original placement was incorrect.

Arbitrarily, change your place on the line. If you were all the way in the back, come to the front. Now try to justify your new place on the line. If you were all the way in the front, come to the back. Now try to justify your new place on the line to the person in front of you; to the person behind you.

You can also focus on the static quality of conventional evaluation. At a certain point in time, give your line some life: have the line begin to move. Can you break up the line and move to a different level?

How about working on form? Come together in a circle according to your involvement in the group. How static and unidimensional can evaluation remain when you are all the same?

Of course, you can apply these techniques to any issue you choose. It is better to select an issue relevant to most persons in the group, and you can certainly go beyond matters dealing with the use or impact of this book. Try to select specific issues, and work with one at a time.

Discussion

Working alone, reflecting on where you find yourself, assessing your situation and state realistically, was probably difficult. Did you find that the energy you devoted to this effort reappeared as a source of understanding about yourself? Did you put enough in to have something come out? Did you take time to be clear enough in your writing to make the writing clarify your thoughts and feelings?

This self-assessment process is difficult, but it can be rewarding. The conventional evaluation approach is difficult but *can't* be rewarding— *it* can only reward or punish you. You are placed on a scale with static categories: high and low, good and bad; and when you are high, someone else must be low. The scale must yield a normal curve—some high, some low, and lots in the middle. During the various lineup procedures you probably had more of this evaluation than you wanted. Boredom, restlessness, frustration, and anger are common reactions. During the exercise, they can be expressed; during an exam or interview, they usually must be suppressed. Did you stay within the conventional evaluation system so as to see its limits more clearly? Could you use the various lineups to make more explicit what we do all the time— manipulate others through arbitrary evaluations of them? Since most of us are indirect in our relationships, we usually don't say we manipulate others. Instead we merely "comment" on others or "express an opinion" of them.

The emptiness of the conventional evaluation approach is pervasive. It goes well beyond problems inherent in all attempts at assessment. Valid assessment requires you clarify your intentions and take into account what have been unnoticed, unfamiliar aspects of behavior. You probably experienced this during your work alone. Certainly it is a common feeling during work on the lines in the group:

In the discussion that followed, it became apparent that there is a fear of defining what has occurred, both because of the vagueness of the terms and because most of us are not on sufficiently familiar ground, even at this point. . . .

The exercise suggests to many people three fundamental sources of this emptiness in conventional evaluation. We let others tell us who we are; they make these judgments in terms of arbitrary and superficial categories; in making these judgments, they assume a competitive win-lose model—if I get an "A," someone must get a "C."

The various lineups highlight the evaluative pressure cooker, sealed and heated up by ourselves and others. Many say they find it very difficult to do the exercise because they don't know how others define terms. They are caught between trying to evaluate themselves with their own standards exclusively, and constantly trying to second guess those of others. Too many remain dependent on others for their source of evaluation. They cannot place themselves without knowing what others think of them or where others place themselves.

This tendency of others to decide for us who we are takes many forms. It is encouraged primarily by our own inability to look honestly inside ourselves and accept what we find, and only secondarily by the persuasiveness of others or their need to be judgmental or their desire to exert power over us.

Does that person really belong there?

Several members announced surprise at finding others of the class in their group, expecting them to be either higher or lower. This was true of the middle group and of the high group: However, as concerned the lower group, not one person even commented on his position there, as if to reassert their group's feelings of noninvolvement with the course.

There is concern about how others evaluate themselves. Sometimes there is hostility, envy, or jealousy, especially toward those who place themselves high on the continuum.

I was not surprised, but felt a bit of hostility toward certain people who had classified themselves in the high involvement group. From talking with others, I found that this anger, or at least, mistrust, may be quite a common phenomenon. I, personally, felt that these very few people were not being honest with themselves—that they had been pushy leaders all semester who were more concerned with leading than learning.

Even though you thought you had good reason to question others' placement, did you spend more time thinking about what they were doing than trying to assess yourself accurately? Did you lose yourself by constantly looking around? Very often this occurs because we all assume there is a limited quantity of attributes or qualities: if I have high involvement someone else must have low.

Our conventional evaluation system demands this type of competitive thinking.

I was prepared to move fairly high on the continuum, and so, it seemed, was everyone else. However, several of us were confronted by the same ten or so people who stay in one group for most of the exercises. They were discussing among themselves who they thought should be placed where along the line. About five of us stepped away at this point and formed a sort of "tie" of people just below that group.

One of its key symbols is "first place."

Essentially what resulted was a bunching together or numerous ties, with, however, only one person uncontested for first place. To have stepped ahead of number one would have been to challenge him, and yet he alone can judge the degree to which he has been affected.

Were you able to step a bit outside these win-lose constraints? Did you create ties? What did first place mean to you?

Can I really express to others how involved I am? Were you reluctant to say you hadn't gotten very involved, perhaps for fear of disappointing the others? Or were you afraid of placing yourself too high along the continuum? Though some people may really feel they belong there, they're not sure others will agree with them. And they will hold back.

I didn't feel I wanted to enforce my own opinion if it conflicted with that of a person I placed myself in front of or in back of; and nobody else seemed any surer than I was about how to arrange the specifics of the continuum.

Did you immediately or finally give up on the need to place yourself in relation to others and work simply on placing yourself?

The only people who avoided the "where to place myself" hassle were those who placed themselves in a spot and let others do the figuring. But I don't think that is a solution that would work for the group as a whole.

But what does it mean to "place" yourself? Do you belong in a place; a place designated by whom? Evaluating yourself in terms of others seems intrinsically unsatisfactory.

I hesitated to place myself on the continuum. I can measure the effect the course has had on me, but have no means of measuring an inner quality for others. I have no basis on which to make, no way in which to make, no right to make a judgment of how I rank in relation to them, as I have no way of knowing where someone started, or how much his alertness has changed. How do you measure yourself for yourself, or how do you measure others, and how do you measure you against them?

When you were alone—trying to establish some perspective, clarifying where you've been, thinking about where you're headed—were others still there? When you were alone, did you react to a group pressure? Did you form your conclusions in reaction to what others say or would say? Or did you consider what others say as just another piece of data from which you eventually conclude certain things about yourself?

The issues you assess remain hard to grasp because they are fundamental: How involved am I, how much have I learned? But the categories used in the exercise to rate these issues are hard to grasp because they are so superficial. Think of all the energy wasted trying to figure out what is meant by "high," "medium," or "low"; "first" or "last"!

These seem to be clear groupings when viewed from the outside; they become more slippery when you have to place yourself in one or the other. For many the middle is the most ambiguous.

Those in the middle group were most controversial since there seemed to be different concepts of "middle involvement." Some considered themselves able to join in class activities but unable to relate their experiences to their "non-class" life. For others, "medium involvement" entailed outside activities related to the course, whereas inside there was only partial participation.

Others find the middle the most appropriate.

With a self-evaluation that contained high and low involvement, I thought it most satisfying to categorize myself in the medium involvement group. I had preconceived notions of what was meant by involvement. Everyone has a stereotypic image of what constitutes a "highly involved" person. Such an image is the goal toward which all conscientious students strive. Similarly, the other extreme of "low involvement" also exists as a preconceived idea in our minds. Very few people, if any, can truthfully place themselves at either of the two extremes without certain inhibitions. No one considers himself totally perfect or totally imperfect, and since the dividing lines between low and middle and middle and high are vague, the safest grouping is middle. Neither of the two extremes was closest to my personal experience, so I was convinced that the medium involvement group was most appropriate.

Still others insist that they felt between two groups and couldn't make up their minds. This problem seems to intensify when the continuum is used because there are no set categories you can fall back on.

The arbitrary quality of the conventional evaluation system is based on a competitive, nonsynergistic model of society. If we assume there is only a limited quantity of "involvement" or "learning," then when I am very involved someone else must be very uninvolved. And if what I do determines how much is left for you, then we keep our eye on each other. We continually compare, we constantly compete. To keep up this frantic effect, we usually resort to simple scales which are quick and easy to rate: high, medium, or low. Any more meaningful effort and we would lose our competitive edge. Obviously, this picture characterizes the grading system in most schools. Can we accept the fact that, in a much more subtle and pervasive way, it also characterizes much of our daily life?

Then the crucial question becomes whether you could begin to move beyond this competitive bind. Is it possible for you to assess yourself in a group setting? Did forming a circle help? How about doing the exercise with your eyes closed? When you worked alone, could you generate a realistic picture of your present situation? Could you assess yourself as you exist in a social context, rather than waiting for the context to tell you who you are and what you're doing? Consider that time alone carefully. If we can't create an honest view of ourselves, for ourselves, we must look again—into ourselves. The reasons lie there.

APPLICATIONS

Try to transform the conventional system of evaluation. Observe various lines in our society and how you behave on them. What are some of the issues raised by standing in line? What does being on a

line do to your mood, your internal state? What kind of a culture do
these lines imply and support? For example, waiting on line to buy a
ticket to the movies, an orderly line. Each person's place on the line
is fixed. There is nothing to do but move up to the box office one by
one. What do you do on such a line? How do you deal with all that
time? By being bored?

What about more active lines, where there is little order, where
people push and shove, sometimes literally, to get to the front. The
fast-service luncheonette where you have to shout out your order; the
traffic jam where cars dart out ahead, trying to gain an extra inch. How
do you deal with these lines? When there are power struggles and
competitions to get the extra edge, where are you? And what does this
type of jostling for a better position imply about our society?

Try changing the atmosphere of one of the competitive lineups. As
all around you shout their orders, as cars nudge and jam you, try to be
still for a moment, reach a point of strength and calm within, and move
at your own pace. Can you do this? Can you go beyond the edict that
only fiercer competition on your part will prevent your being overwhelmed, run over, pushed aside? Consider these issues on a different
level: nonviolent resistance. Where do you stand on the matters of nonviolence, what do you do? Do you find yourself doing violence to
others, in subtle, psychological ways, while espousing nonviolence?

Can you create a synergistic system, if only for a brief time and in
a limited area? Can you create a situation where you and others can
work together on something? Where each person's efforts help the
other? Where one person's "success" encourages another's "success," so
that success and failure become meaningless? Think of a situation
where that which is worked on and valued is not scarce. Psychological
and emotional attributes can have this expandable quality. Try, for
example, creating a situation where there is more warmth or openness
among people. The more open you are, the more others can be open,
the more openness there is. How can you sustain such a synergistic
situation in our manipulative, win-lose society? Try often to establish
such situations and you'll learn many of the answers. You might even
introduce some changes.

If you want to work specifically with the "Line Up" exercise, try it
at home or on the job. For example, at home, have you and your family
line up according to who is most important in the home, most responsible, sensitive, lazy, loud, etc. Place yourself on these lines, place each
other. Pick criteria which seem to express the underlying dimensions
of your family. Make these dimensions explicit with the lineups so all
can recognize them more clearly. Then you all have the opportunity to

change them. What does it mean if the father places himself as being most important yet is placed by his children as being least sensitive?

To make self-assessment work, you must work at it. If you hope to gain some perspective on what has happened and some guidance about what can happen, you have to understand where you are now. Try regularly to assess your situation and state. Your efforts at assessment should become more a part of your everyday functioning.

Begin your day by trying to come to a central point in yourself. Do this early in the morning, before you're overwhelmed by the concerns of your daily routines, including your washing and breakfast routines. Select times in the day when you will check in on yourself and try to come to a place of substance within. Consider what you wish for the day. Then follow through as much as possible on your intentions. By doing this you can create a real day, where time doesn't merely pass you by. Start your days on a high level; see how long you can sustain that level.

In the evening, before going to bed, again consider your day. This time reflect on how much of what you intended to do you did. Most important, did you have moments when you came to yourself?

Through these morning and evening reflections, you can add life to your days. You can also see more clearly what kind of a person you really are; not what you intended to be, but what you in fact are. We are what we do, every day.

Mirror Talk

Every day we stand before a mirror, glance at how we look, and alter our appearance according to where we are going and whom we are going to see. Sometimes this fixing up is a very routine process; at other times it is long and deliberate. We change what we don't like, improve upon what we like. But do we ever stop and consider what the mirror simply shows: a realistic reflection? It is realistic at all stages, before and after you've altered your appearance. Mirrors don't lie; they simply reflect us. In disregarding this reflection, wishing it would disappear, we begin to lie. Do you ever view yourself as you are rather than as you are trying to appear?

In this exercise you can work more specifically with both evaluating and trying to be realistic about yourself. We have very little experience in being realistic. We are rarely unbiased about who we are and what we do. We are experts, however, in subjectivity, easily forming likes and dislikes about aspects of ourselves, quickly clouding over the simple facts about ourselves. But only if we begin accepting these facts, accepting ourselves as we are, can we begin to grow.

We use the mirror only on a *temporary* basis. It may help us with our ultimate goal: to create inner "eyes," to develop *inside ourselves* some ability to be honest with ourselves and accept what we find.

LABORATORY PHASE

Structure

This exercise can be done wherever there is a mirror. A full-length mirror is preferable but not necessary. There are two parts: the first taking approximately ten minutes, the other about five minutes.

Instructions

Stand alone in front of the mirror for approximately ten minutes. As you look at yourself, first congratulate yourself, then reprimand yourself, and finally talk honestly to yourself (for approximately three minutes each). Try to keep each phase as pure as possible. In congratulating yourself, express what you like about yourself without inhibition. In reprimanding yourself, really express what you dislike about yourself, what you find unattractive. In talking straight, be simple and simply honest about yourself.

After a brief period, go back in front of the mirror, and, for the next five minutes, describe your body. Keep the description as unbiased as possible. Focus on your body, avoiding, for example, inferences about your personality.

Remember. Keep going beyond your mirror image; keep going beneath a literal description of your body. Search for your own breadth and depth; come to yourself.

Extension. When discussing this exercise with others, at times institute this ground rule: Use the third person in talking about yourself and your experience. Don't use the word "I." For example, instead of Dave saying "I am. . . ." he would say "Dave is. . . ."

Discussion

Upon receiving the instructions to "Talk to myself in a mirror," I thought this exercise would be useless. During my daily activities I often talk to myself, not casual bantering, but hash and re-hash various problems. It was not until I said "Good Morning" to the mirror that I realized the "purpose" of the exercise.

This exercise is deceptively simple; it's almost too familiar.

I looked in the mirror and my first reaction was to straighten my hair; half out of embarrassment because I felt like I was looking at a specimen through a microscope, and half because that is what I habitually do when I look in the mirror.

The challenge is to get out of our mirror-looking habits so we can actually see what's there.

Often people experience a sense of separation from themselves.

After staring at myself for a while, the mirror image seemed to become a different person. My features looked strange as if I were becoming familiar with them for the first time. I also felt much freer to reprimand because the mirror self had somehow come apart from my inner self. I didn't feel very strongly about it and it somehow seemed more objective. It became a two-way conversation between myself and the image. The reprimand thrown back at me made me stop and think. The double reflection (physical and mental) made it more possible to become alert to how I might seem to others.

Different selves emerge. It can become confused and complex.

I became you as she looked back at me from the mirror. Then there was us, she and me talking to her, at her, and things were very filled up. It was as if there was a crowd, and for that while there was no room for anyone else. If anyone else had entered the relationship at that point they would have been intruding, for we were very involved in each other, yet separate.

The question remains as to the direction and quality of this separation; in some cases it can lead to seeing ourselves more realistically, in other cases to idle daydreaming.

For many, one immediate reaction is a disbelief that the reflection in the mirror is them—the person they are viewing is not the one they thought they were.

I was self-conscious and somewhat embarrassed to do this exercise before my reflection as if it was another person—this was at first uncomfortable.

This unfamiliarity of the mirror image can be a clue that you are beginning to realize something, maybe for the first time.

It is not hard to achieve this feeling of separateness from a mirror image, for I am not used to seeing my whole body in action, talking and gesturing, most of all, looking at myself in the eye.

For a while the more I looked at myself, the more strange and unfamiliar I appeared.

Did you overcome the strangeness of the situation so you viewed yourself from a slightly new perspective? Did you use the unfamiliarity to get beyond habitual perception and see something new? Were you able to transform this experience of separation into an experience of self-understanding?

Your attitude is important.

The exercise was like having a talk with a good friend or somebody that cared a lot about you and knew a lot about you. Only this was better, because it was you—and you knew most about it, and it doesn't lose in the translation from one person's eyes to another. There was a giving of information in a very direct way—with any interpretation being a function of the information itself. On the level that you admitted what you knew—that was the level and the degree to which you permitted interpretation. . . . Because I controlled what was said and what wasn't, I was dealing with as much as I could. Again, the exercise being a slightly different way of opening up and examining what I saw and permitting me slightly greater opportunities to see.

It is helpful to enlist the mirror reflection as an ally, helping to keep you on the right track, zeroing in on yourself.

What you say becomes more important, more crucial, because someone is looking at you, and you just can't drift off and retract what you're saying to yourself. Just involving your eyes, forcing them to focus and including them as part of this interior dialogue shifts the whole thing from a daydream into an encounter. You are encountering you as you see you, and you have the chance to make you so much more yourself.

The real issue is whether there was some increase in self-knowledge, slight though it may be.

Our eyes are always outwardly fixed . . . and I realized that a good deal of the reason I may feel inferior to others is that I can watch them and not myself. They look confident, knowledgeable. *I* may look this way but I certainly don't feel this way. And possibly, they may not feel the way they look either.

It was as if the me that is presented to the world became external to myself. And the inside "mees" that know what's going on (whether I like it or not) did more than just converse with each other, or send messages to each other; they got to confront each other, and so make the total me more in tune with myself.

You can approach the mirror and your image in many different ways. Is the image a mere physical replica or yourself? How does the reflected me relate to *me?* Did I talk to myself or with myself? Again, the key remains: Did being somewhat separate from yourself allow you to be more unbiased about yourself? Can you begin to distinguish more clearly between what you dislike or like *about* yourself, and who you *are?* Did you find some selves without the mirror?

As you begin listening to your own inner voices more, you not only move from evaluation to acceptance but also from being evaluated by others to assessing yourself. Yet the overwhelming force of others' evaluations of you is not easily dissipated. As you talked to yourself, did your words lose their meaning, did you lose interest? Often people say things that others had said about them—you are bright, easily angered, far out, friendly, unpredictable, etc.

After a while, however, I found myself slipping into the clichés and handy phrases that my friends and I throw around in describing each other. I became very frustrated because I couldn't force myself to concentrate on the image I was getting bored with. One point that I brought out to my image was that much of my self-evaluation is greatly determined by other people's evaluations of me. This lack of clarity between what I want and what others have made me feel I should want, began to concern and confuse me.

Many have this difficulty because, never before experiencing them-selves in quite this way, they may be saying things they're now not sure they believe or feel. We have an image in the eyes of others, and for many it becomes the most convenient way of looking at ourselves.

Any physical attribute I mentioned had already been mentioned and cate-gorized by someone else. Their categories were the ones that seemed to come naturally to me.

For many, the message is clear.

I was realizing that I was judging myself too much by external standards and too little by my own.

There is a world of difference between others' impressions of you and you seeing yourself *as if* from the outside. In the final analysis, only you can really see yourself as you are. Getting outside yourself, approaching yourself *as if* you were an unfamiliar person can help in the beginning. A woman who separated herself from her mirror reflection, experiencing it as if it were another person, describes what she learned:

I saw more clearly why I had given the impression of being definitely a set person, inflexible, and aloof. When I talked, I had a way of making an

opinion of mine sound final and exact. As if they were the final truths to be
spoken about the matter. I had a set facial expression, very sober without
any sign of doubt. My tone of voice was assertive and steady.

But developing the capacity for self-assessment is not simply a matter
of working from the inside out. You must contact the "real" inner voices.
Self-assessment demands valid, truthful assessments. We are seeking
facts. Congratulation and reprimand are one and the same; they are
evaluations, judgments, opinions. Fame and shame are one and the
same. Could you begin collecting facts about yourself when you tried
to talk honestly with yourself?
Many find it easy to congratulate themselves.

I congratulated myself a lot. I didn't say much; only that I was really together and really liked myself. This is because I have pulled myself together
a lot in the last month, and having finally regained peace with myself I liked
what I was and was happy to be that.

Many find it hard.

The "praise" experience was the most difficult; punctuated by silences and
laughter, it was "uncomfortable," embarrassing. A nonautonomous person
praises himself as he perceives others would praise him; and, therefore, he
feel, "I feel socially uncomfortable in the presence of compliments."

Many find it easy to reprimand themselves. Many find it hard.
But everybody should find it hard to talk honestly with themselves.
Congratulations and reprimands are formed from opinions and evaluations, what you like or dislike about yourself. Generating them is
easy when compared with the search for facts about yourself.

I couldn't get outside of myself to see myself in a totally first-hand, first-
time experience.

Talking honestly to myself made me somewhat tense, for the first time
that day. I realized that this reflection I was gazing at was real and material,
and that wherever I am present, it too is present.

Could you move toward collecting simple facts about yourself?
Could you begin accepting truths? Several things *can* be misleading,
taking you off the mark; the sincerity of your own efforts, for instance.

The subjectivity of the first two phases seemed hypocritical at times—I
knew the self-adulation was just as false as the self-deprecation, but I kept
on for the full required time so as to experience the full effect. The third

phase seemed all the more sincere after the four minutes of opposing and extreme evaluations.

Or desire for self-improvement:

Talking straight wasn't negative, but rather reassuring—opening up slightly new directions to move in, and offering a slightly different conceptual framework to work things through in.

Or, perhaps, too quickly taking the familiar for the real.

The only time I felt the least bit comfortable or honest was during the last three minutes of the exercise. Then I was able to look at myself in the same way that I do each day. I saw myself as I really am and although it may not have been as flattering as the first three minutes, it was infinitely more satisfying. I didn't have to pretend anything about myself. I was honest and straightforward. The person I saw in the mirror and the person I was talking about were finally the same. I was again aware of my own identity. For the six minutes before I was talking about another, someone I didn't know. Now I could talk about myself, someone I knew well.

Were you more able to be honest about certain aspects of yourself? People generally find it easier to state facts about their bodies and physical appearance than their thoughts, emotions, or personality. Was the second part of the exercise, when you described your body, more fruitful? For some, it can be a high point.

As I was describing my facial expression, a very different feeling developed. I felt more detached from my usual concerns. Then, my face changed its expression, my mouth forming a smile. I saw this, but not with my eyes. I saw that smile, and through it, came right to my core. I was there, simply there, at that moment!

But collecting facts about "your body" is only relatively easier. We remain quite attached to our body. We can become alienated, not detached from it:

I realized that to me, on most occasions I was only a mind—no body—just a mind, and on second thought a heart or an emotional component. In other words I was nothing tangible, just something ephemeral. That is, I conceive of myself in terms of my thoughts and feelings rather than in terms of my height, weight, or other physical characteristics.

The goal is not a "split personality" where, alienated from yourself, you watch yourself from the outside, perhaps generating self-images or pictures. Rather, we strive toward developing a capacity *within* us which, functioning beyond the five senses, could have a truer perspective on our selves.

APPLICATIONS

Listen to yourself talk. Recognize how often you are evaluating yourself and others. "He is good," "He is bad"; "I had very little trouble with this"; "Don't you think this came out well?" Note how you use evaluative statements to put others down and, in the process, place yourself up. Be perceptive about yourself. Catch your evaluative remarks which are meant to sound fair and neutral: "Oh, I didn't know you were going to do it *that* way." Can you increase the degree to which you talk honestly to and about yourself, to and about others?

Bring these efforts into your relationships. Is there anyone you know who is as a reflector, who lets you see yourself more clearly when you relate to him? If so, seek him out more, relate to him more deeply. If he allows you to grow, he is also probably growing.

Are there relationships where you are overwhelmed; where all you can perceive is the other's image and all you feel is his influence? Perhaps he inspires you; more than likely he manipulates you. Try working within these relationships. When you are being manipulated, is it possible to talk honestly?

Make an explicit agreement with one of these manipulating persons to change the relationship so it is more harmonious and allows for growth. First, for several minutes, ask him to physically follow your actions; he must do whatever you do, faithfully, immediately, and precisely. Does this interaction help him understand something about how you feel? Can he appreciate more what it is like to be controlled by another? Use this brief mirroring exercise as an opening to a more extended discussion of your relationship. Together, plan ways to create more harmony. Do what you plan to do.

Hopefully, the mirror exercise can help you relate more honestly to yourself. But don't keep looking at the mirror; begin to look through it and beyond it, into yourself. Apply the exercise; try relating honestly to yourself at moments during your day. You don't need a mirror. You do need yourself—which means that first you must find yourself. You have to develop within yourself the capacity for honest viewing.

Seek this honesty with yourself as a part of your everyday behavior. Try to increase your honesty at different times, in different places. Many, many times, try to contact yourself, directly and simply. Keep remembering; keep reminding yourself. Make efforts in everyday situations to accept what you are really doing. Don't immediately worry about whether you like or dislike the way you talked to your assistant, the way you dress, or the way you relate to your wife. Likes and dislikes arise without any help; they get us nowhere but feeling in a good mood then a bad mood, then good, then bad, etc. Spend your energy trying to be realistic about your actions. Before you attempt to change anything, first realize what you are *in fact* doing.

FURTHER READING

Hermann Hesse, *Magister Ludi* (*The Glass Bead Game*), Frederick Ungar Publishing Co., New York, 1949.

All goes well for Joseph Knecht, very well indeed; at least on the outside. But within him, the seed of self-questioning exists and grows. Hesse leads us deeply into Knecht's world, and then leaves us with him. Though this novel's setting may seem exotic, it can provide a useful metaphor for your everyday life.

Eugen Herrigel, *Zen in the Art of Archery*, Pantheon Books, a division of Random House, Inc., New York, 1953.

Herrigel describes in specific and moving terms an aspect of his Zen training. Though his account is practical and straightforward, his book is not a manual for Zen training. Rather, it is a vivid reminder of how easily external success distracts us from the essence of growth, namely, the condition of our inner life; and, paradoxically, of how work on our inner life can evoke "external success" without our being personally caught up in it. Zen training may seem far afield. Look beneath the form for principles about human growth.

John Neihardt, *Black Elk Speaks*, Bison Books, University of Nebraska Press, Lincoln, Nebr., 1961.

Black Elk speaks, and through John Neihardt, he speaks strongly and poetically. He is reflecting on his life, recontacting his roots, reexperiencing his development. Black Elk still continues meeting the religious or spiritual dimension. He searches for the meaning of that dimension; what it was for him, what it is now. One man's journey expands into material for us all.

Educating for Personal Growth

Creative Alertness in Your
Everyday Life

THE issue is living, not doing exercises. The challenge is to grow beyond our individualistic selves, not to increase the skill with which we repeat ourselves. We want to erase the dichotomy between exercises and living, and not worry about applying what we learned because we *are* trying to live it. We work with the material of our day and bring that material into focus through an exercise, which is really an opportunity. Throughout our day, we intentionally create opportunities to see ourselves more honestly. Perhaps for moments we can even transcend ourselves.

STRUCTURE: YOUR LIFE

INSTRUCTIONS: HOW WILL YOU APPROACH IT?

And so this is not a particular exercise, to be fitted into your day. It is an invitation to make your life more a journey of self-discovery. It asks you: How do you now approach your life? Do you create opportunities where you dare to grow? Do you seek what is beyond all our individualistic selves?

How would you answer such questions? Or better, how do you meet such questions? Actually take time to raise such questions for yourself, and take time to consider them. Write down some of your thoughts and hopes. Establish some ways in which you can actualize these hopes, and put them into action. Keep track of what you wished for and what you did; then you can become more realistic about who you are. A diary or journal can be helpful here.

I would suggest a certain ordering of priorities. Simply, try to keep your feet on the ground, doing first things first. Before leaping into considerations of the transcendent, consider first who you are—right now. Learn more about yourself as you presently exist. This is a very important stage because you can't really find something beyond yourself until you have discovered your present self. You try to get yourself together, and explore your strengths and weaknesses. The exercises in this book can be helpful in this exploration. First, you see yourself as you are, going about your everyday affairs, and you accept what you see. Then, when you can realize the limitations of this "you," this person, the wish for something beyond yourself, beyond persons, emerges.

How might you develop this kind of approach to your life? I think raising and considering fundamental life questions is important. Even more important is applying your ideas and plans. The approach develops as you begin *doing* things in a certain way.

But now, first things first. Not what do you want to be, or what do you wish for, or what do you try to be; but what *are* you now? Can I rely on you? When I need support, will you be there? Are you worthy of trust? Do you do what you say? When I come to you, will I meet someone of substance or is there a hollowness inside? But it's not a matter of me asking you. Only when you honestly ask yourself does it become important; and when you can honestly answer yourself, it becomes very important!

Start to take note of the quality and character of your days, the force and direction of your life. You examine yourself, and if your vision is clear, you see what we all must see—that, right now, we are all very unreliable, undependable, and insubstantial. We are at the mercy of our environment, reacting to the whims and wishes of others. If you can establish that fact for yourself and accept it, then you can begin to do something about it. I'm not suggesting that free will springs full-blown from a reacting personality. But you could begin to change the quality or flavor of your days ever so slightly. You could begin to be more intentional and start to stand up because you're strong inside.

I'm feeling really down tonight, I just can't seem to get started even though I know I have to get that thing written. . . . I'll go to bed early, and then I'll get up early in the morning with a fresh start and really begin to write. . . . Oh, shit, I can't get up now, it's too cold, and I'm still tired. Jesus, it's already 10:00 o'clock. . . .

Can you do what you intend? When you realize clearly you must do something, do it. Don't give yourself the "excuses of tomorrow." Tomorrow will be a good day to do something else. Now is the time to do what is to be done today.

Demonstrate to yourself that you have some ability to carry out your intentions. For example, get up a half hour earlier each morning for a week; for several meals, eat to satisfy your physical hunger rather than your psychological needs; avoid idle chatter or evaluating comments the next time you visit others. Do each of these things not because they are "good" or "healthy," but because you told yourself to do them. Generalize your ability as you develop it. Be more intentional in all aspects of your life.

I hope that guy doesn't ask me for help—how could I give him something, what would I say. . . . He looks agitated but if I sort of look the other way maybe he won't come over. . . . What a spot . . . here I am anxious as hell because someone in trouble may ask me for some understanding!

Are you solid enough to support another? Are you in touch enough with your own needs to accept the needs of another? Some people are points of strength in the midst of disorder. You're at a large, open gathering, perhaps a coffee house, and a fight is ready to break out. Who moves forward to stop it, and who moves away to ignore it, hoping it will go away, not wanting to get involved? Or you belong to a group and some work has to be done on the meeting room. Who accepts the responsibility despite the fact that, like everyone else, he is busy? Who looks down to the ground, trying to become "unnoticed," waiting until someone else assumes the responsibility? Or you're talking with someone who has some "power" over you—your teacher, your boss, or your friend who represents your ideal of being hip. Who talks straight, not aggressively and insultingly, but honestly? Who changes his words as he changes his environment, never daring to say what he feels? Try moving, in your actions, toward being more substantial and responsible.

Keep reminding yourself to come to yourself. Leave notes to yourself, in your pocket, on your mirror: "Stop! Where are you *now*? Can you *be* here?" During the day, change your rhythms, break through the inertia. Select times when you shift your emphasis and try to re-establish contact with yourself—every two hours; or on rising, at noon, and before going to bed, etc. Use the exercises in this book to suggest other ways of creating these opportunities for coming to yourself. Remember you are developing an approach. Avoid doing something here, there, and everywhere, and in the process forgetting why you're doing it in the first place.

Try to rediscover the life in you. Keep your efforts alive—vary them, reestablish them. Keep shaking yourself out of your sleepwalk, which is your ordinary everyday walk. There you are, talking to your room-mate, and you realize that for the past hour your intention to be more open with him has been unrealized; it's even vanished. At that point, reestablish your intention, try to be more open. You have to intention-ally overcome your usual state where it's only "business as usual."

This approach is hard. There are many forces keeping you asleep on your feet. So marshal your resources to bolster your efforts. Try to create opportunities in supportive environments. For example, pick situations where you're not expected to maintain a certain image—when you are alone, or with strangers or with accepting friends. In these situations you can afford to take a moment to seek yourself or try something out. You're not surrounded by others who will be surprised or critical or disappointed when you do something slightly different. From these more protected situations, you move toward situations throughout your day.

As you learn about yourself, you can become more sensitive and helpful with others. Opportunities you create may well be opportunities for those around you; at the very least they should not take away from others. You're not a callous psychologist, experimenting on the world, enlisting others as your guinea pigs.

Before your day starts, come to yourself. And from that perspective, consider your day: what do you want for that day, what do you wish for yourself, what do you hope for others? Previsualize your day: what will you be doing, who will you be with, when can you make efforts to see yourself? Then, as often as possible, as honestly as possible, try in fact to see yourself as you are in your various activities. At the end of the day, reflect on what has actually happened, and consider the next day and what you would like it to bring. As with your days, so with your weeks, months, seasons, etc. Your birthday may become a point for reconsideration and reflection, a point for hopes and aspir-ations, and a time for recommitment. Spring may become a period when you consider the potentialities in yourself and others that seek expression. Thanksgiving may become a time when you really consider what you are thankful for, and what you can give to yourself and others.

As you start becoming more honest, intentional, and substantial in your ordinary day-to-day life, you begin to lay the foundation for the extraordinary. For just as you try being more honest, you realize even more clearly your limitations. Your honesty remains subject to your personality and to the conditions around you. But from the strength of these efforts to be more honest and substantial, you become more alive as a person. And as you contact the life within you, you can realize it seeks expression beyond you, beyond others. The wish can develop for a higher, more transcendent order of experience to guide and inspire you. The wish can develop for real, lasting honesty. The wish can develop to move beyond the preludes to growth.

You search for ways to meet this wish. I believe each of us must create within ourselves the capacity to transcend ourselves. It would take much work and effort to create this capacity, which would exist on an entirely different level than our ordinary functioning. It would exist on a vertical plane above and beyond the horizontal of our ordinary lives. We must create something in ourselves that is separate from our ordinary selves—something that would enable us to see those ordinary selves as they truly are. Put another way, we must recontact and participate in that aspect of ourselves which has been called transcendental or spiritual. For moments, we create a place in ourselves where the cosmos can live.

Your feet are on the ground, and you are alive and questioning; and so your arms almost instinctively reach for the sky. You've known enough of yourself to realize you want something more, something which can see you more as you truly are. With that more transcendent perspective, you could enter a new phase of growth. Through exploring your own particular terrain, you yearn now to venture more into the common unknown. Your journey begins again as you move toward a path.

FURTHER READING

Hermann Hesse, *Siddhartha*, New Directions Publishing Corporation, New York, 1951.

Personal growth takes place within a person's day-to-day activities, and over his lifetime. Siddhartha changes his external activities and situations, but his quest for an inner life continues. Try to read this little book in one sitting. As you finish the last page, where do you find yourself? For me, at that moment, life had expanded beyond me and throughout the world.

René Daumal, *Mount Analogue*, City Lights, San Francisco, 1971.

This book remains unfinished. Daumal died before completing it. I think he might have preferred it to remain so open at its end. He's talking to us about personal growth—our growth—and each of us must write his own story, which also has no end. Through a challenging "mountain climb," Daumal offers the prospect of moving from earth toward heaven. The climb is difficult. It requires strenuous and sincere effort on your part in order to participate.

Section Two:

Photograph by the author

. . . *I* was at perhaps the highest point of my academic career. . . . In a wordly sense, I was making a great income and I was a collector of possessions. . . . I wasn't a genuine scholar, but I had gone through the whole academic trip. I had gotten my Ph.D.; I was writing books. I had research contracts. . . . But what all this boils down to is that I was really a very good game player.

My lecture notes were the ideas of other men, subtly presented, and my research was all within the Zeitgeist—all that which one was supposed to research about . . . the theories I was teaching, which were theories of achievement and anxiety and defense mechanisms and so on, weren't getting to the crux of the matter.

. . . Something was wrong. And the something wrong was that I just didn't know, though I kept feeling all along the way that somebody else must know even though I didn't. The nature of life was a mystery to me. All the stuff I was teaching was just like little molecular bits of stuff but they didn't add up to a feeling anything like wisdom. I was just getting more and more knowledgeable. And I was getting very good at bouncing three knowledge balls at once. I could sit in a doctoral exam, ask very sophisticated questions and look terribly wise. It was a hustle.

. . . there was that horrible realization that I didn't know something or other which made it all fall together. And there was a slight panic in me

167

that I was going to spend the next forty years not knowing, and that apparently that was par for the course. . . . The whole thing was too empty. It was not honest enough.[1]

Suddenly: "What am I doing?" "Am I to go through life playing the clown?" "What am I doing, going to parties that I don't enjoy?" "What am I doing, being with people who bore me?" "Why am I so hollow and the hollowness filled with emptiness?" A shell. How has this shell grown around me? Why am I proud of my children and unhappy about their lives which are not good enough? Why am I disappointed? Why do I feel so much waste?

I comes through, a little. In moments. And gets pushed back by other I.

I refuses to play the clown any more. Which I is that? "She used to be fun, but now she thinks too much about herself." I lets friends drop away. Which I is that? "She's being too much by herself. That's bad. She's losing her mind." Which mind?[2]

I am a composer. Music has always been for me the "talent" of the New Testament, given to me by God and demanding that I develop it and work on it unceasingly. It was clear to me long before I met Mr. Gurdjieff, however, that to be able to develop in my creative work something was necessary, something greater or higher, which I could not name. Only if I could possess this "something" would I be able to progress further and hope to have any real satisfaction from my own creation, and not be ashamed of myself. The words of Beethoven often came to my mind: "Music is a higher revelation than philosophy or science," and I always remembered, when composing, the wonderful words of a Russian fairy tale: "Go—not knowing where; bring—not knowing what; the path is long; the way unknown: the hero knows not how to arrive there by himself alone; he has to seek the guidance and help of Higher Forces. . . ."

And so my life was a search.

. . . I made a great effort and forced myself to say to him that I wished to be admitted to his Work. Mr. Gurdjieff asked the reason for my request; perhaps I was not happy in life? Or was there some other special reason? I answered that I was perfectly happy, happily married, that I had enough money to live on, without having to earn my living, and that I had my music which was the center of my life. But I added, all this was not enough. "Without inner growth," I said, "there is no life at all for me; both my wife and I are searching for a way to develop."[3]

---

[1] Baba Ram Dass (Richard Alpert), *Be Here Now,* Lama Foundation, San Cristobal, New Mexico, distributed by Crown Publishing Company, 1971.

[2] Carl Rogers and Barry Stevens, *Person to Person: The Problem of Being Human,* Real People Press, Walnut Creek, Calif., 1967, p. 11.

[3] Thomas deHartmann, *Our Life with Mr. Gurdjieff,* Cooper Square Publishers, New York, 1964, pp. 3 and 5.

What is this desire for change; this yearning for something deeper and more meaningful; this seeking of a level beyond one's personal, individualistic life? Where do such desires and searchings originate? Are they all phases of the same process? Does each of us experience them? I want to approach these questions through a discussion of personal growth.

Personal Growth: Conceptual Groundwork

Personal growth is not easy to talk about; it is even more difficult to write about. In a very important sense we can know it only by experiencing it. But writings about growth may encourage us to begin to have such experiences.

There are moments when we become more aware of our own nature and the nature of the universe. During these moments we are more able to choose freely and to act intentionally. Personal growth evolves when these moments begin to cumulate and intensify. Therefore growth deals with the quality and direction of one's life.

Two Phases of Growth: Preludes and Paths

The process of personal growth has many different phases. There are at least two major phases—preludes to personal growth and paths toward personal growth. In the former preliminary phase, growth deals more with issues in personality. It is oriented to changes at a psychological level. In the advanced phase of a path, growth deals more with the essential core beneath personality, what is common to mankind and the universe. It is oriented more to changes at a spiritual level. Working on a path, one can begin to guide the evolution of (his) consciousness.

When functioning as a prelude, the process of growth is more possibility than reality. At this phase, a person may realize that he can change, that his personality and life-style can assume a new direction and quality. He may become open to the influx of more meaning into his life. He may accept the fact that honesty with oneself and others can lead beneath the superficial. At this preliminary phase, a person can catch a glimpse into the possibility of personal growth *for himself*. He can establish a vision that he can go beyond his apparently individualistic self toward more transpersonal existence.

When functioning as a path, the process of growth is progressively realized. Personal growth is more than a few moments of insight; it is a lifelong journey dedicated to self-understanding.[4] Working with a path over a long period of time, a person can begin a journey into more spiritual realms. He can begin to transcend himself. A person involved with the preludes to growth can generate a vision of transcendence for himself. Working with a path is one way to begin actualizing this vision.

In their purer forms, there is a qualitative difference between these two phases of growth.[5] In practice, however, the distinctions are not always clear-cut. It is never simply a matter of certain techniques dealing with preludes and other paths. It is one thing to consider the technique or teaching, and another thing to consider how the technique is used or the teaching applied.

There are techniques which focus on preludes to growth. Examples would be achievement or competence training, with its emphasis on self-control; sensitivity training, with its emphasis on encounter; Outward Bound, with its emphasis on stretching limits; Women's Liberation consciousness-raising groups, with their emphasis on biological-cultural identity; and many of the communes, with their emphasis on community issues.

There are teachings which focus on paths of growth. Examples are Hatha Yoga, with its emphasis on the physical approach; the teachings of Meher Baba, with their emphasis on the devotional or emotional approach; Zen meditation, with its emphasis on the intellectual approach; and the teachings of Gurdjieff, with their emphasis on a wholistic approach.

This book focuses on the preludes to growth, and it also points toward paths of growth.

Persons can take from a technique or teaching what is offered. At times, someone can even move beyond a technique. For example, someone can have a transcendent experience while engaged in a prelude; and the *rare* individual who becomes a master is no longer dependent on a particular path.

This "going beyond the technique" blurs the distinction between prelude and path on the practical level. More frequent, however, is

---

[4] The experience of a journey is beautifully presented by R. Daumal in *Mount Analogue*, City Lights, San Francisco, 1971; and H. Hesse, *Siddhartha*, New Directions Publishing Corporation, New York, 1951.

J. Campbell in *Hero with a Thousand Faces*, 1956, and H. Zimmer, in *The King and the Corpse*, 1960 (both Meridian Books published by World Publishing Company, Cleveland), present myths of this journey from diverse cultures and epochs.

[5] For a fuller discussion of these two phases of growth and various approaches to growth, as well as other points in this overview, see R. Katz, *Transformations: The Meaning of Personal Growth*, Prentice-Hall, Inc., Englewood Cliffs, N.J., 1974.

the blurring which occurs with the person who is unable to apply or use what is offered. A person with strong therapeutic needs may not be able to use opportunities a prelude may offer. A person who has yet to pose fundamental questions to himself may miss opportunities in a path. When preludes are continually, almost repetitively tried, with no higher or larger aim, they can become deadening ends. Rather than opening doors, they close them or set up blind alleys. Many persons who go from one sensitivity group experience to another eventually realize they are going nowhere. Also, paths do not magically transform people. Persons grow when actively engaged in a journey of self-discovery and stagnate when merely enamored of their membership in a "spiritual" group.

Now it may seem that I have too strong a bias, as if the preliminary phases of growth were important only because they can lead to a path. By nature I am an idealist and always seek what is beyond. Therefore I stress the more advanced phase of growth—it can give us all something to work toward. I believe we must be guided by a vision of what is possible though not necessarily probable.

But I've written this book, which deals with the preludes to growth, for a reason. Though there is a qualitative difference between preludes and paths, they are intrinsically related. They can be part of the same process.

I am idealistic, but I am beginning to learn from my experience. It is becoming increasingly clear to me that first things must come first. Before you reach for heaven, your feet must be on the ground. In a transcendent experience, you transcend something you are, you give up what you have. First we must be mature as persons, know ourselves in an ordinary psychological sense, and be able to communicate with others. Only then can we begin to transcend this ordinary existence. It's quite simple. A dedicated search for a more transcendent existence can only grow in a person who is alive and questioning, who realizes for himself that he must go beyond himself. Time and energy must be devoted to being alive and questioning, to the preludes to growth.

I believe this preliminary phase is very important in itself. During it, we can become more alive, more open to ourselves, others, and our environment. Also, if this phase leads to an involvement with a path, that is important at a different level.

Not Therapy

Regardless of the phase at which growth is occurring, there are certain characteristics to that process. For example, growth techniques do not ignore a person's neuroses or personal deficiencies, but neither do they

focus on these deficiencies. This is in contrast to the therapy approaches. By focusing on these deficiencies, therapy tries to teach a
person to function (at least) adequately. Growth techniques assume
a person who already functions adequately, but *only* adequately. Their
focus is on enhancing this adequate quality so that a person can live
more beyond his individual self. When the agitated young student seeks
enlightenment at the door of the Zen master, he is often told: First
straighten out your day-to-day situation, get more stability there so you
aren't so nervous. How could you possibly meditate when in the most
ordinary sense your life is so fragmented?

Again, the distinction between therapy and phases of personal growth
is not always present. Theoretically, one would say there is an ordering from therapy to preludes to paths. But persons become involved
in growth techniques for various reasons, some of them therapeutic.
Also, certain therapy approaches are particularly interested in raising
possibilities of personal growth. The Jungian approach emphasizes
involvement with archetypal images and transcendent symbols. The
existential approach works on paradoxes of existence which are at the
heart of growth. For example, Laing tries to transform the schizo-
phrenic experience into an opportunity to get beyond oneself; he tries
to appreciate the sanity of madness.[6] He treats the classic double bind,
the origin of much of schizophrenia, as if it were a Zen koan—which
in a sense it is. Frankel meets the condition of boredom and meaning-
lessness head on and strives for a sense of purpose with his therapy.[7]
But the main emphasis in most therapy is for a person to attain an
adequate level of functioning. Toward the end of therapy, as one moves
toward issues of fullness and meaning in life, one raises issues of
personal growth.

CREATIVE ALERTNESS AND AWARENESS

"Creative alertness" and "awareness" occupy special places in the
process of growth. They refer to different "levels of consciousness,"
different kinds of "altered-states-of-consciousness."

Given the ordinary course of a man's life, inertia is one of the major
forces. He can't seem to get started. He puts off until tomorrow what
must be done today. And, of course, it is nearly impossible for him to
change. But when he becomes actively concerned about the direction
and quality of his life, he seeks to do something about it. I believe the

[6] R. D. Laing, *The Politics of Experience*, Pantheon Books, a division of Random
House, Inc., New York, 1967; and *The Divided Self*, Penguin Books, Inc., Balti-
more, 1965.

[7] V. Frankel, *Man's Search For Meaning*, Washington Square Press, a division
of Simon & Schuster, Inc., New York, 1963.

only way he can begin to do something about this life is to begin creating moments of alertness and awareness in his life. In these moments he attains some distance from his ongoing activities. He starts to have perspective. And he begins to see himself more as he in fact is. As he accepts himself as he really is, he begins to grow.

Here again the difference between preludes and paths comes in. During the preludes to growth, there can be moments of creative alertness. One aspect of the personality tries to examine other aspects perceptively and sensitively—but it all remains at the same level of personality. The perspective that results is not especially universal. The information about oneself that emerges remains slightly biased. Still, these moments of alertness can be in the direction of growth. They can introduce a questioning, searching attitude which can be the invitation to further growth on a path.

When involved in a path, there can be moments of awareness. The perspective they generate is more universal, the facts which emerge are more essentially accurate. After much work and time on a path, these moments can result in the creation of a capacity to see oneself as one really is. It's as if one has inside himself a capacity which is wholly apart from him, which is eternal where he is temporal, which is unbiased where he is biased. As this capacity grows, personal growth exists.

Do We Really Want to Change?

The first step in the process of personal growth is both simply and essential: do we want to change? This may sound almost absurd, it is so obvious. And too quickly one says: "Of course, I do!" But, do we *really* want to change? When it comes down to *in fact* making a change, can I? *Do* I? *Do* you?

Let's back up a bit. Is there any reason why you would want to change? Surely you've met people who say: "I'm satisfied with things as they are." Apparently they don't want to change. Now either they don't see that their lives are sorely in need of change—they are blind to the emptiness; or they realize the need but don't feel they *can* change; or they *are* where they are, existing at peace with themselves, perhaps even at a high level of consciousness; or . . . or. The possibilities are endless.

SEARCHING FOR SOMETHING HIGHER

Sometimes these same people will say: "Why do you always want more?" And here is a key: A person must initiate the process of growth in himself. I don't mean to imply that one must manipulate things and force growth to occur. I do mean that one must assume responsibility for his own growth. Benoilt has written a book on Zen entitled *Let Go!*[8] The paradox is, of course, that "letting go" of those things which prevent growth is not a case of passive relaxation. Instead, you must focus on what is essential and eternal so that you can let go of all else—so that it can drop away from you.

I want to go soon and live away by the pond, where I shall hear only the wind whispering among the reeds. It will be success if I shall have left myself behind. But my friends ask what I will do when I get there. Will it not be employment enough to watch the progress of the seasons?[9]

Put simply, we must seek something more for our lives if growth is to occur. We must be questioners, searchers. And we must seek something beyond in a yielding fashion rather than grasping for it.

MECHANICALITY IN LIFE

Certainly there is ample reason for seeking more. If I can honestly describe my usual state and my usual day, more than likely I will realize the absence of a center. Where is the place inside me which remains an island of peace amid an undependable and, at times, stormy day? My usual day has good moods and bad, likes and dislikes. One moment I'm riding high, in a "good" state; and then I criticize myself or someone criticizes me, or I get tense, my mood changes, and there I am at a lower ebb. And what is more subtle but equally unreliable—a good piece of news, a positive feeling, a favorable reaction to my work, and I am off again into a "good" state. But I have no control over these states. Too often I'm on a roller coaster, going up and down regardless of my will or intention.

Consider yourself. Take time, *now*. Does this picture of my usual day capture some of the quality of your days?

I think that most of the time we are like mechanical men, responding to a set of controls which operate randomly. We think we can control our lives. We say, for example: "I'll change, I'll keep my negative moods from consuming me; just wait, starting tomorrow, whenever I feel a negative mood coming, I'll . . . etc., etc." Dr. W. A. Nyland has talked amout the "disease of tomorrow." There is a story he tells about "tomorrow":

[8] H. Benoilt, *Let Go!* (translated by A. Low), George Allen & Unwin, Ltd., London, England, 1962.

[9] H. D. Thoreau, *Journal* (December 24, 1841), Riverside Press, New York, 1906.

A restaurant had a sign on it "Enjoy your meal today, because tomorrow it will all be free!" A man passed by, stopped, of course, and couldn't resist going in—"Will this food be good enough to eat again tomorrow?" he wondered. He ate a hearty meal, even more enjoyable with the thought of his free meal tomorrow. The next day he returned and quickly went in, sat down and again ate heartily! As he slowly sipped his tea and had his last bite of dessert, he leaned back, content. Then the waiter brought him the check, which was also substantial. He could hardly believe what was happening, and quickly asked, now with some hesitancy: "But the sign said 'Enjoy your meal today because tomorrow it will all be free,' didn't it?" The waiter cheerfully replied: "Yes, that is what the sign says, *every day!*"

NEED FOR A CENTER

It is clear that as we paint the portrait of ourselves in everyday life, there is a hole in the center—it is empty. There is no center, no place where we live more essentially, no point from which awareness can exist, no opportunity to participate in the eternal in each of us. We miss a center which is unchanging in the rushing stream of chaotic and mechanical happenings. We miss an ability to step aside from everyday concerns; and a capacity to consider these concerns honestly, seeing ourselves as we really are. In accepting this as the condition of our lives today, we can become truly motivated toward growth.

At this point you may very well be asking: "Eternity? Yes, certainly, I need a center, and I wish freedom; but 'eternity' and 'freedom in eternity'? Is this religion or growth? I want to change, be more effective, become a better person, relate more openly, be more honest and considerate. Where does 'eternity' come in?" Let's deal with this question later, but for now let me say this. I've talked about phases of growth. Participation in a moment of eternity characterizes paths toward growth. It occurs at a spiritual level of growth. In preliminary phases of growth, eternity is not the immediate issue. The issue is more common-sense, psychological self-knowledge. But I believe that unless we eventually contact what is eternal in each of us, we cannot fully grow. To grow in the fullest sense, we need moments when we *are* in the most essential sense; and that is when we are in a moment of eternity.

OBSTACLES TO GROWTH

Growth can't be taken for granted. But again I would ask: Do we want to change? Really? Consider first some of the obstacles to growth. We cannot merely go along with the way things are, assuming that some force toward growth will carry us on.

A number of thinkers believe there is a force toward growth. The educator Neill[10] sees a natural tendency to explore for deeper understanding; the psychotherapist Frankel[11] finds a need for meaning in man; the psychologist Rogers[12] sees man as seeking genuiness and authenticity in his relations with others and himself; the psychologist Maslow[13] posits a drive toward self-actualization; and the philosopher de Chardin[14] writes of man's spiritual evolution toward God. But each of these thinkers stresses that man must be open to this growth force; he must accept his nature. And it is very clear to me that this acceptance involves much struggle and self-discipline. It is difficult to be at ease with one's self. The exquisite paradox of the effortless effort finds a home in very few.

Moreover, others say that man's nature also leads him against this growth force. There are countless and vivid demonstrations of man's inability and unwillingness to change, let alone grow. Man is most often a creature of habit, feasting on the illusion of his freedom (and control) as he is unknowingly contained by the limits of his routines. The ethologist Lorenz[15] feels that as man becomes more himself, he *can* become more competitive and aggressive. Freud spoke of two basic instincts which are in dynamic tension in man: the death instinct and the life instinct. Maslow attempted to marshal evidence for the assumption that man is naturally good and growth-oriented; but he found the evidence inconclusive.[16] In working on his theory of man, Maslow felt he had to consider evil more objectively and comprehensively. He didn't want to underestimate the power of the devil in man.[17]

I think it comes down to our own experience and the experience of those whom we trust. From that we develop our assumptions about our own nature and the nature of man. I believe that man does have a need for meaning and honesty, a drive toward self-actualization and transcendence. But meaning, honesty, self-actualization, and transcendence are only *potential* conditions. Before they can be realized in a person, he must first, be ready, and second, work to bring them about. He must cultivate the seeds if growth is to occur. The inertial force of habit

[10] A. S. Neill, *Summerhill*, Hart Publishing Co., New York, 1960.
[11] V. Frankel, op. cit.
[12] C. Rogers, *On Becoming a Person*, Houghton Mifflin Company, Boston, 1961.
[13] A. Maslow, *Towards a Psychology of Being*, 2d ed., D. Van Nostrand Company, Inc., Princeton, N.J., 1962.
[14] Teilhard de Chardin, *The Divine Millieu*, 1965, and *The Phenomenon of Man*, 1961, both Torchbooks, Harper & Row Publishers, Incorporated, New York.
[15] K. Lorenz, *On Aggression*, Harcourt Brace Jovanovich, New York, 1966.
[16] A. Maslow, op. cit.
[17] A. Maslow, personal communication, 1968.

must be overcome. It is like the recurring miracle of the bulb pushing through the earth, sometimes capped with snow, to meet the sun.

Of course I'm growing. . . . That's what it says I'm doing. There is an inevitable tendency to equate form with essence, words with actions, expectations with experience. Someone says he's much more open with others now—that encounter group really worked. Funny, you hadn't noticed any change in your relationship with him. Someone else says, with the appropriate look of beatific calm, that he is more centered—after all, he is now meditating three hours a day. Strange, since as he says this he seems tense, as if he were forcing an image on you and himself. This spiritual pride afflicts us all and blinds us to our actual condition. Encounter groups or meditation can be just another way of repeating ourselves; they may merely encourage us to form new habits. We cannot vault over personality problems by meditating; we work through them. And one is not meditating merely because he is putting in the hours in a meditating position.

An old Chinese folk novel—*Monkey*—reveals that truths keep reappearing. As we enter the fairy tale, Monkey, Pigsy, and Sandy have just secretly eaten the offerings placed "reverently" in the temple by the three Taoists—Tiger Strength Immortal, Deer Strength Immortal, and Ram Strength Immortal.

Monkey pinched Sandy with one hand and Pigsy with the other. They understood what he meant and both sat stock still, while the three Taoists advanced, peering about in every direction. "Some rascal must have been here," said the Tiger Strength Immortal. "All the offerings have been eaten up." "It looks as though ordinary human beings have been at work," said the Deer Strength Immortal. "They've spat out the fruit stones and skins. It's strange that there is no one to be seen." "It's my idea," said the Ram Strength Immortal, "that the Three Blessed Ones have been so deeply moved by our prayers and recitations that they have vouchsafed to come down and accept our offerings. They may easily be hovering about somewhere on their cranes, and it would be a good plan to take advantage of their presence. I suggest that we should beg for some holy water and a little Elixir. We should get a lot of credit at Court if we could use them to the king's advantage." "A good idea," said the Tiger Strength Immortal. And sending for some of his disciples, he bade them recite the scriptures, while he himself in full robes danced the dance of the Dipper Star, calling upon the Trinity to vouchsafe to its devout worshippers a little Elixir and holy water, that the king might live forever.

"Brother," whispered Pigsy to Monkey, "there was no need to let ourselves in for this. Directly we finished eating we ought to have bolted. How are we going to answer their prayer?" Monkey pinched him, and then called out in a loud, impressive voice, "My children," he said, "I must ask you to defer this request. My colleagues and I have come on straight from a peach banquet in Heaven, and we haven't got any holy water or Elixir with us." Hearing the deity condescend to address them, the Taoists trembled with religious awe. "Father," they said, "you surely realize that for us this is too good an opportunity to be lost. Do not, we beseech you, go back to Heaven without leaving us some sort of magical receipt." Sandy pinched Monkey. "Brother," he whispered, "they are praying again. We're not going to get out of this so easily." "Nonsense," whispered Monkey. "All we've got to do is to answer their prayers and give them something." "That would be easier if we had anything to give," whispered Pigsy. "Watch me," whispered Monkey, "and you'll see that you are just as capable of satisfying them as I am." "Little ones," he said, addressing the Taoists, "I am naturally not keen on letting my congregation die out; so I'll see if we can manage to let you have a little holy water, to promote your longevity." "We implore you to do so," they said, prostrating themselves. "All our days shall be devoted to the propagation of the Way and its Power, to the service of our king and the credit of the Secret School." "Very well then," said Monkey. "But we shall each need something to put it into." The Tiger Strength Immortal bustled off and soon re-appeared carrying, single-handed, an enormous earthenware jar. The Deer Strength Immortal brought a garden-vase and put it on the altar. The Ram Strength Immortal took the flowers out of a flower-pot and put it between the other two. "Now go outside the buiding, close the shutters and stay there," said Monkey. "For no one is permitted to witness our holy mysteries." When all was ready, Monkey got up, lifted his tiger-skin and pissed into the flower-pot. "Brother," said Pigsy, highly delighted. "We've had some rare games together since I joined you, but this beats all." And that fool Pigsy, lifting his dress, let fall such a cascade as would have made the Lü Liang Falls seem a mere trickle. Left with the big jug, Sandy could do no more than half fill it. Then they adjusted their clothes, and sat down decorously as before. "Little ones," Monkey called out, "you can come and fetch your holy water." The Taoists returned, full of gratitude and awe. "Bring a cup," said the Tiger Strength Immortal to one of his disciples. "I should like to taste it." The moment he tasted the contents of the cup, the Immortal's lip curled wryly. "Does it taste good?" asked the Deer Strength Immortal. "It's rather too full-flavoured for my liking," said the Tiger Strength Immortal. "Let me taste it," said the Ram Strength Immortal. "It smells rather like pig's urine," he said doubtfully, when the cup touched his lips. Monkey saw that the game was up. "We've played our trick," he said to the others, "and now we'd better take the credit for it." "How could you be such fools," he called out to the Taoists, "as to believe that the Deities had come down to earth? We're no Blessed Trinity, but priests, from China. And what you have been drinking is not the Water of Life, but just our piss!"[18]

---

[18] Wu Ch'eng-en, *Monkey* (translated by Arthur Waley), Grove Press, New York, 1958, pp. 224–226. Copyright © 1946 by the John Day Company. Reprinted with permission of the John Day Company and George Allen & Unwin Ltd.

Readiness for growth. I talked of being "ready." Maslow developed a fundamental concept of the hierarchy of needs.[19] Man fulfills his needs more or less according to a ranking of priority. Before he can really attend to his higher needs, such as transcendence, he must have satisfied his basic lower needs, such as hunger, warmth, and security. Though the ranking cannot be rigid, it is clear that someone who is struggling to make ends meet financially has little energy left for contemplative, meditative efforts. This is in contrast to the spiritual seeker who will purposely deprive himself in order to transcend himself. The Plains Indians, for example, fasted during their vision quest so they could evoke a visionary experience.[20] Also, a person who is very insecure or nervous often cannot move openly toward another; he cannot go beyond his self because he is too preoccupied with himself. And so there seems to be a time, and perhaps a place, for growth. Before transcendence can occur, these earlier growth needs must be fulfilled.

Ambivalence toward growth. And even when you feel you are ready for growth, when your basic needs seem sufficiently satisfied, still it is not clear and easy. For there is the paradox that while we seek to discover the unknown, we fear it. The Kalahari Zu/wasi seek a trance state which gives them curing power but which also throws them into fearsome and unknown states of consciousness. As they express it, a person dies when he first enters trance, and the fact that it is a psychological death of the ego makes it no less painful and feared.[21] Maslow wrote a fascinating essay entitled, "The Need to Know and the Fear of Knowing."[22] There is the pull and tug, back and forth, toward the edge of discovery and back from that frightening precipice. Late in his life, Maslow had renewed respect for this constant battle:

Human life will never be understood unless its highest aspirations are taken into account. Growth, self-actualization, the striving toward health, the quest for identity and autonomy, the yearning for excellence (and other ways of phrasing the striving "upward") must now be accepted beyond question as a widespread and perhaps universal human tendency.

And yet there are also other regressive, fearful, self-diminishing tendencies as well, and it is very easy to forget them in our intoxication with "personal growth," especially for inexperienced youngsters. I consider that a necessary

[19] A. Maslow, *Motivation and Personality*, rev. ed., Harper & Row Publishers, Incorporated, New York, 1970.
[20] Ruth Benedict, "The Concept of the Guardian Spirit in North America," American Anthropological Association Memoir, 1923.
[21] Richard Katz, *Boiling Medicine: Trance Curing with the Kalahari Zu/wasi*, in preparation.
[22] Abraham Maslow, op. cit., p. 6off.

prophylactic against such illusions is a thorough knowledge of psycho-pathology and of depth psychology. We must appreciate that many people choose the worse rather than the better, that growth is often a painful process and may for this reason be shunned, that we are afraid of our own best possibilities in addition to loving them, and that we are all of us profoundly ambivalent about truth, beauty, virtue, loving them and fearing them too.[23]

BALANCE POINT

The question is: "Where is the balance point?" How strong is the urge to look into the unknown? How strong is the desire to pull back? We know that it is important for a person to maintain the integrity of his own personality. As Lecky and Sullivan have postulated, there is a need for self-consistency.[24] Usually, we don't want to accept more new information than we can comfortably and conveniently handle. But if growth is to occur, we must be one step ahead of ourselves rather than one step behind. We must always be learning something more than we expect, and seeing something about ourselves we were not quite ready to accept. Personal growth is a path for an explorer; an alive explorer, I would add, because the risks involved in discovering the unknown are not to be undertaken frivolously or carelessly.

And we are back to the first step: Do we want to change? We have to admit our strong desire to appear as though we are growing—"growth is good." We also have to appreciate some of the obstacles, subtle and paradoxical, to growth. And now we can ask ourselves even more simply: Do I want to change? Each of us can know only for himself. The proof is in the doing. Are we trying to make growth a reality in your day-to-day functions?

Pause to Reflect

Let's stop here for a moment. I've used many terms already in try-ing to write about awareness and personal growth; and I'll use several more in the following pages. Perhaps I can consider these terms in relation to each other and thereby present a more coherent picture.

We can start with our ordinary everyday life; what we usually do,

[23] Abraham Maslow, *Motivation and Personality*, rev. ed., Harper & Row Pub-lishers, Incorporated, New York, 1970.
[24] Prescott Lecky, *Self-consistency in Personality*, Anchor Books, Doubleday & Company, Inc., Garden City, N.Y., 1969.
Harry S. Sullivan, *Theory of Interpersonal Psychiatry*, W. W. Norton & Com-pany, Inc., New York, 1953.

think, and feel; our roles, expectations, habits, and characteristics. Lower or basic needs abound. Once we have more or less fulfilled our lower needs—for example, having a sufficient income, adequate home, and reasonable job—we can begin to look more carefully at our ordinary life. We are struck with its mechanical, unfeeling, unthinking quality. We see ourselves enmeshed in ordinary affairs which are unpredictable, unreliable, and insubstantial—in brief, dishonest. And in seeing this, we could realize the possibility of something beyond, something which could exist more in our extraordinary life, something which is closer to our essential being—moments of creative alertness and possibly moments of awareness.

We create these moments from the aliveness within us. This alertness and awareness give perspective to our mechanical ordinary life, which is only a reflection of this aliveness within. From that perspective, we can consider our ordinary, everyday activities and thoughts more as they really are. As we see ourselves, we begin to understand ourselves.

Moments of alertness and awareness arise and grow from a center in us, a point of strength and tranquillity in the midst of our insubstantial and chaotic daily life. This center leads us to our essential being. It leads us to freedom as it participates in eternity. It simply brings sensitivity and understanding into our everyday lives. This center is more or less extraordinary, depending on the phase of growth one is engaged in. The process of personal growth consists of moments of awareness cumulating into an extraordinary center within ourselves.

In each of us there is a balance between forces of growth and conservation. Self-consistency has to be sacrificed somewhat if we venture into the unknown. The motivation for growth is an expression of our aliveness, a questioning attitude, a desire to change, a searching for more. This motivation for growth varies in strength and depth, and it consequently leads to different phases of growth.

We can distinguish, broadly speaking, two phases: preludes to growth and paths toward growth. When we are involved in preludes to growth, the focus is on personality. This is the process of psychological growth. There can be moments of creative alertness where we begin to get some idea of who we are—though our perceptions are still biased. We begin to find some place inside from which we can see ourselves more honestly, an ordinary center from which we can judge the wheat and the chaff. We are still at the level of personality. There is a horizontal separation within the personality; for example, a more conscious aspect may examine more habitual aspects. But with these ordinary moments of alertness and from this ordinary center comes an aliveness. In an ordinary sense, a person can be more alive and questioning, more responsible and honest. Something has definitely happened. He can then also begin a search for more transcendent experiences, for an existence beyond his individual, ordinary life. He can begin a journey along a path. Something *else* can now happen.

When we are involved in paths toward personal growth, the focus is on essential being. This is more the process of spiritual growth. The more we deal with our essential self, the more unfamiliar the territory becomes. Now we try to have moments of awareness. In such moments we try to create an extraordinary center within our ordinary selves. We try to create something from within ourselves which is completely different from and higher than ourselves. This extraordinary center generates a universal perspective on ourselves. It enables us to see ourselves as we really are, without embellishment. It establishes the fact and facts of our existence. The concepts of truth and true perceptions become appropriate. A vertical separation now exists—something which is eternal sees us in all our temporal "glory." This paradox—that *we* create something in *ourselves* which is *higher than* ourselves and can be aware of *us*—must remain. It is the paradox of the very human man seeking to contact the universal or cosmic or Godlike principle in himself.

As these moments of awareness become more complete and frequent, the extraordinary center becomes more permanent. Transcendence exists at this level of growth. The freedom which one can experience is increasingly more complete. It is the ultimate freedom of participating in a moment of eternity. And from that all flows, including living life in the ordinary sense as a truly responsible and understanding person, worthy of respect.

I feel like I've said as much as I can. For the key emphasis must remain on the *experience* of growth; it is more alive and real than any written discussion could be.

What Are Your Goals?

BEING A GOOD MAN IN EVERYDAY LIFE

I've spoken at length about inner space, the realm of our fears and desires, our fantasies and aspirations. Certainly I respect the importance of these motivations. But when you ask yourself, "In what ways do I want to change?" you would probably talk quite a bit about everyday life. And I would agree with that focus. I think a goal for personal growth is simply to be a full-grown person in our day-to-day activities. To be a good father or daughter or mother or husband or wife or teacher or mechanic or son or salesman or artist—and I use the word *good* in the best, unmoralistic sense. I mean someone who lives from his center or what could become a center. Someone who approaches whatever he does with perspective and honesty. Someone who is alive and questioning. Simply, for example, a father who is growing as a person. I'm using classical role descriptions—"father," "lover," "mechanic," "student"—only for brevity. The emphasis is on the growing person.

Part of this aliveness is a freshness in one's approach, a newness in one's attitude. It's almost as if one were born again for a moment, rediscovering a deep well of clear water. Thoreau describes those infrequent times when he could begin again, as he is affected by a nature which is always beginning again.

There are from time to time mornings, both in summer and in winter, when especially the world seems to begin anew, beyond which memory need not go, for not behind them is yesterday and our past life; when, as in the morning of a hoary frost, there are visible the effects as of a certain creative energy.

. . . The world has visibly been recreated in the night. Mornings of creation, I call them. In the midst of these marks of a creative energy recently active, while the sun is rising with more than usual splendor, I look back . . . for the era of this creation, not into the night, but to a dawn for which no man ever rose early enough. A morning which carries us back beyond the mosaic creation where crystallizations are fresh and unmelted. It is the poet's hour. Mornings when men are new-born, men who have the seeds of life in them.[25]

And there is no conflict between growth and effectiveness. Schumacher has written a fascinating article entitled "Buddhist Economics."[26] He describes how, when work is approached openly and honestly, it becomes a path toward growth *and* one becomes an effective worker. In Hesse's novel *Siddhartha*, we see that as Siddhartha is growing, he continually masters and goes beyond particular jobs and professions, whether it be merchant or ascetic or lover.[27] Herrigel's book *Zen and the Art of Archery* reports his own discovery of this same principle—when one is aware, one is most effective in an ordinary sense.[28] He learns not to try to be effective, but to *be*, in the

---

[25] H. D. Thoreau, op. cit. (January 26, 1853).

[26] E. F. Schumacher, "Buddhist Economics," *Manas*, vol. 22, no. 33, April 13, 1969, Los Angeles. (Reprinted from *Resurgence*, vol. 1, no. 11, January–February, 1968, London.)

[27] H. Hesse, *Siddhartha*, New Directions Publishing Corporation, New York, 1961.

[28] Eugen Herrigel, *Zen and the Art of Archery*, Pantheon Books, a division of Random House, Inc., New York, 1953.

fullest sense. The Russian mystic-philosopher Gurdjieff tells of how, when he was least identified with his own activities, when he neither liked nor disliked them and didn't care whether or not he became well-known in them, that was when he was most effective. For example, he practiced spiritualism for the higher purpose of finding out about himself and about the nature of man—not so that he, Gurdjieff, would become a successful spiritualist. Not only did he learn something about himself and man's nature, but also, to his chagrin, he was soon beseiged with clients.

I must stress the day-to-day context of growth. I want to create a difference where it makes a difference—in my everyday ordinary life. I'm not interested in withdrawing from life but living my life fully *and* with some wisdom. I want to be less insistent on my opinions and more caring for others—more detached and less alienated. Joseph Knecht in *Magister Ludi* apparently has everything as he reaches the pinnacle of his chosen spiritual path. He has everything but opportunities to be spiritual outside of his retreat setting. He (willingly) gives up his life for the chance to test his spirituality in the crucible of everyday emotions and situations.[29]

It is important to be a good father or daughter or mechanic in all the specific, concrete situations which make up a lifetime; not merely in your philosophical attitudes. It is also important to be this way in a variety of situations, including the stressful ones. The best and worst of a person always seem to come out during a crisis, whether it be during an automobile accident, a friend's intense depression, a family argument, or a difficult drug session. You discover who you can really count on because he or she is real. Too often we want only nice feelings such as joy; or, if the feelings are "bad" ones, then we want them only intensely: "I can really feel anger for the first time." But what about times of frustration or boredom or ordinary feelings— what about our day? We need perspective then, even more so. We need perspective on what we do regardless of whether we like it or not.

And, finally, it's important to be a good person over time. Too often, someone rises to the occasion, but when the immediate crisis subsides, he is no longer there. I'm talking about a good father, I would almost say whenever and wherever he's needed. Siddhartha, over his lifetime, through his many occupations and roles, brought a special quality to his actions and thoughts. Hesse's story *Siddhartha* provides a lovely access to this lifelong journey.

[29] Hermann Hesse, *Magister Ludi* (translated by M. Savill), Frederick Ungar Publishing Co., New York, 1949.

Now all this is quite idealistic. As I have done throughout this essay, I'm stressing the further goals toward which growth could lead. The steps toward these goals, however, are practical, small, at times unnoticeable. Honesty can be deeply woven into everyday affairs.

Free Man in Eternity

There is another goal of personal growth that is even more ultimate. Here we look to the heavens, to an extraordinary level of existence. In an ultimate sense, we seek moments of freedom from the confines of the human species and the boundaries of earth. We seek participation in moments of eternity, going beyond our individualistic selves to a union with the cosmos. At moments like that there is a possibility to guide, to some small extent, the evolution of our own consciousness. De Chardin examines this possibility when he talks of man developing to the point where he participates in the evolution of the spirit.[30] Buckminster Fuller takes a more pragmatic approach, considering man's possibility for controlling his own evolution through technological innovation.[31] But Fuller is not naïve, and beneath the smooth surface of his technology is free-flowing consciousness. He is talking fundamentally of an evolution in consciousness.

Now if the goal of being a good person sounded idealistic, this extraordinary goal must seem especially idealistic *and* abstract. But again, it is expressed in simple, day-to-day activities. And the two goals are related. Suzuki reports a Zen parable:

Before a man studies Zen, to him mountains are mountains and waters are waters; after he gets an insight into the truth of Zen through the instruction of a good master, mountains to him are not mountains and waters are not waters; but after this, when he really attains to the abode of rest, mountains are once more mountains and waters are waters.[32]

We are on earth, this is where we start and end. Before growth can occur, we must have our life free of turmoil, our feet must be on the ground. In meeting the responsibilities of a man, we can become honest with ourselves and others. It also can lead us toward eternity. And from the standpoint of an eternal moment, we can become truly honest in our everyday life.

[30] T. de Chardin, op. cit.

[31] Buckminster Fuller, *Ideas and Integrities*, Collier Books, The Macmillan Company, New York, 1963.

[32] D. Suzuki, in W. Barrett (ed.), *Zen Buddhism*, Anchor Books, Doubleday & Company, Inc., Garden City, N.Y., 1956, p. 14.

Again we see the two phases of growth—insights gained in the preliminary phase can stimulate embarking on a path, and being on a path deepens those beginning insights. As our center becomes more extraordinary, we can see ourselves "as we really are" in more varied situations, and for longer periods of time. As we continue to accept these facts about ourselves, our consciousness begins to change in the most fundamental evolutionary sense.

Self-knowledge! Is That All? That Is All!

I have purposely emphasized self-knowledge. We must attend first to what's at hand, to what we know best, namely, our selves. We are always too willing to offer opinions on others, sometimes to others. In becoming open and honest with ourselves, we can become open and honest with another. Rogers documents the need for the therapist to be genuine and authentic if the therapy is to be effective.[33] The therapist must be himself if he expects his patient to regain normal functioning, that is, to be himself. Even the psychoanalysts now find this to be an important condition for therapeutic success. And this quid pro quo holds for interpersonal relationships generally. Jourard has done research on self-disclosure and openness.[34] His finding is simple: People talk about themselves openly to the degree that the listener has also talked about himself openly. Buber writes eloquently of how one man can have an elevating effect on another. If you relate to another from the Godlike principle of your being, respecting the God principle in the other, the God in him emerges. The I-Thou encounter washes away the I-It subject-object relationship which dehumanizes us all.[35]

On a larger scale, the issue is the same. What holds for interpersonal relations holds for social, economic, and political realms. Persons engaged in self-development at critical times and places, and in critical numbers, can introduce valuable and lasting political and economic changes. The history of man is a history of unrealized good intentions and realized bad ones. Wars seem inevitable except when enough men in a particular area and period have reached a certain spiritual level. Then a critical mass of peace seems reached. In recent times Tibet exemplified this condition. But as Gurdjieff maintains, war and

[33] C. Rogers, op. cit.
[34] Sidney Jourard, *The Transparent Self*, D. Van Nostrand Company, Inc., Princeton, N.J., 1964.
[35] Martin Buber, *Between Man and Man*, Beacon Press, Boston, 1955; *I and Thou*, Charles Scribner's Sons, New York, 1958.

the enumerable less dramatic human failings will continue as long as we change only the form of human existence without changing that existence itself.[36]

Suppose, for example, many persons become truly honest with themselves and others; suppose they changed their human nature to some degree. Such a change could have a revolutionary impact on all aspects of life—individual, political, perhaps even cosmological.

At this point in time, the obverse is true. Those with the most influence on large numbers of people remain television "personalities" and "newsworthy" persons, and invariably they operate on a double standard. How convincing is a President who calls for peace between disputing students and the military as he is waging war right across the ocean? How real is the sparkling woman who praises the dryness of her underarms as she breezes through three floors of vacuuming? The media figures are not doing what they're saying.

But, of course, a return to honesty will not easily develop into a revolutionary force. Our mechanical and mechanized society has too much to lose. Consider, for example, the tremendous increase of interest in personal growth. Does this represent the "last gasp" of the humanists in their battle against a more mechanized society? Or is this but an early indication of a major change in the structure and nature of our society? Is there enough substance in the techniques and systems people are turning to, enough substance to make real growth possible?

What is going to happen when the young people who have grown up seeking love, warmth, and understanding begin to reach the "age of responsibility"? How much of this utopian quality will remain? How many of them will be willing to assume responsibilities appropriate to their age? If they do assume positions of power in the political, economic, and social worlds, how humanistically oriented will they remain? How humanistically oriented *can* they remain without changing the structure of power?

The potential for a change in nature, a raising of consciousness, may exist. But there is already a polarization around the individual's rights to personal growth reminiscent of the polarization swirling around the individual's civil rights. Revolutionary forces can hardly expect the way to be freshly paved and cleared of obstructions.

In the final analysis, the emphasis on self-knowledge is the only emphasis possible. It is through truly understanding ourselves that we can contact the ultimate ground of existence. As we honestly meet

---

[36] G. I. Gurdjieff, *All and Everything: Beelzebub's Tales to his Grandson*, E. P. Dutton & Co., Inc., New York, 1950.

our own everyday responsibilities, we are attending to the business of the universe. Eastern philosophy-religion has made this crystal clear. In each of us is the cosmos of which we are a part. We are each a microcosmos. That which is eternal resides in us, waiting to be realized.

The world existed first as seed, which as it grew and developed took on names and forms. As a razor in its case or as fire in wood, so dwells the Self, the Lord of the universe, in all forms, even to the tips of the fingers. Yet the ignorant do not know him, for behind the names and forms he remains hidden. When one breathes, one know him as breath; when one speaks, one knows him as speech; when one sees, one knows him as the eye; when one hears, one knows him as the ear; when one thinks, one knows him as the mind. All these are but names related to his acts; and he who worships the Self as one or another of them does not know him, for of them he is neither one nor another. Wherefore let a man worship him as the Self, and as the Self alone. The perfection which is the Self is the goal of all beings. For by knowing the Self one knows all. He who knows the Self is honored of all men and attains to blessedness.[37]

The Beginnings of Growth

Before seriously considering our own personal growth, we must first put our everyday house in order, our feet must be on the ground. We can't begin while still overwhelmed by anxieties, or embroiled in family tensions, or depressed by a shortage of money, or *preoccupied* with deciding who we want to be. We have to step beyond these entanglements, if ever so briefly. We need a time of relative calm. Then we begin, simply and directly with ourself. I try to keep certain principles alive in me:

Be honest with myself about myself. Who am I now? Do I want to change? What am I doing with my time, in the morning, at noon, before I go to bed? Honestly!
Focus on my essential being. Concentrate on what is substantial inside me. When I am all alone, I can meet myself without adornment. I'm talking not about idle introspection but about an encounter with myself. My public behavior, my role-influenced thoughts and feelings, are the insubstance of ordinary life.
Accept what I honestly see about myself. How can I see something

[37] *The Upanishads* (translated by Swami Prabhavananda and F. Manchester), Mentor Books, New American Library, Inc., New York, 1957.

about myself honestly unless I can also accept that self-knowledge?
When I accept aspects of myself, I am less attached to them and
can more easily give them up—in short, grow.
Respect my day-to-day activities. When I bring perspective into my
daily life, I can see myself more as I really am. I can also begin to
change where it matters, in the realm that I exist in almost all the
time.
Don't believe anything without testing it out in my own experience
—especially when someone tells me about "principles" to keep in
mind.

There are several other points important for the beginnings of
growth. Self-directed learning is necessary both to initiate the process
of growth and to substantiate its effects. An open, experimental approach is needed. We are exploring our own apparent limits; we put
ourself in an unfamiliar situation in order to see ourself more clearly.
Self-discipline is critical. Without it, "freedom" becomes mere chaos.
Sincere and serious effort is necessary, though somberness isn't. Our
life *does* depend on our beginning to grow.

And don't look for big, dramatic changes. It's the small, subtle
changes which are often most substantial and enduring. They cumulate
into growth. Dramatic breakthroughs are transient experiences unless
there is some follow-through. What are the long-term effects of Leonard's "learning environment"?[38] I think that environment postulates
young people who will want more and more stimulation rather than
seeking growth. I question the depth of the experience of ecstacy described by Leonard. Can it contact our essential being, repeatedly?

Kapleau's rich material on Zen students documents our misguided
obsession with the dramatic breakthrough to enlightenment.[39] For
matters only begin with these deep experiences of awareness. The issue
soon becomes: What does that experience mean in and for your life?
What do you make of that experience? You say that "you've had an
experience of enlightenment." What does that mean the next morning
when you rise from bed and face the people you live with; and so on
into that day and the next day and the next. . . .

As always, each of these points mean something different depending
on what one brings to them. When a man is honest in an ordinary
sense, at a psychological level, that is quite something. When a man
is honest in an extraordinary sense, at an essential level, that is another thing entirely.

[38] George Leonard, *Education and Ecstacy*, Delacorte Press, Dell Publishing Co.,
Inc., New York, 1969.
[39] Philip Kapleau, *Three Pillars of Zen*, Beacon Press, Boston, 1967.

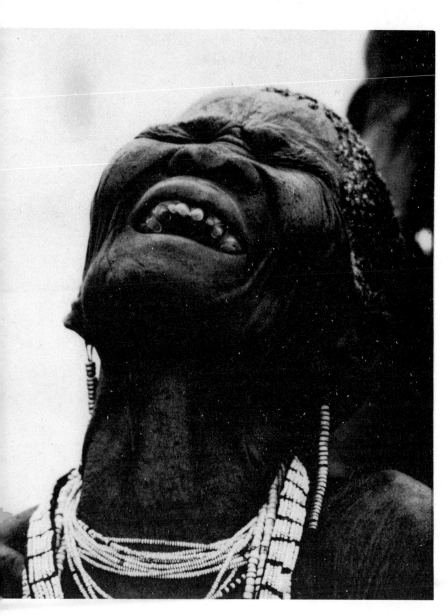

Case Studies

A Solo Survival Experience[1]

Solo Survival Experiences and Growth

*H*ISTORICALLY, and in its rarer contemporary forms, the solo survival experience has been a critical aspect of individual development and societal functioning. It usually functions as a "rite of passage," very often as an initiation rite. Some of its more important forms are the vision quest of the North American Plains Indians,[2] religious retreats

[1] Revision of an article entitled "A Solo-survival Experience as Education for no. 4, Fall, 1969, New York State Department of Education, Albany.
Personal Growth," originally published in *Educational Opportunity Forum*, vol. 1,
  I want to thank for their help the directors, staff, and students at the Colorado, Hurricane Island, and Minnesota Outward Bound Schools in the summer of 1966, especially Colin Bolton, Joe Nold, Bob Pieh, Jed Williamson, Eugene Check, S.J., John Hertzog, Mary Maxwell Katz, Francis J. Kelly, Josh Miner, and David Tresemer.
  Research for this article was supported by the Center for Research and Development on Educational Differences, Harvard Graduate School of Education, and the Office of Juvenile Delinquency, Health, Education and Welfare Administration, Grant #66013.
  [2] Ruth Benedict, "The Concept of the Guardian Spirit in North America," American Anthropological Association Memoir, 1923.

such as the Jesuit Spiritual Exercises,[3] and the *sesshin,* or periods of intense meditation, in Zen Buddhist training.[4] More recently, the Outward Bound Schools in America have been working with still another form of solo survival.

A solo survival experience *could* lead toward personal growth. During the solo experience you are alone and have to rely on your own resources. Existing in that condition, your sense of space, time, self, and the subject-object distinction changes significantly. Whether this altered state of consciousness is an experience of fantasy or creative alertness or even awareness, it is influenced by your preparation for and reaction to the altered state. For example, your altered sense of time can evoke an experience of timelessness, or a feeling of boredom and anxiety. An experience of timelessness, with its transcendent perspective, has greater potential for growth than an experience of anxiety or boredom.

An Outward Bound Solo Survival[5]

Outward Bound is a school offering a twenty-six-day residential course in an isolated wilderness setting. Typically, the course is for males aged sixteen to twenty-three from a variety of racial, religious, educational, and socioeconomic backgrounds. The curriculum consists primarily of physical activities such as wilderness travel and camping, mountain climbing, canoeing, and seamanship. Activities are meant to become increasingly difficult for students, both physically and psychologically. The school challenges students to go beyond what they considered their psychological and physical limits. In the process, it is hoped they will increase their knowledge and appreciation of themselves and others.

Kurt Hahn, the founder of Outward Bound, said:

[3] *Spiritual Exercises of St. Ignatius* (translated by L. J. Puhl, S.J.), Newman Press, Westminster, Md., 1962.

[4] Daisetz T. Suzuki, *Manual of Zen Buddhism,* Rider and Co., London, 1950; Philip Kapleau (ed.), *The Three Pillars of Zen,* Beacon Press, Boston, 1967.

[5] A more detailed study of the Outward Bound solo, and in particular what students do, feel, and think during the solo, appears in my paper "Solo-survival experience as education for personal growth," Monograph #7, Center for Research & Development on Educational Differences, Harvard Graduate School of Education, 1969.

The description of my solo in this section was written in 1966 and was based on journal notes I made immediately after completing the solo. I haven't revised this description; an experience stands on its own as an experience.

the purpose of Outward Bound is to protect youth against a diseased civilization. Three decays surround the modern youth: The decay of care and skill; the decay of enterprise and adventure; and the decay of compassion.[6]

He saw Outward Bound as a response to William James' call for a moral equivalent to war.[7]

For approximately three days and three nights, each Outward Bound student is physically alone in an isolated wilderness setting, eating only what he can forage, with warmth and shelter supplied by the clothing on his back, a 6- by 6-foot waterproof cloth, and a half-dozen matches. This is the "solo."

Outward Bound presents this solo survival experience as one of the high points of the twenty-six-day course:

. . . [during the solo] every student has his hours of self-appraisal, of seeing himself in unique perspective. Properly done, [the solo] can be one of the unique experiences of your life.[8]

According to Outward Bound ideology, the solo demands that you examine certain aspects of yourself. As with the entire course, there is an emphasis on "character-training" during the solo. Character consists primarily of initiative, self-confidence, responsibility, compassion, self-discipline, determination, leadership, and understanding. The development of character is Outward Bound's concept of personal growth.

The ideology continues: "The solo is a test of the mind and the spirit, of boy against himself and against the raw components of his environment."[9] The solo is presented as an opportunity to test oneself. Many students look upon it as an initiation rite, a not particularly pleasant but "real" way of finding out who they are. It looms as a challenge to their self-definition. Mastery of nature and mastery of oneself are two forms of this challenge. Testing yourself through a mastery of nature is often akin to "winning warmth from nature." There is an emphasis on struggle with nature; it becomes an ordeal. There is another part to the idea of the solo: ". . . The contest is not with nature around you, but with yourself." Here the emphasis is on cooperation with nature so as

[6] Outward Bound Schools brochure.

[7] For a fuller discussion of Outward Bound and the place of challenge and adventure in education, see Richard Katz and David Kolb, "Challenge to Grow: The Outward Bound Approach," in Saxe (ed.), *Opening the Schools: Alternative Ways of Learning,* McCutchan Publishing Corporation, Berkeley, Calif., 1972.

[8] Hurricane Island Outward Bound School literature.

[9] Ibid.

to satisfy physical needs. The issue then becomes, "can you live with yourself?"

I was intrigued by the concept of the solo before I began my Outward Bound course, and my anticipation increased as the course progressed. This was in spite of the fact that I was put off by the Protestant ethic quality in Outward Bound's idea of a solo. And the solo truly became a high point in my course. As I left for my solo site, I felt in part like a wilderness expert and in part like a psychic explorer. At Outward Bound, I learned how to make shelters, build fires, catch and forage food. In reality I had achieved a very modest proficiency in these skills, but subjectively I felt ready. At Outward Bound I had not learned how a solo can alter your state of consciousness, or how the solo experience relates to personal growth. But I had come to Outward Bound already prepared for experiencing, accepting, and using altered states to evoke moments of creative alertness, and perhaps even awareness. This kind of psychological preparation was a resource few students had available.[10] But since I had no idea about the psychological characteristics of this particular experience, I was exploring like everyone else.

My solo site was a beautiful island in the middle of a secluded lake, several days by canoe from people. The clear, bright air made it all magical. I bathed in this idyllic atmosphere, then I bathed in the smooth, crystal waters. Then I became serious. The wilderness expert emerged; the child of nature vanished. The shelter was constructed, the wood pile collected, and the fire started—with one match. And there I sat. During the next three days and nights my shelter and my fire became very important parts of my world. I had no idea how important they would become that first sun-filled afternoon.

But the night changed things. The night was long and hard to get through. It was cold. The woodpile became small so quickly. As the fire burned down to white coals, the cold air brought me out of my shelter and I built the fire back into flames. I stayed by the flames for awhile and got warmed up. Sitting there, lit up by the flames in the dark silence, I felt completely alone but not lonely. I realized that information about myself was now emerging in bold relief. There were no other persons or institutions around to confuse the issue, no convenient ways to project feelings on others or lay blame on an institution. In the uncomplicated environment of the solo, my thoughts and actions paraded about, expressing "me" in an obvious fashion. If I decided to structure my day in the usual manner, this would be me "speaking," me seeking a certain kind of order in my existence. The solo could be an unusual chance to see myself and gain some understanding—provided, of course, I could refrain from projecting and, in fact, confront myself. That was not so easy to do.

---

[10] In addition to my prior personal experience with altered states and research in that area, I was in my late twenties when I took my solo. Most other Outward Bound students are between sixteen and twenty-one.

The environment was powerful, and it had its own intrinsic ordering principles, its own rhythms. By the second day, I found myself functioning more and more in accord with them. I began to sleep when it was warm, not when it was nighttime. It was warm during the day and—*when* my fire was hot—at night. My diurnal rhythm was altered but I was getting enough sleep from the frequent shorter periods of rest. I also felt an intimate part of my environment. As I bathed in the water, I felt it soaking up the sun's warmth. At night the sudden sharp slaps of the beaver's tail on the water first frightened me, then they became a rhythmic counterpart to my heartbeat and my breathing.

There were the rhythms of the wilderness and the rhythms I brought with me from urban society and intellectual activities. Well into the second day, the degree to which I was importing an order became astounding. I realized I was beginning to fill up my day with "rituals": stocking the woodpile, walking down to the lakeshore, "reading" the clocks of the sun and moon. Some of these rituals were, of course, necessary. But when I saw myself scratching two lines into the large boulder behind the shelter, my eyes opened. Counting the days! It was hard to avoid. But seeing those two lines on the boulder brought my ordering attempts into clear focus. It also encouraged me to minimize the importation of order.

The first day you set things up, the second you live there, and the third you prepare to leave. It seems simple enough, except boredom can become a key issue. There is lots of time available. I thought about many things. I learned some things; but not for twenty-four hours a day. I didn't want to do things *just* to fill up time. And that would have been difficult to do even if I had tried; there wasn't that much material at hand. So time was everywhere.

The weather was good, but the nights were cold. I had many cups of rose-hip tea and some frog's legs, but food was scarce. Basic needs are important. They shaped the quality and level of my consciousness.

I was exploring the far side of the island on the third day. I was also seeing myself, an animal covering his territory. It was very quiet, even still. Suddenly a thunderous sound in the leaves. The stillness had become noise, and since I was alone on the island, my fantasies at that instant were elaborate. Simpler yet, there was a flushed grouse frozen in fear 3 feet from my face. I wasn't sure whether I looked as scared; I certainly had been deeply frightened. But I unfroze and the grouse did not. The myth of man the primitive hunter began to unfold as I reached for a stick. But before I took any action, another myth took hold and there was no taking of life. The basic need of hunger; the basic force of life. I can't forget that encounter.

As the third night was reaching into dawn, I thought more about the simplicity of my island environment. Soon I would be back with other Outward Bound students: added complexity. And there was the world outside Outward Bound's wilderness course: incomprehensible complexity. We work hard to make it so.

The return from my solo site was too abrupt. There was too much small talk too soon. The quiet seemed destroyed rather than savored and built upon. My vocal cords needed retraining; three days of silence made a difference. And there was too much food too soon. Hunger was no longer a live issue.

The solo felt over, and I relaxed. I wanted time to gather up energy for the canoe trip back to camp. It would be hard and exhausting. We had this day off. Then suddenly there was confusion and concern. A student had just cut his foot badly on a sharp rock. He had to receive medical attention. A two-man rescue party was organized; I was one of the two. All the necessary energy welled up. A couple of chocolate bars, some more pancakes, and we left. It was a long, long day of hard paddling before we reached the hospital. During the rescue my solo faded into a strong appreciation of our enormous reservoirs of energy, our vast resources for action.

I've talked with many Outward Bound students about their solo experiences. There are many different solos; there are many different students.

Developing Solo Survivals which Educate for Personal Growth

The Outward Bound solo is a unique, even anachronistic experience. Therein lies much of its power. Nevertheless, there are some features which keep it from being a clear stimulus to personal growth and other features which limit its relevance in contemporary society. I want to examine aspects of the Outward Bound solo in light of three other forms of the solo experience: the vision quest, the Jesuit spiritual retreat, and the Zen *sesshin*. Perhaps this examination can bring us closer to the core of a solo survival experience. It could also produce guidelines for developing effective solo survivals for today. Since such a solo experience would deal with fundamentals of human nature, it might also, in its essence, be effective for "yesterdays" and "tomorrows."

THE SOLO AND THE SURVIVAL ASPECTS

During a solo survival you are alone and have to rely primarily on your own resources. You can be alone in both a "subjective" and "objective" sense. Subjectively, you may feel or think you are alone; objectively, you may be physically unable to perceive another. The extent to which a person must rely on his own resources depends on the accessibility of certain elements: food, warmth, shelter, companionship, and general stimulation or "having something to do." The solo and survival aspects can have a variety of forms, more or less literal, depending on the individual. Where one person may undergo withdrawal symptoms when the TV tube blows, another may feel he is on his own only at the perimeter of the Antarctic Circle.

The most important element in a solo experience is the subjective sense of being alone, on your own. Even on Outward Bound solos, visual contact sometimes occurs between students. Sometimes you can see another student or the smoke from his fire across the stream. More importantly, you know that each day you are checked by the staff, since safety must be maintained. This is done inconspicuously, without unnecessary verbal or visual contact, yet you feel protected. If there is an emergency, you blow your whistle and aid comes. The solo is not a true survival situation, yet what is most essential is there—you feel alone and on your own.

These subjective states which are critical to the success of a solo experience can be created through metaphors of that experience. You could function for a period without talking, or without sight or hearing, or in an unfamiliar setting. You could have periods of "alone time" or do without certain luxuries which have now become essentials. There is great variety possible in the setting and nature of solo experiences, but the goal remains to induce the feelings of being alone and dependent on your own resources.

The Phase of Personal Growth

The solo survival can intensify the examination of self and its relation to the environment. But our selves are many and varied. How will this examination proceed? Depending on the level of one's understanding, the focus could be on preludes to growth or on a path.

Personal growth is understood in different ways. For Outward Bound, it means character development. In the vision quest, growth occurred when, in contacting something higher, one realized his own identity; this helped to determine his role in the society. In the Jesuit retreat, the participant grows as he renews his communion with himself and others through a renewed and expanded communion with God.

The methods employed vary accordingly. The Outward Bound solo tests one's character by challenging one's limits. The vision quest also tested individuals through an ordeal (fasting, sometimes flagellation). The Jesuit retreat emphasizes the path of detachment from external concerns and of concentrated reflection. In planning solo growth experiences, we must be clear about what phase of personal growth is our goal. Only then can we be clear about the best methods to employ. Above all, it is important to remember that experiences of creative alertness and awareness are critical, not the particular structure which evokes those experiences.

CHARACTERISTICS OF PARTICIPANTS

Solo survival experiences are often reserved for persons at developmental crisis points. They mark the passage from one developmental stage to another. The vision quest for the East Woodlands tribes was associated with puberty rites and occurred only at that stage. For the Plains tribes, however, the vision quest was continually available, but only after the person reached maturity.

Each developmental stage presents particular problems and opportunities for the solo survival. The Outward Bound solo seems very appropriate for its typical participant, the adolescent. For example, Erikson has described the adolescent's search for identity and need for intimacy.[11] The testing of limits and self-confrontation during a solo can clarify an adolescent's state of identity diffusion. His movement from the loneliness of the solo toward intimacy can be a major developmental juncture. In general, the goals and methods of any solo should reflect the characteristics of the participants.

UNDERLYING STRUCTURE OF THE EXPERIENCE

There are three major interrelated aspects of a solo survival experience: preparation for the experience, the experience itself, and the return of the participant from the experience. Each aspect deserves special attention, although in the functioning of a solo experience they become a continuous process.

Van Gennep describes a similar sequence underlying *rites de passage* which mark transitions between developmental stages: the person *separates* from his family, *participates* in the rite, and is *incorporated* back into his family.[12] Campbell says the same kind of sequence underlies myths about the hero's adventures in unraveling the (psychic)

---

[11] Erik Erikson, *Childhood and Society*, W. W. Norton & Company Inc., New York, 1963.

[12] Arnold van Gennep, *The Rites of Passage*, Phoenix Books, University of Chicago Press, Chicago, 1960.

unknown.[13] A solo survival experience is very much a *rite de passage* and a reenactment of such heroic myths.

Preparation

If you are not prepared to learn from your solo, the experience is less meaningful and it becomes more difficult to sustain its impact. At Outward Bound, physical preparation is handled well, psychological preparation less so. The altered states of consciousness induced by a solo must be accepted and worked with, otherwise they work against you. You must be psychologically ready for these dramatic changes in your sense of time, space, and self. Often Outward Bound students are not prepared to experience these changes in a manner conducive to personal growth. For example, it is hard to retain the normal diurnal rhythm during a solo. If you accept the changes in your consciousness evoked by a new rhythm, you can begin to see things about yourself. But instead of accepting these changes, students often are distressed by them to the point of trying to counteract them. This is like swimming upstream. Culture shock can become the main response to their new environment.

Goals of an Outward Bound solo are not sufficiently discussed, nor is enough attention paid to different parts of the experience. There is a difference between the first day and the third, the warm days and the cold nights, the moods of elation and boredom. A sense of such differences could prepare one to make better use of each part of the experience. Outward Bound students often develop a private sense of purpose at odds with the official purpose of self-understanding. Many enter their solo determined "to make it through" the three days and three nights. It becomes "How can I get through the solo?" rather than "How can I productively use this opportunity for self-examination?" They can mark time because they know the solo will end after a specified period. At the end, you know you can "do a solo." But you don't really know much more—e.g., something about those strengths and weaknesses which were revealed during the solo.

The vision quest provides an instructive contrast to the Outward Bound solo in this area of preparation. The vision quest was comprehensively, specifically, and effectively programmed. Traditions and myths existed about what happened during the quest. Before going on the quest, these traditions and myths were exchanged in group sessions with other members of the tribe. There were rules about how much

[13] Joseph Campbell, *The Hero with a Thousand Faces,* Meridian Books, World Publishing Company, Cleveland, 1956.

you tortured yourself, traditions about the content and significance of your visions. Visions of certain guardian animals indicated a deeper experience and entailed more important roles for the participant in his tribe. The criteria of success were clear and understood before the quest began. The participant had a sense of mission when he went on the quest. He sought an important favor from supernatural forces in the form of a vision which "allowed" him to progress in the developmental sequence.

Yet for all its comprehensiveness, the preparation did not detract from the experience of the vision quest. Persons were not bored or disappointed by their experience, because they knew what to expect. The preparation didn't substitute for the experience; it prepared one to have the experience more fully.

It is possible, however, to overprepare or prepare people in the wrong direction. If expectations are unrealistically high—for example, that the experience will be dramatic, revelatory, and life changing—then the actual experience may seem trifling and disappointing. Such expectations can generate passivity by subtly indicating to participants that "it will all happen *to* you." And valid experiences of self-understanding can be overlooked and not sustained because they appear so simple. The best preparation is both realistic, extensive, and specific with regard to the purposes of the solo.

Out on the Solo Survival

A critical relationship out on solo is that between deprivation and altered states of consciousness. How deprivation is handled helps determine whether the altered states evoked are creative alertness or awareness, or intense boredom or anxiety. The Outward Bound solo functions according to a need-deprivation model, especially in the area of hunger, shelter, companionship, and "having something to do." Rarely does a student eat well on the solo; few eat much at all. You may be given some wire to make a snare or a fish hook. Sometimes you have a supplement, e.g., enough Bisquick for a biscuit each of the three mornings. But food is scarce. A cold night and a poor fire can make warmth a problem. If the weather is bad, a solo can be focused upon trying to master nature. This happens frequently. But providing for food and warmth usually does not occupy much of a student's time or energy. There is little to do on the Outward Bound solo unless you help to create it.

A negative orientation toward these deprivations occurs more often in those Outward Bound solos I would call unproductive. These were the solos in which students felt little challenge or commitment, made little effort at work (e.g., building a fire or good shelter), had fewer insights, wanted to quit, and evaluated the experience negatively.[14]

Outward Bound students report minor perceptual alterations and changes in their sense of time and usual sleeping patterns. But these changes usually are felt as disruptive. At times there may be distressing hallucinations. Students worry about losing control and try to impose an order by establishing familiar patterns. When this reaction occurs, there is less insight during the solo. Quite different were the rare instances when students accepted the order unique and intrinsic to the solo, the order of the wilderness. Then there are enhanced perceptions of self and environment, not hallucinations. Living according to an unusual order can provide excellent opportunities to transcend yourself, getting beyond the rituals you so identify with. Moments of creative alertness, and even awareness, are then more likely.

In the vision quest, the approach to altered states was also through need deprivation. A period of fasting was a part of every vision quest. The purpose of the fasting was to cast the participant in the role of the "pitiful suppliant," weakened by lack of food. He was then more likely to establish contact with the supernatural forces. The participant focused on his need deprivation. Feeling one's hunger as intensely as possible was the way to contact the supernatural.

In the Zen *sesshin,* the emphasis is on being able to control the need for food and thereby to transcend it. Hunger is manipulated so the meditator can learn about its various permutations. There may be times of fasting, but care is taken so that the meditator is not distracted or weakened by hunger. One cannot become aware when in a state of need. A focused mind and a strong body are necessary for meditation. Most often, simple food is provided. The meditator may be encouraged to eat no more than half of what he normally does, to eat neither too fast nor too slow, and to eat in silence.

In the Jesuit religious retreat, participants receive simple meals. The assumption is that basic needs must be modestly fulfilled so they can become inconspicuous. Unfulfilled basic needs would interfere with the ability to attend to "higher" concerns, such as reflecting on religious themes. Maslow's concept of "hierarchy of needs" becomes relevant here.[15] He feels that the "lower" needs such as hunger must be fulfilled (not overfilled) before higher needs such as reflection, love, or

---

[14] These kinds of solos *could* become productive. An enduring realization could result *just because* the solo experience was so empty and difficult.

[15] Abraham Maslow, *Motivation and Personality,* rev. ed., Harper & Row Publishers, Incorporated, New York, 1971.

transcendence can become functional. A proper attitude toward deprivation, instilled during the preparation phase, is important to the success of the solo.

Reentry

If there is to be personal growth, moments of creative alertness and awareness experienced during the solo must have a relationship with one's ongoing life situations. A goal could be to have these solo experiences inspire moments of awareness in everyday life.

Alterations of consciousness are intrinsically hard to describe; often they are ineffable. Subtle and sensitive procedures must be available so one can understand the significance of these alterations. It is important that the participant be encouraged to work over his experience, to begin to grasp its significance. It is even more important that he be encouraged to apply his experience to his daily life, to begin to extend its significance.

At Outward Bound, this critical reentry phase is usually short-circuited. There is more attention paid to what one *did during* the solo than to how one can build on the solo experience. Success in the solo becomes translated into physical accomplishment: How little equipment or assistance did you have? How rough were your solo terrain and weather conditions? Catch any animals? Any matches left? Discussions about loneliness or boredom or insights are infrequent. There are few structures available for building upon such psychological or emotional experiences.

Issues raised in the solo are not usually worked on during the rest of the Outward Bound course; rarely are they worked on after the course ends. As a result, few students can relate their solo experience to their day-to-day functioning at home. The solo setting and experience are too unusual. Where does a wilderness retreat fit into an urban environment? Bridges must be constructed into the individual's subsequent ordinary functioning. Otherwise insights generated during the solo will have short half-lives.

The reentry phase in the vision quest received careful attention. The reciprocity between the solo participant and his society was reenacted. The content of the vision was described in a group setting. Clarity prevailed because the imagery and content of the visions followed along traditional patterns. There was societal affirmation and confirmation for the vision and its developmental implications. The participant's self-uncovering was also encouraged because his visions were important to the community. His insights were integrated into his society's patterns and needs. For example, his vision might signal his movement to a new developmental stage, thus celebrating the tribe's socialization patterns; or it might contain information about curing some sick tribesman, thus caring for the community.

In the Zen *sesshin* and Jesuit retreat, there is a "continuous exchange" model of reporting solo survival experiences. The student describes his state of consciousness to the master at various times. The student thereby clarifies the nature of his state and gains direction for future work.

The temptation after solo survival experiences is to dwell on the physical aspects—the suffering, the sensations, and the reactions. These are easy to talk about. But the growth potential is more in the subtle quality of the experience and the glimmerings of self-understanding. These are hard to talk about. But extending these glimmerings into substantial personal growth requires more than a discussion after the solo. The reentry must reestablish the relationship between the individual and his day-to-day existence. He must be reborn into an environment, so he can live again, now possibly in a different way. The reentry phase must express the reciprocity between the individual and his culture—both value the solo experience as each realizes its potential for changing them.

Education for Transcendence

Transcendence and Growth

*T*HE experience of transcendence has been approached from many perspectives.[1] Maslow has offered a psychological perspective. He has described "peak experiences" in life which are

felt as self-validating, self-justifying moments . . . (during which) There is a very characteristic disorientation of time and space. Perception is richer and tends strongly to be idiographic and non-classificatory. The experience, or object, tends to be seen as a whole, as a complete unit, detached from relations, from possible usefulness, from expediency and from purpose . . . many dichotomies, polarities and conflicts are fused, transcended or resolved.

Cognition during the peak experience is much more passive and receptive than active. The emotional reaction in the peak experience has a special flavor of wonder, of awe, of reverence, of humility and surrender before something great. Perception can be relatively ego-transcending, self-forgetful.[2]

[1] See for example the essays in Richardson and Cutler (eds.), *Transcendence*, Beacon Press, Boston, 1969.
[2] Abraham Maslow, *Toward a Psychology of Being*, D. Van Nostrand Company, Inc., Princeton, N.J., 1962.

Transcendental religious experiences are also documented. James presents reports of both conversion experiences and mystical experiences.[3] R. M. Bucke describes the concept of "cosmic consciousness" which is primarily a consciousness of the cosmos, or the life and order of the universe.[4]

There is also the yogic state of samadhi and the Zen Buddhist state of satori. Suzuki[5] describes the experience of satori or enlightenment as an "intuitive looking into the nature of things" as opposed to an analytical or logical understanding of it. Figuratively expressed, satori is "the opening of the mind-flower," or "the removing of the bar." Practically speaking, it means the "unfolding of a new world hitherto unperceived in the confusion of a dualistic mind." Suzuki quotes Zen masters as they speak of satori. Stressing the sense of the beyond in satori, one master says: "There is not a fragment of tile above my head, there is not an inch of earth beneath my feet." Another, stressing the spiritual revolution produced by satori, says: "The bottom of a pail is broken through."

Complementing these considerations of transcendence as an outcome of individual growth is a consideration of transcendence as expressed in myth. Myth can be viewed as a level of reality transcendent to a particular culture or society. Campbell has extensively described this function of myth in a variety of cultures.[6] Jung, in his analysis of archetypes, describes the reappearance of these myths in an individual's deepest thoughts, feelings, and fantasies.

There is always a tendency to rank these experiences of transcendence according to their depth or purity or intensity. For example, Maslow's peak experiences may seem more a question of going beyond the ordinary self, while the experience of satori may seem more a question of participating in eternity. This difference in emphasis would lead one to place satori on a higher level. But I would like to focus on transcendent experiences in general, rather than on the differences between them. Huston Smith expresses this approach to the study of transcendence:

Transcendence should be defined neither quantitatively as "more of the same" nor qualitatively as "better than anything previously experienced" but in

[3] William James, *The Varieties of Religious Experience*, Mentor Books, New American Library, Inc., New York, 1958.

[4] R. M. Bucke, *Cosmic Consciousness*, E. P. Dutton & Co., New York, 1923.

[5] W. Barrett (ed.), *Zen Buddhism: Selected Writings of D. T. Suzuki*, Anchor Books, Doubleday & Company, Inc., Garden City, N.Y., 1956, chap. 4, pp. 83–110.

[6] Joseph Campbell, *The Masks of God*, volumes I–IV, Compass Books, The Viking Press, Inc., New York, 1969.

terms of the *kind* of value it designates. The effect of its appearance is to counter predicaments that are ingrained in the human situation. . . .[7]

I've taken this approach because I want to consider issues in education which depend on the fact of transcendence, not its degree or level. A proper education can evoke a transcendent experience and transform it into an experience of growth. Certainly different experiences of transcendence have different implications for growth. Experiences of satori may produce spiritual revolutions, leading to the birth of a new man, while peak experiences may produce intense awe or joy or reflection, leading to a change in emphasis or direction. I will not discuss such different implications in this case study.

Central to any discussion of education for transcendence is the idea that man, or an aspect of man, seeks something beyond himself. I am assuming such a need for transcendence. Huston Smith puts it this way: "Man lives forever on the verge, on the threshold of 'something more' than he can currently apprehend."[8] He quotes Nietzche's Zarathustra, who says that "man is a bridge and not an end." Philip Wheelwright has proposed a "metaphysics of the threshold" to deal with the fact that "we are never quite *there*, we are always and deviously on the verge of being there."[9]

Education for transcendence must deal directly with an experiential threshold. It must teach how one can cross the threshold of fear into the state of transcendence. This education must also bring transcendence into ordinary life and ordinary life into transcendence if personal growth is to occur.[10]

Trance-Curing with the Zu/wasi[11]

I want to describe the Zu/wasi trance-curing, an experience of transcendence, and their education for this trance-curing.[12] The word

---

[7] H. Smith, "The Reach and the Grasp: Transcendence Today," in Richardson and Cutler (eds.), op. cit., pp. 2–3.

[8] Huston Smith, op. cit., p. 1.

[9] P. Wheelwright, *The Burning Fountain*, Indiana University Press, Bloomington, Ind., 1968, p. 272, quoted in H. Smith, op. cit., p. 1.

[10] See Richard Katz, *Transformations: The Meaning of Personal Growth*, Englewood Cliffs, N.J., Prentice-Hall, 1974, for a discussion of personal growth and transcendence.

[11] This section is based on fieldwork I did while living with the Zu/wasi in the Kalahari Desert, in northwest Botswana, Africa. The group of people I lived with have been called the !Kung Bushmen elsewhere in anthropological literature. Zu/wasi is a more accurate and honest word; it is the word they use to describe themselves. Zu/wasi means "only or just people," or "true people," or simply "us."

"trance" may be the best available, but it is not clear enough. I'm using it to suggest the transcendent rather than somnambulistic quality of an experience. I believe important insights into education for transcendence can emerge from this study of the Zu/wasi Bushmen. For example, the Zu/wasi are a hunting and gathering group living primarily in the Kalahari Desert. Since their existence is less overlaid with "civilization," certain aspects of their education for transcendence becomes more apparent. Many Zu/wasi—approximately half the older adult males and one-third the adult women—become trancers.[13] During the trance state, they cure and fulfill many religious functions. Trancing is harmonious or synergistic with maintenance and growth on both the individual and cultural levels. The fact that large numbers of persons can experience transcendence in a way harmonious with their own and their culture's growth is somewhat unique and certainly significant. Though the Zu/wasi are in one sense remote from contemporary civilization, this becomes less important when we emphasize education for transcendence. That process of education seems more related to fundamental human characteristics than particular cultural settings.

THE TRANCE DANCE

The primary structure for the occurrence of trance is a dance which usually lasts from dusk to dawn and may occur once or twice a week. The entire village comes to such dances, including children and old persons. The women gather around the fire, singing trance songs and rhythmically clapping their hands. The men dance in a circle around the women, some working themselves into a trance state.

The trance, and its setting of the trance dance, serves many functions. It is the Zu/wasi's primary expression of religion and cosmology. It provides curing and protection, being a magico-medical mode of coping with illness and misfortune. The trance and the dance also increases social cohesion and solidarity. It allows for an individual and

---

My research was supported by an N.I.M.H. grant, #MH 13611. I am indebted to Richard Lee, who was my colleague, collaborator, and interpreter in the field. His help continues to be invaluable.

[12] A more extensive presentation of data on trance-curing, and a discussion of their implications for personal growth will appear in my book, *Boiling Medicine: Trance-Curing with the Kalahari Zu/wasi*, in preparation. For another view of Zu/wasi trance, see Richard Lee, "The Sociology of !Kung Bushmen Trance Performance," in R. H. Prince (ed.), *Trance and Possession States*, R. M. Bucke Society, Montreal, 1968.

[13] I won't be talking here specifically about the Zu/wasi women. The process of educating for trance is fundamentally similar for men and women.

communal release of hostility. Finally, the dance alters the consciousness of many members of the community. As individuals go into trance,
others at the dance, participating in various ways and to various degrees, themselves experience an alteration in their state of consciousness. An atmosphere develops. at a dance whereby individual experiences of trance can have a contagious effect on others.

ONSET OF TRANCE

The Zu/wasi say that trance is due to the activation of an energy,
which they call medicine. Medicine resides in the pit of the stomach.
As the trancer continues his energetic dance, becoming warm and
sweating profusely, the medicine heats up and becomes a vapor. It
then rises up the spine, to a point approximately at the base of the
skull, at which time a trance state results.

Bo[14] talks about the trance experience:

You dance, dance, dance, dance. Then [medicine] lifts you in your belly and
lifts you in your back, and then you start to shiver. [Medicine] makes you
tremble; it's hot. Your eyes are open but you don't look around; you hold
your eyes still and look straight ahead. But when you get into trance, you're
looking around because you see everything, because you see what's troubling
everybody. . . . Rapid shallow breathing, that's what draws medicine up . . .
then medicine enters every part of your body, right to the tip of your feet
and even your hair.

The action and ascent of medicine is described by Tsau:

In your backbone you feel a pointed something, and it works its way up.
Then the base of your spine is tingling, tingling, tingling, tingling, tingling,
tingling, tingling . . . and then it makes your thoughts nothing in your head

This medicine or energy is held in awe and considered to be very
powerful and mysterious. It is this same medicine that the trancer
"puts into" somebody in attempting to cure him. So, once heated up,
medicine can both induce trance and combat illness.[15]

TRANCE AS A TRANSCENDENT EXPERIENCE

Trance can be considered a state of transcendence because during
the trance a Zu/wasi experiences himself as existing beyond his or-

---

[14] Throughout, I'm using pseudonyms for the Zu/wasi who speak in this paper.
[15] This medicine seems analogous to other phenomena such as the Kundalini in
Yogic approaches.

dinary level of existence. The trance itself is a very intense, emotional state. Emotions are aroused to an extraordinary level, whether they be fear or exhilaration or seriousness. Also, a Zu/wasi practices extraordinary activities during trance. He performs cures, handles and walks on fire, claims x-ray vision, and at times says he sees over great distances. He doesn't even attempt such activities in his ordinary state.

Moreover, he can go beyond his ordinary self by becoming more himself, more essential, or by becoming more than himself. For example, there hadn't been a dance for a number of weeks at a particular waterhole. One of the important trancers who lived there said he wanted to have a dance soon so that "I can really become myself again." I think he meant that he wanted to experience again what he felt was his more essential self. Tsau, a blind man who is one of the most respected trancers, describes his own transformation:

... God keeps my eyeballs in a little cloth bag. When He first collected them, He got a little cloth bag and plucked my eyeballs out and put them into the bag and then He tied the eyeballs to His belt and went up to heaven. And now when I dance, on the nights when I dance and the singing rises up, He comes down from heaven swinging the bag with the eyeballs above my head and then He lowers the eyeballs to my eye level, and as the singing gets strong, He puts the eyeballs into my sockets and they stay there and I cure. And then when the women stop singing and separate out, He removes the eyeballs, puts them back in the cloth bag and takes them up to heaven.

During the trance state he becomes more than himself because he can now see, and he meant that both figuratively and literally.

Through the trance, the Zu/wasi participates in the religious dimension. Transcending himself, he is able to contact the supernatural, a realm where the ghosts of dead ancestors live. Sickness is a process in which these ghosts try to carry off a chosen one (the sick person) to their supernatural realm. The ghosts are strong but not invincible. Trancers may struggle with ghosts and may often win. While in trance, a trancer argues and contends with these ghosts. He carries on a sometimes heated dialogue: "Don't take this person yet, he's not ready to go." In his ordinary state, a Zu/wasi is in awe of the supernatural and avoids talking about it; certainly he does not deal directly with it. If a trancer's medicine is strong, the ghosts will retreat and the sick one will live. This struggle is at the heart of the trancer's art, skill, and power.

Trance can be viewed as an altered state of consciousness, altered to the degree and quality where it becomes a state of transcendence.[16]

---

[16] See Tart (ed.), *Altered States of Consciousness*. John Wiley & Sons, Inc., New York, 1969, for a survey of theory and research in this area.

A Zu/wasi's sense of self, time, and space are significantly altered. There is a feeling of ascent during trance; a trancer says: "When I pick up medicine, it explodes and throws me up in the air and I enter heaven and then fall down." During trance others feel they are "bursting open, like a ripe pod" or "opening up" so that something more important can come out.

EDUCATING FOR TRANCE

Socialization for Trancing

One of the most striking things about Zu/wasi education for trancing is that it is very much a normal process of socialization. Every male tries to become a trancer, though he may try more or less hard. Long before a person seriously tries to become a trancer, perhaps in his late teens or early twenties, he is playing with trancing. A group of five- and six-year-olds may perform a small trance dance, imitating the structure of the dance, the dance steps, and the trance gestures, at times falling as if in trance. Through play, the child is modeling; as he grows up, he is learning about trance.

Furthermore, education for trancing occurs within the context of the family, which, of course, is the major vehicle for socialization. The primary source of information about trance as well as the experiential teacher of trance is likely one's father, perhaps one's uncle or an older brother.

Seeking Trance

But this strong and supportive context for trancing is not enough. A Zu/wasi must seek trance—he must be willing and ready to receive medicine which can evoke the experience of trance. Medicine is not "put into" someone who cannot accept it. This seeking of trance usually occurs when a young man reaches twenty or so. He becomes a "student"[17] and may express his search by going to as many dances as possible, perhaps two or three a week; in a sense he is pushing himself to get more experience with the trance dance, to get closer to the trance experience. Also his dancing itself becomes more serious, more oriented toward trancing: eyes are focused straight ahead, distractions are ignored or screened out, he dances hard and intently.

---

[17] I'm using the term "student" to signify someone who has yet to trance and who is seeking medicine. I'll also use the term "potential trancer." It signifies someone who may trance during a particular dance, including students who for the first time may get medicine during that dance, as well as persons with varying experience in trancing.

Predisposition for Trancing

Who is it that seeks medicine? And who finds it, or rather who is able to accept medicine? Though approximately 50 percent of the adult males do trance and cure, 50 percent don't. There were several variables which I found increased the likelihood one would become a trancer. First, trancing families seem to exist—if your father has medicine, it is likely that you will get it.[18] Also, there were individual predisposing factors. For example, if you are very emotional, you're more likely to become a trancer. Experience with intense emotions would be good preparation for the intensely emotional trance experience. Moreover, Zu/wasi who have a richer fantasy life, who have more access to their fantasies and are more able to accept them, are more likely to become trancers. Since fantasy is an altered state of consciousness, these qualities could again be excellent preparation for contacting and accepting another altered state, i.e., trance. Though I have no data on this, there might also be predisposing characteristics of a more physiological and biochemical nature. Reaction to stress, brain rhythm activity, and blood-sugar level are among the variables which can affect the appearance and nature of an altered state.[19]

The Trance Experience

Socialization for trancing and seeking trance are prepatory phases in education for trancing. At the heart of this educational process is the experience of trance itself. There is consensual agreement and clarity about the concept of trance and the action of medicine. Most Zu/wasi, whether they trance or not, can describe how medicine works and what it feels like to be in trance. But during the trance experience itself, these concepts and descriptions are not available. While there is conceptual clarity, there is experiential mystery. This is the case with one's first trance experience; it is also, though usually to a lesser degree, the case with subsequent trances. And when someone who has tranced over the years experiences trance with a new intensity or quality, the experiential mystery is again great. At its core, the education is a process of accepting a trance *experience* for *oneself*. This is especially difficult because trance is painful as well as unknown; it is a greatly feared experience.

Along with feelings of release and liberation, trance also brings profound feelings of pain and fear. In describing the onset of trance,

[18] Richard Lee has collected data which shows a significant relationship between a father's having medicine and his son's getting medicine, whether or not the father actually teaches the son. Could there be some inheritability of a predisposition toward trancing?

[19] Tart (ed.), op. cit.

trancers referred again and again to pain and fear. They describe searing pain in the area of the diaphragm and spleen, and at the pit of the stomach. A trancer, recalling his first experience with medicine, says: "Medicine got into my stomach. It was hot and painful, like fire. I was surprised and I cried."

But as I thought about this pain and fear, I couldn't understand their depth and profundity only in physical terms; or, put another way, the physical symptoms seemed also to be metaphors for other nonphysical processes. Finally I talked with one of the two most knowledgeable and powerful curers. His description of trancing was both clear and subtle. He said that as a person enters trance, the fear is that not only will he lose himself, but he may never come back. To paraphrase it, the fear is of psychological death without an experience of rebirth. This fear evokes its own special and profound pain. When the potential trancer can face the fact that he must die to himself, *and* feel assured that he will be born again, then he can face the fear, overcome it, and break through to the trance state.

One of the older trancers describes this death and rebirth:

[In trance] your heart stops, you're dead, your thoughts are nothing, you breathe with difficulty. You see things, medicine things; you see ghosts killing people, you smell burning, rotten flesh; then you cure, you pull sickness out. You cure, cure, cure, cure . . . then you live. Then your eyeballs clear and then you see people clearly.

Here we get some idea of why the trance remains an experiential mystery and why it's feared. We can say that to enter trance, the Zu/wasi must give up his familiar identity and assume a new trance-identity. He gives up the familiar and enters the unknown. Looked at from another viewpoint, he must experience psychological death before he can be reborn into trance. This passage into the unknown is frightening for the Zu/wasi, as it has been for persons in every culture.

THE DANCE STRUCTURE.   How do the Zu/wasi educate for this critical passage into trance? Of primary importance is that the person himself seeks trance, and if it comes to him he must accept it. Various structures and techniques at the dance support his efforts and encourage them.

At any dance, the potential trancer can receive support and encouragement from a number of people. First and foremost for the student is his teacher, who has agreed to train him and give him medicine. This teacher, perhaps with one or two other trancers, will likely be the one who tries to put medicine into the student during a dance. There are also a number of people who can become guardians. They may give the potential trancer physical support when the onset of trance makes him shaky and unstable, or hold him when he trembles during trance, or lead him to others so he can cure them. The guardians serve another crucial function since the potential trancer may do things which can be harmful to himself or others. For example, he may want to get closer to the fire to help his medicine boil up; but when he tries to put his head in the fire or throw hot coals in the air, someone at the dance will usually leap up and restrain him. These guardians, who are there to support and protect the potential trancer, can be anyone at the dance. Another supportive and at times inspirational group is made up of the women who are singing and clapping the trance songs. Their singing and clapping stimulates the medicine to boil and rise up the spine. The intensity of their singing can help to determine and regulate the depth of one's trance. Finally, there is the entire community that's present at the dance; friends, family, neighbors, all participating to some degree and by their physical presence offering support.

THE THERMOSTATIC APPROACH. As one continues to dance into the night, ever more seriously, his medicine may begin to boil and trance becomes imminent. At this point, another critical element in the educational process occurs. Almost as with a thermostat, the potential trancer tries to regulate his condition. As he feels trance coming on, he may involuntarily draw back from and, at times, actively resist this transition to an extraordinary state. His teacher, the guardians, and the singing women help him overcome this resistance. They try to help him balance his fear of trance and the intensity of the oncoming trance. If his trance is coming on so fast that his fear escalates and prevents him from experiencing the trance, his teacher may make him stop dancing for a while, or drink some water, or lie down, all to "cool down" his too rapidly boiling medicine. The medicine must be hot enough to evoke trance but not so hot that it provokes debilitating fear. Also, it's never a question of merely putting medicine in the student. The correct amount is critical. Experienced trancers, for example, are encouraged to go as deeply into trance as they can, provided they maintain enough control over the medicine to use it for curing.

Tsau tells what he does during a dance with someone who is learning to trance:

You must do the [student's spleen area] properly. You've got to fire arrows into that area; fire them in and fire them in and fire them in until these arrows of medicine, which are a lot like thorns, long thorns, are sticking out of the spleen and stomach area like a pincushion, sticking out in all directions. So you see why we rub [the person's body] like we do, because the arrows are popping out of his body and we're rubbing them back into his body. And that's why we take our sweat, and then we try to work the arrows around to the back. When we do that, his breath and soul returns properly to his body; but if we don't do that, then he might die, he might die if we just left those things [sticking out].

When the student is too fearful, Tsau ceases to focus the medicine inward and upward, and instead allows it to subside:

. . . If I come up to [someone at the dance who is learning to trance] and he fears it, and he says: "please don't put your hands on me because I might die," and he just says: "take your hands off me," then I leave him because he fears it. . . . When a person says he is afraid, I remove [the arrows] I've put in.

Throughout this work at the dance, there is extensive physical contact between the potential trancer and his teachers and guardians. Much of the sensitivity to these subtle thermostatic considerations comes from this intimate contact. Physical support complements the psychological support offered the potential trancer.

Drugs are not used on any regular basis to induce trance. There is, however, one indigenous drug which apparently is used infrequently and in a specialized manner.[20] If a student is having considerable difficulty learning to trance, he may be given this drug at the beginning of a dance. The drug is offered as a training device, which may vault him over his intense fears as well as bringing him closer to the trance state. The drug experience itself also becomes a preparation for trance, since both experiences are forms of altered states of consciousness. As with other techniques used at the dance, the dosage and time of ingestion of the drug are carefully regulated by the teacher. The drug is supposed to help the student over the barrier of fear and into trance, not catapult him into yet another unknown and potentially frightening altered state.

There are specific and sometimes idiosyncratic signs that someone is approaching that threshold of fear and/or trance. The signs must then be interpreted: is the fear so intense that he must sit down; or is the fear such that if he stays with it, he can overcome it and enter a trance

[20] The drug is awaiting botanical identification and analysis. It appears to be a psychoactive substance which has not yet been reported in the literature. I never observed the use of this drug during any of the trance-dances I attended.

state? Some of the signs used to determine the balance between fear and trance in a particular dancer might be: Is his body shaking? Does he have a glazed look, or are his eyes downcast? Is his face impassive? These are signs used not only by the person himself but also by his teacher, guardians, and the women who are singing and clapping. If the women sense that someone is ready to go into trance, they may intensify their singing and clapping to give him an extra push.

An example may describe the subtlety of this thermostatic idea. One young Zu/wasi, who was new to trance, had a look of tremendous fear as he was dancing. The singing and clapping, the dance in general, was at a high intensity. Trance was threatening to overwhelm him. But instead of taking him away from the dance, two persons went to him, one holding him from the front, the other from behind, and physically brought him back to the dance. The three of them then continued dancing, in close physical contact, as the singing reached new levels of intensity and excitement. In a sense they brought him back to what he most feared, but they were now physically with him. He became able to go through his fear and into trance. The approach to each potential trancer depends on his history with trance and present readiness for trance.

As the person experiences the beginnings of trance, those who are teaching and working on him can confirm the validity of his experience. They can acknowledge his entrance into trance.

TRANCE MANAGEMENT. As trancing occurs at a dance, the atmosphere becomes more electric and the dance more focused. One person going into trance is in a sense an incentive or stimulant for others to do likewise. At one dance there were fifteen dancers, and twelve of them were potential trancers. I tried to imagine what would happen if all of them were to go into a trance at once. Certainly the process of education for trancing would be severely strained. But no more than two or three were in trance at any one time. What happened was a process of trance management. The more experienced trancers hold back their trance until those who need more help are either under control or able to function in trance. Rarely are there people in a state of trance who need help and cannot get it.

THE TEACHER. The teacher is a Zu/wasi who is a trancer. He remains an ordinary person during his nontrance state, rather than an intimate of the gods or a chosen instrument. He does not demand obedience nor a long apprenticeship. The period of learning is focused during the dance itself. The emphasis is on experiential education. The core of the teaching is at those points when trance is about to and does

occur. The teacher is with the student at the threshold of the latter's
fear and trance, trying to help him over his fear and into trance, and
then guiding him to use that trance for curing.

The blind, powerful trancer Tsau said to me:

> . . . I ask God for medicine and put it into you. And I say to God: here's
> my child, give me some more medicine so I may put it into him . . . even
> today I'm going to put it into you, and you'll dance, dance, dance, dance:
> I'll put it into you . . . one of these days soon, when the women start sing-
> ing, you'll start shivering . . . let's dance tonight, let's dance tonight and
> . . . and dance tomorrow night and then I'm going to dance you again . . .
> I'll dance you tonight and dance you tomorrow night . . . I'm going to
> do you . . . and you will be trembling like leaves in the winds . . . when I
> cure you, I will feel medicine trembling in your body, and then I'll say: oh,
> today this fellow has drunk medicine.

Though originally from the gods, medicine now passes regularly
from man to man. Teaching is primarily by example. The teacher has
been there before. He may be trancing at that particular time; certainly he has tranced many times before. He recognizes the student's
progress, interprets his condition, and confirms that he is in trance.

As he works with his student, the teacher combines many functions.
He is likely a parent or close relative, and therefore he is responsible
for the student's socialization in general. The teacher is a guide in that
he leads the student through the barrier of fear. He is like a priest in
that he has had contact with the ghosts and can guide the student to
that realm. He's very much a therapist in that he tries to help the
student accept his fear rather than be overcome by it. And he has been
an academic teacher because very likely he taught the student the
conceptual framework of trance.

MEDICINE AS A SPECIAL GIFT. The process of educating for trance
has consistent and constant features. For example, though medicine
originally came from the gods, men now teach or give medicine to
other men. Also, they usually get medicine in their mid-twenties, oc-
casionally in their early twenties or early thirties. Certain exceptions
to this usual educational process seem associated with especially powerful medicine. Certain special conditions seem to stimulate the appearance of powerful medicine and to signify its continuing availability.

!Cum is considered by other Zu/wasi to be a powerful trancer. He
agrees. I asked him how others get their medicine; he said, "How do
I know they got it? So they dance and do it; but do they *really* know
what they're doing? I don't know. Maybe it's the singing of the women
that does it." I then asked him whether he cures with the other medi-

cine men in the village; he said, "What other doctors? You think there are other medicine men in the village?" !Cum loves to joke but he nonetheless means what he said.

!Cum's father had medicine, but did not give it to him. !Cum received medicine directly from God. He describes it this way:

When I was about fourteen or fifteen, I was asleep, and God grabbed me by the legs and sent me out into the bush at night, and out there, He gave me a small tortoise and told me: "This tortoise, leave it here and then in the morning, get your father to degut it, and put medicine into it and that will be your medicine." And then God took me farther and I was crying in the dark, and my father came looking for me and found me crying, and carried me back to the fireside. Then in the morning I said: "Father, come and see this tortoise; fix it for me and put medicine in it, and give it to me because this is what God has given me. Fix it and give it to me so I may keep it; so that when you are dying, I can use it and I'll save you." But my father refused. He just killed the tortoise, roasted it and ate it; and then the skin of his throat parted and we could see his windpipe exposed. Then God told me: "For what your father has done, I'm going to kill him. The thing I gave to you that he ate is killing him." And I refused, and I said: "My father won't die." And I took another tortoise with medicine in it, and dropped burning coals into the shell. And then I put the shell to his lips and he drank the smoke, and the same day the skin above and the skin below came together and closed, and he lived. Then God said to me: "See what your father's arrogance has done to him; you tell him to stop that and not to do it again or else I will *really* kill him next time." And that's how I got what I have. That's where I started it and today I carry the people in the different villages. If someone is sick, I go to them.

This vision and gift of medicine is both unusual and startling. So were some of the immediate effects. !Cum says, "I only danced after this [vision] experience, and only tranced after this experience; but *right* after!" He then says that twice after the vision, God took him out to the bush alone, and he tranced. First trances are times of especially strong fear, fear of the hot medicine and the unexpected intensity of the experience. But his solo, God-induced trances were different. He says of these two experiences:

How [could I] be afraid during these trances like [the others are during their trances]? God killed every thought. He wiped me clean. Then he took my soul away whirling, my thoughts whirled.

Tsau is considered an even more powerful trancer, perhaps one of the two most powerful ones in the area. And he also describes himself as such. He talked about how he got medicine:

When I was a tiny thing, sucking at my mother's breast, I took medicine, I
drank medicine. It was medicine . . . it was at the breast, I was about three
or four years old. I would cry, and cry and cry; my mother would sing to
me; and I would cry and suck the breast and cry. I just sat in my mother's
lap and danced. I was afraid of the medicine; it was hot and hurt. . . . That
is my story. Others [who trance] are much older than me, but they started
their medicine later than me.

Others were understandably surprised at this early onset of trancing
ability. As Tsau put it, people would say, "What's this baby still at
the breast doing?"

Kau is a youngster of only eleven or twelve years. And yet already
there is something special about his relation to trancing. He is an
especially talented dancer, and dances more frequently than his peers.
Most unusual, he seems already to have drunk medicine. In the view
of others, he has great potential for becoming a powerful trancer.
!Cum describes a particular dance:

I've looked at this kid, Kau, and didn't see anything until recently. But a
few months ago we had a dance in the bush, and the kid started crying and
was carried around [the dance] crying by his playmates. . . . He was
witless. . . . His father was away. I said, "This kid's already drunk medicine."
Then I told the women, "Stop singing because this kid's father [who is
teaching him about medicine] is far away, and I'm not going to work on
him, and you're going to give this boy a lot of pain if you keep singing."
Then the ladies stopped.

!Cum then tried to figure out why Kau is so special:

. . . what is it that has made Kau trance while such a young boy? I'm trying
to figure it out in my own mind what it is that sets him apart. . . . When
I see a little kid like that I say, "His heart is full, full of dancing" . . . it's
his heart. He loves to dance. When the singing starts, he's not the least bit
afraid of people, so he dances full out and that's what helps him trance.

Where others approach trance with fear and caution, Kau's enthusiastic
and devoted approach is striking.

TRANCE IN CONTEXT. The Zu/wasi do not seek trance for its own
sake. They experience trance in order to cure others. If they were just
to trance without curing, this would be seen as a misuse of these
trance-related powers. Also, trance is not cultivated as a long-term
state. A Zu/wasi has to maintain his responsibilities as a member of a
hunting and gathering group. He is a hunter and gatherer who also

happens to trance. Trancing generally should occur within the period of a dance. One of the older and more experienced trancers didn't come out of trance when the dance ended the next morning. This extended trance wasn't seen as a privilege or an extra source of curing power; it was seen as a mistake. The trancer himself was quite upset and tried as hard as he could to come out of the trance. When he returned to his normal state later that morning, he was able to resume his ordinary, everyday responsibilities.

The intrinsically valuable experience of trancing remains thoroughly functional. Trancing always occurs in context. One way I've tried to describe this is with the concept synergistic consciousness. Trancing is a state of synergistic consciousness, harmonious with both the individual and cultural levels of existence. Trancing supports the functioning and growth of the individual trancer. It allows him to transcend himself and develop extraordinary powers during certain periods. It reaffirms his relationship with the supernatural and leaves him with a feeling of well-being. For a few of the most powerful curers, trancing also seems to raise their level of consciousness; their ordinary lives take on a special quality. And trancing does not interrupt or disrupt the Zu/wasi's carrying out his basic everyday responsibilities. Trancing also supports the functioning and growth of the culture. When a Zu/wasi becomes a trancer, everybody gains. With its religious, medical and social dimensions, trancing is a major force in the culture. Also, there is no limit on medicine; no zero-sum game is involved. One Zu/wasi becoming a trancer does not mean another Zu/wasi cannot become one; often, especially if they know each other, it can mean just the opposite. Medicine is an expandable substance. What is good for the individual is good for the culture is again good for the individual. This is a synergistic relationship.

Educating for Transcendence

Perhaps we can extract from the Zu/wasi's experience with trance certain more general ideas about education for transcendence. As I've already said, there are important reasons why the Zu/wasi can be an especially significant source of such ideas.

BEYOND TRANSCENDENCE

The experience of transcendence is momentary, though in another sense timeless. The emphasis is not so much on having a transcendent experience but on what you do next—what effect does this experience have on your life? The Zu/wasi trance in order to cure and to participate in the religious dimension. Trancing has an integral place in the ongoing life of the individual and his group. As documented so vividly and so often, Westerners too easily place all the emphasis on the experience of transcendence.[21] They look harder and harder for this one transcendent experience, the breakthrough. The farther they feel from that experience, the harder they look, the more desperate they can become. If they are fortunate enough to stop grasping and allow the experience to occur, then they are faced squarely with the crux of the matter. After the exhilaration and relief which can follow the experience, there is often a letdown. Instead of having found the answer, they are usually faced with a perplexing question: What do I do now? Without a context for transcendence, it is a transitory experience, with uncertain implications for personal growth. The explorer of consciousness temporarily leaves himself and his society. But after experiencing a truth, he returns to himself and to his society and attempts to live this truth with himself and others.

Certainly there have been dramatic instances where one transcendent experience changes the course of a life and begins a path toward growth. Religious conversions, for example, do occur. But there was a fertile soil from which the experience could arise and in which it could subsequently grow.

There is another aspect to this issue of transcendence in context. What is an experience of transcendence for a particular person? How does his life, as a context, affect the nature of that experience? Put another way, is the Zu/wasi experience of trance analogous to other more familiar experiences of transcendence—such as the Zen satori or the mystical religious experience? My feeling at this point is that more than likely they are similar. This doesn't deny the fact that *within* any culture (or spiritual discipline), there are differences in degree or level between experiences of transcendence.

I think that each culture transcends itself in a way specific and organic to that culture. The mode and metaphors of transcendence can be quite different, but I think the state is similar. For example, one culture may have an *apparently* more sophisticated or elaborated set of metaphors. But these may be merely a more literate representation of a universal experience of transcendence, and the emphasis certainly belongs on the experience.

---

[21] See, for example, the first-person accounts in P. Kapleau, *Three Pillars of Zen,* Beacon Press, Boston, 1967.

The Student Seeks

As was clear with Zu/wasi trance, the individual himself seeks the transcendent experience. But this seeking is not a grasping after trance; it is making oneself ready to receive trance. This is in contrast to a situation where someone sits back, waiting for it to happen *to* him, waiting for a teacher to *give* him an experience of transcendence. The saying that the teacher finds the student when the latter is ready can also be applied to the experience of transcendence. Transcendence grows in fertile soil.

An Experiential Passage

I've been talking about the experience, not the concept of transcendence. Entering into a transcendent state is an experiential passage. Conceptual clarity about that state may give one a feeling of confidence or some comfort, but when it comes down to the moment of transcendence, it's of no help at all. In his book *The Teachings of Don Juan,* Castaneda describes how his need for conceptual clarity about transcendence denies him the very experience of transcendence.[22]

But inevitably there is a strong desire to find out what will occur during a transcendent experience: "What will happen to me? How will I feel?" We all want to hold on to something, something known when we face the unknown of a transcendent moment. But, just as inevitably, there can be no conceptual clarity in that moment because there are no concepts. The experience is transcendent because it has gone beyond such concepts, beyond the mind.

Psychological Death and Rebirth

The Zu/wasi describe a process analogous to a psychological death and rebirth as critical to entering trance. This is not surprising. There is a broad range of evidence suggesting this is the process which characterizes the entrance into a transcendent state. During an experience of psychological death, you give up who you are, what you are accustomed to. And in the process of giving up your identity, you can enter the state of transcendence. The conviction that you will be reborn encourages you to enter this state. You can accept the fear; it's no longer immobilizing, as when you fear that you will become nothing

---

[22] C. Castaneda, *The Teachings of Don Juan,* Ballantine Books, Inc., New York, 1968.

or that you can't come back again to yourself. Rebirth for the Zu/wasi is being reborn into the trance state; also, after the dance, being reborn as an ordinary, fully functioning Zu/wasi. Having a conviction about rebirth is helpful. But the basic process is being able to accept the unknown, willingly going into fundamental mysteries. The hero's passage is a journey into the unknown; facing the unknown, the boy becomes a man, the man a hero.[23]

Today, particularly among adolescents, many people are trying to establish their own identity.[24] Many of them would also say they are looking for an experience of transcendence. But being in a state of identity diffusion—at loose ends, not particularly invested in anything—is not equivalent to being in a state of transcendence. You give up your identity when you experience transcendence, but before you give up an identity, you must first have one. The Zu/wasi for the most part know who they are and sense their place in their universe. They have an identity which they can transcend.

The Teacher

I talked about the idea of the teacher of Zu/wasi trance as being someone who is there at the crossroads, at the point of no return, who by his presence encourages you across fear into trance. The emphasis remains on your being prepared for trance, ready to receive the medicine he puts in you. Also, the Zu/wasi teacher is someone who is initiating you into areas he's had experience with. In one sense, he performs the classic role of initiating persons into the (cultural) mysteries, teaching others about the nature of their existence.

But the Zu/wasi model is too rare today. There are few supposed teachers of transcendence who are encouraging others to go where they themselves have already been. There are few teachers who are relatively complete: very few parents are teachers, and very few teachers are parents. Also, teachers operate too often without a context. The Zu/wasi education for trance is effective primarily because it occurs within a context which is actively interested in this education. It's almost as simple as that. When transcendence is pursued in isolation of any cultural supports, if it's experienced, it quickly dissipates, with very little effect on a person's daily behavior. Transcendence needs to be educated toward growth.

[23] Campbell, in his book *Hero with a Thousand Faces* (Meridian Books, The World Publishing Company, Cleveland, 1956), demonstrates the depth of man's commitment to this process.

[24] See, for example, E. Erikson, *Identity: Youth and Crisis*, W. W. Norton & Company, Inc., New York, 1968.

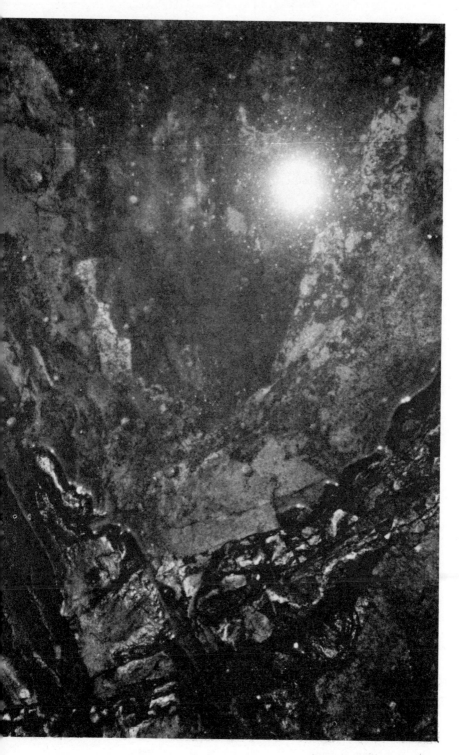

Photograph by the author

Index

Barnes, Cary F., 60
Barrett, W., 185, 207
Benedict, Ruth, 179, 193
Benoilt, H., 174
Berzon, Betty, 32
Bolton, Colin, 193
Buber, Martin, 51, 118, 186
Bucke, R. M., 207

Campbell, Joseph, 118, 170, 200–01, 207, 224
Carpenter, Edmund, 26
Castaneda, Carlos, 118, 223
Check, Eugene, 193
Cutler, D. R., 206, 208

Erikson, Erik, 200, 224

Frankel, V., 172, 176
Fuller, Buckminster, 139, 185

Goffman, Erving, 60
Gurdjieff, Georges I., 78, 163, 168, 170, 184, 186–87

Herrigel, Eugen, 157, 183
Hertzog, John, 193
Hesse, Hermann, 157, 162, 170, 183, 184

James, William, 78, 195, 207
Jourard, Sidney, 186
Jung, Carl Gustav, 207

Kahn, Kurt, 194–95
Kapleau, Philip, 189, 194, 222
Katz, Mary Maxwell, 193
Kelly, Francis J., 193
Kolb, David, 32, 109, 194, 195

Laing, R. D., 172
Lecky, Prescott, 180
Lee, Richard, 209, 213
Leonard, George, 189
Lorenz, K., 176

McKelvey, William, 95
McLuhan, Marshall, 26
Manchester, F., 188
Maslow, Abraham, 78, 176, 179, 180, 203, 206–07
Miner, Josh, 193

Neilhardt, John, 157
Neill, A. S., 176
Nietzche, Friedrich Wilhelm, 208
Nold, Joe, 193
Nyland, W. A., 174–75

Ouspensky, P. D., 78

Pieh, Bob, 193
Prabhavananda, Swami, 188
Prince, R. H., 209

Richardson, H. W., 206, 208
Rogers, Carl, 103, 168, 176, 186
Rubin, Irv, 109
Rudolfsky, Bernard, 137

Sartre, Jean Paul, 51
Schachtel, Ernest, 26
Schumacher, E. F., 183
Schwitzgabel, Ralph, 32
Smith, Huston, 207–08
Solomon, Lawrence N., 32
Stevens, Barry, 168
Sullivan, Harry S., 180
Suzuki, Daisetz T., 185, 194, 207

Tart, Charles T., 211, 213
Teilhard de Chardin, Pierre, 176, 185
Thoreau, Henry David, 174, 183
Tresemer, David, 193

van Gennep, Arnold, 200

Wheelwright, Philip, 208
Wilhelm, Richard, 60
Williamson, Jed, 193
Wu Ch'eng-en, 178

Zimmer, H., 170